# Golf for Everybody

# Golf for Everybody

## A Lifetime Guide for Learning, Playing, and Enjoying the Game

Brad Brewer and Steve Hosid

*Chandler House Press*
WORCESTER, MASSACHUSETTS

1998

**Golf for Everybody: A Lifetime Guide for Learning, Playing, and Enjoying the Game**

ISBN 1-886284-15-6

Library of Congress Catalog Card Number 97-77503

First Edition

ABCDEFGHIJK

*Published by*
**CHANDLER HOUSE PRESS**
335 Chandler Street
Worcester, MA 01602
USA

*President*
Lawrence J. Abramoff

*Publisher/Editor-in-Chief*
Richard J. Staron

*Vice President of Sales*
Irene S. Bergman

*Editorial/Production Manager*
Jennifer J. Goguen

*Editor*
Joan Paterson

*Book & Cover Design*
Marshall Henrichs

*Photographs*
Steve Hosid

Chandler House Press books are available at special discounts for bulk purchases. For more information about how to arrange such purchases, please contact Irene Bergman at Chandler House Press, 335 Chandler Street, Worcester, MA 01602, or call (800) 642-6657, or fax (508) 756-9425, or find us on the World Wide Web at **www.tatnuck.com.**

Chandler House Press books are distributed to the trade by National Book Network, Inc.
4720 Boston Way
Lanham, MD 20706
(800) 462-6420

# Contents

# Foreword

I take particular pride in commending the pages that follow to anybody searching for a competent golf game and everything that goes with it. In fact, I feel a bit like a collaborator in this book since Brad Brewer has been an associate of mine for 14 years in various roles as he pursued his career as a golf professional and teacher to his present position as director of our Arnold Palmer Golf Academy program. It is certainly no accident that this text reflects much of my thinking, not only about the basics of playing golf but about all aspects of the game.

For you young people and others being initiated into golf for the first time, Brad Brewer traces the game's history from its creative roots to the present day as you become part of it and urges you to share your enjoyment with others, passing it along to the players of the future. He deals with the traditions passed down to us, the etiquette and sportsmanship that must be maintained and fostered to preserve the game as we know it. He discusses the bugaboo of slow play and offers the remedy of "ready golf," the care our beautiful courses can and should receive from their users.

Brad achieves with this book what he set out to offer—a lifetime guide for learning, playing and enjoying the game.

*Arnold Palmer*

# Introduction

Golf is very special to me. I've been fortunate to be associated with one of the most respected legends of the game, Arnold Palmer. His inspiration, love of the game and its traditions combined with the thrill of competition provided a strong motivational factor in the creation of *Golf for Everybody*.

Writing a golf book to appeal to every golfer is a staggering task. We've tried to include all sorts of information that will help you increase your enjoyment and understanding along with instruction segments to help you cut strokes even before you work on correcting your swing faults. I'll show you how to play a golf hole and how to avoid trouble and lost balls. We'll deal with challenging lies and tell you how to shape your shots around trouble, just like the pros. Have you ever thought sand play was as simple as hitting a "Donut" out of a bunker?

I believe that improvement comes from understanding, so we've included chapters explaining how to use your home video camera to improve your game, just like the pros and their instructors. You'll learn how to set up your camera correctly to videotape your swing, and then how to view it and identify your swing faults. You'll become your own coach! Whenever you want to begin building a new consistent golf swing based on mastering five simple fundamentals, the information in Part 7 is waiting to help.

Golf affords my family the quality time we need together. I'll share some of the ways I'm teaching my four children to learn and play the sport. Our lines of communication are open as we enjoy each other as friends as well as parents and children. If you have junior golfers who dream of playing professional golf, we have a chapter that deals with how you can help and outlines what it takes for the child to develop his or her competitive game.

Don't feel you have to use every bit of information in this book today to play golf. It's a reference that will help you improve and its timeless nature ensures that you can go back to it over and over again. Just remember, golf is a game—so enjoy it!

*Brad Brewer*

# Acknowledgments

To Steve and Jill Hosid for their competence and dedication in the preparation of this manuscript. To my Mom, Dad, and wife: Rita, Paul, and Wanda Brewer for their ongoing support and unwavering belief. To my four children: Kenna, Carli, Tori, and Bradley Jr. for being great models for how to enjoy the game. To the late Patrick Shortridge Sr. who taught me as a junior golfer how to hit it hard and have fun. And to my mentor, Arnold Palmer, for personally giving me so much and, most importantly, for his infectious passion for the game and its traditions.

To the many people who have touched my life and made a difference with the book. To mention just a few—Dick Tiddy, Jim Miller, Bill, Patrick, and Robert Damron, Ian Baker-Finch, Scott Hoch, Doc Giffin, Ed Seay, Doug Wherry, John O'Leary, Rolf Deming, Fred Settle Jr., Doris Killian, and the entire "Bay Hill Shoot-Out."

# PART 1

# Golf's a Game— So Enjoy It!

Whether you're just taking up golf or have played for 20 years, you'll learn more than you ever knew about the sport from this book. And it's a lot easier to enjoy something you truly understand. Golf is a lifetime sport, and you'll discover how to maximize your enjoyment from all facets of the game. You'll read about golf's wonderful traditions and learn how all of us can do our best to eliminate slow play. You'll find out how to get your own handicap and how to play various fun formats that add variety to this wonderful game.

Golf is the corporate sport of American business and you'll learn how to use it to your advantage. Including golf as part of corporate entertaining and seminars can enhance team building.

# How to Enjoy the Lifetime Sport of Golf

*A Good Walk Spoiled*
   title of **John Feinstein's** best-selling book about golf

*"Golf is a good walk with enjoyable and challenging opportunities!"*
      **Brad Brewer**

**D**oes it seem strange to start off a golf book by encouraging you to have fun? I'll be the first to tell you that golf requires a strong sense of humor along with a good sense of perspective. While playing in the Los Angeles Open one year, Arnold Palmer shot an unbelievable 12 on a hole. After the round, someone asked the "King" how he could have possibly shot the 12. Arnold answered, "Easy! I missed a 20-footer for an 11!"

How's that for a sense of humor from a man who personifies everything that's good about the sport? Let me assure you, there's no one on the face of the earth who enjoys golf more than Arnold Palmer. And just like Arnold Palmer, all golfers have to be able to laugh at some of the things that happen because, frankly, golf is an imperfect sport. It's also a game of incredible emotional rewards. The passion you develop for the game brings you back over and over again.

# Enjoyment Doesn't Always Mean Smiling!

Enjoyment is one of those subjective, hard-to-define terms because each of us has a unique sense of what we individually find enjoyable. You may not be smiling, for example, as you read the green for a tricky 10-foot downhill putt, but chances are you're enjoying the challenge of making it. In fact, let's rephrase that to say— you're enjoying the opportunity of taking on that challenge. Maybe my next book will be titled, "Golf is a good walk with enjoyable and challenging opportunities."

## HISTORICAL HIGHLIGHT

The earliest mention of the word golf occurred in 1457 in an act of the Scottish Parliament. King James II passed the "Fiery Face" act, forbidding the playing of *golfe* along with *futeball* so that every ablebodied man could devote all of his spare time to practicing archery. The aim was to protect the realm during the long drawn-out war with England.

King James did not live long enough to see the futility of his decree. He was soon after blown up while inspecting a cannon. Perhaps this was golf's first example of a "blown round."

Some of us may enjoy the thrill of competing while others may find enjoyment by just getting together with friends for a few hours on the course. Some may enjoy the ambiance of a well-groomed and designed country club course, while countless others are represented by the golfers I've seen teeing it up on a trailer park course in the shadow of the majestic Zion National Park in Utah.

By the way, when the Scots invented the game, it was played on fields, not the meticulously groomed courses of today. Do you think they didn't enjoy the game just as much back then? Forget about the occasional spike marks or the bunker that's not perfectly groomed when you play today—you never had to contend with the droppings of well-fed sheep!

# What Do You Really Like about Golf?

What is your answer to this question: "What do you enjoy about golf?" The off-the-top-of-your-head answer would most likely involve a "Tiger Woods"-type long drive or a tricky putt holed. But below the surface lies the true answer, the special magic of unique enjoyment that golf brings to you.

Obviously, you have a passion for golf—or we wouldn't be meeting like this. However, your answers may provide an insight into some of the challenges you face. Being clear about your attitudes will help you learn to enjoy the game of golf even more than you do now. Whatever your answers are, we can turn negatives into positive areas to work on as we improve your game.

## Brad's Golf Enjoyment Questionnaire

1. Can you control your emotions and remain even-tempered while on the golf course?
2. Are you easy on yourself by using positive self-talk and avoiding negative thoughts?
3. Can you keep your confidence level up even when you hit a bad shot?
4. Are you committed to the shot you want to hit?
5. Can you visualize your ball flying, landing, and coming to rest at its intended destination before you pull the trigger?
6. Do you enjoy competing against other golfers?
7. Do you like to practice your game and sometimes roll putts on the carpet at home or practice gripping the club while watching TV?
8. Do you enjoy having someone coaching you?
9. Can you learn by listening to others?
10. Do you enjoy the challenge of having to create a shot to get out of trouble without cursing the gods of golf for giving you a bad lie?
11. Are you friendly with your playing partners, even if they are complete strangers?
12. Do you like to carry on conversations between shots?
13. Do you enjoy the walk or ride between shots, smelling the flowers and looking at the scenery?

# So, Brad, What Do My Answers Mean?

What's important to keep in mind is that all golfers run the full gamut of emotions—but good golfers learn to regain control before their next shot. In fact, it's not that bad to get mad occasionally and get it over with, but keep your temper under control. Getting mad usually means that you enjoy your competitive side and strive to play the best you can. Just be careful of negative self-talk.

**SWING KILLERS**

"Steve, you idiot, why did you do that! How stupid can you be?" Nothing will destroy your confidence more than negative self-talk. (By the way, notice I didn't use "Brad" in my example). Golf is a mind game, and even if you hit a bad shot, try and find a way to encourage yourself to remain positive.

Gaining confidence in your abilities after hitting quality shots is another normal reaction and high up on the enjoyment meter. Confidence allows you to relax and thus frees up your swing, creating better shots. All golfers have bad days—it's a fact of life. It's normal to experience an occasional lack of confidence. Unfortunately, tension is usually the end result, along with a tight restricted swing.

Sometimes even the very best players in the world have to play mind games with themselves. Brad Faxon usually ranks at or near the top of the PGA Tour's putting statistics. He's found a simple way to keep his confidence level high even if he misses some putts early in the round. Brad walks off the green pretending that he made them and reminds himself that he's a great putter.

If you could ask Brad Faxon about the key to becoming a successful putter, he'd answer, "Putt like a kid." Give a child a putter and ball and they putt to make instead of tensing up and becoming preoccupied with working on technique. Kids are relaxed, having fun, and just trying to put the ball in the hole. As we get older, our minds take over and we become too mechanical. In the Stroke Saver section of the book, Part 5, we'll work on restoring the *putt to make attitude* into your game.

Having a clear understanding of the type of shot you want to hit is a positive way to approach the game. Jack Nicklaus decides what he wants the ball to do and then mentally visualizes the flight of the ball before he hits it. This works for him, along with using the same pre-shot visualization while addressing the ball. Great players understand that consistency breeds confidence. Being positive definitely keeps your enjoyment level high.

# Enjoyment Comes from Attainable Goals

All of the positive enjoyment traits are fed and nurtured by the feedback you get from your senses and your mind-set. Without really knowing it, subconsciously you are already practicing one of my favorite aspects of the game—*attainable goals.* On the other hand, if you get easily frustrated and have even thought of giving up golf or actually did give it up, attainable goals may be just the element you need to become a good golfer as well as rejuvenating your enjoyment for the sport.

If you're a high handicap golfer and get easily frustrated by your lack of consistency or improvement, I suggest working on the fundamentals of the game (correct grip, for example) and setting an attainable goal of 30 days to feel comfortable with them. If, on the other hand, you say to yourself that "by tomorrow my grip will be perfect"—that's not going to happen and you'll get frustrated. Most people I know don't equate frustration with enjoyment.

However, if you set a realistic time frame for getting comfortable with your new grip and then do something every day to work toward your goal, you'll accomplish the goal and have fun doing it. Many of the fundamentals of golf can be practiced at home and you'll be surprised at your progress. You can work on a new grip by holding onto a club with your hands in the correct positions while developing a feel for the pressure points as you watch TV at night. Working toward a goal and being able to see and feel your progress will definitely boost and maintain your enjoyment level.

## ATTAINABLE GOALS

*Here's my definition of an attainable goal: goals that are easily reached. Your progress must be easily seen and tracked. Depending on the goal, it should be reachable today or within a 30-day period of time. Set your target on the tasks you are going to do on a daily basis in order to accomplish your attainable goal.*

# Enjoyment Comes from a True Understanding

Most of us enjoy something we understand. If something is a mystery, we may even shy away from it, preferring not to reveal our ignorance of the subject. Using a computer is an example of this behavior. Whether you've played golf for years or are just taking up golf, you are going to really boost your enjoyment level for the game by developing a true understanding of what the sport is all about. What takes place in the swing is an example. Once you understand the simple aspects of a free-flowing golf swing and practice the fundamentals, you will see improvement in all aspects of your game.

To many golfers, the various movements and actions in the one and a half seconds it takes to make a swing are a complete mystery. You may read about them in magazines and see the terminology but, in this book, you'll be able to learn, see, and feel the swing. I'm not going to turn you into a bio-mechanical engineer, just help you develop golf senses you never thought were possible. You'll know what it takes to have a good-quality golf swing that repeats itself. As you develop your new understanding of the complete game, you'll even enjoy watching golf on television a little bit more.

The swing is only one facet of good golf. Course strategy, getting yourself out of trouble, and understanding how to practice effectively will all lead to further enjoyment. And understanding the scoring zone can dramatically cut strokes from your game.

# Enjoyment Comes from Friendships

Golf is usually played in foursomes, so it's not uncommon to be paired up with players you've never met. What an incredible opportunity to make new friends! You may also get to meet golfers from other states or other countries. As a golfer, you are a member of a worldwide fraternity (or sorority). It's funny, wherever I have played around the world, I've met someone who knows somebody I know.

Conversation and camaraderie should be easy to establish since you're sharing a common experience. You're not competing against one another as much as testing the golf course and yourself. When you're out there and walking to the next shot or hole, you have time to make friends with people, share stories, and have fun.

While growing up in Winona, Minnesota, I was often invited to play with the leaders of industry in my hometown at the young age of 15. They enjoyed playing with me, because I could hit the golf ball pretty good and, at the same time, I enjoyed learning about their businesses and about life in general. Golf provided the opportunity to make friends with people who were twenty or thirty years older than I was. We competed against each other on even ground. Few sports allow or encourage that environment to happen. What a great experience for a young teenager!

In the PGA Tour's *Partners* magazine, Arnold Palmer was asked what it is about golf that intrigues him. Part of his answer had to do with friendships made: "Think how many people you've met and made friends with because you play golf. I don't care where you are or the sport you're in, it can't compare. Golf is a world in itself."

# Enjoyment Comes from a Healthy Lifestyle

Being able to get out and play golf in the fresh air and walking, if possible, is going to help your quality of life. Try to adopt the attitude that golf is a game that is fun. Allow this to happen and golf will de-pressurize you. Hitting the golf ball, going and finding it no matter where it ends up, hitting it again and having fun doing it—while enjoying the people you're with—is as good as life gets.

Sometimes, to take even more pressure away, I recommend not keeping score. Forget about the score. Focus on having fun, playing golf, and enjoying your walk. Is there anything more enjoyable than the serenity of a beautiful environment?

# Enjoyment Comes from Being Part of the History of Golf

Golf is a sport that has been passed down from generation to generation. It's a sport with an illustrious past. All of us, regardless of our skill level, who uphold the traditions of golf and have its passion in our souls are part of the lineage of golf.

We are not only participants but witnesses to the evolving history of the sport. It's a game with great players of the past, present, and future. You may have watched or read about the great amateur Bobby Jones, seen the legendary charges of Arnold Palmer, or the incredible victories of Jack Nicklaus.

On television you may have seen the unforgettable chip shot of Tom Watson's winning the 1982 U.S. Open and Tiger Woods' amazing performance as he won his first Masters. The battles between Annika Sorenstam and Karrie Webb will be part of golf's history. All of it is there for us to enjoy.

# Golf: The Next Generation

Just as it was passed on to us, we all have the responsibility of passing on our enjoyment of the sport to the next generation. Part 6 deals with teaching children to play golf, but I think the best way for them to develop a sense of enjoyment for the game is to observe us.

I've had the incredible opportunity of learning the traditions from one of golf's strongest pillars, Arnold Palmer. He's someone who has made golf history. He's someone who believes in traditions and etiquette, and for me to be able to be in his presence and learn firsthand has been an unbelievable experience. He lives the passion of the game and it's infectious when you're in his aura.

As a result, I will continue to pass that on to my children and the people I work with. This is what makes golf a special sport and game.

# Golf's Wonderful Traditions

*"In the fields called the Links, the citizens of Edinburgh divert themselves at a game called Golf, in which they use a curious kind of bat tipped with horn and small elastic balls of leather, stuffed with feathers."*

**Tobias Smollett Humphrey**

*"How could golf survive and flourish through the centuries, being passed down from generation to generation? The answer—tradition."*

**Brad Brewer**

Some scholars trace the origins of golf back to the time of the Roman Empire and a game called *paganica*. The French developed a game called *jeu de mail* and the Dutch played *kolven*. However, most golf historians believe the Scots should be credited with the game we know today as golf. In Scotland, golf was originally played on seaside links. The Scots took their skills, along with their passion for the game, with them all over the world. They developed the first golf clubs and balls and established standards and rules that are still observed today. Reading about the fascinating origins of the sport is time well spent. (Included in the Resources is a list of interesting books on the subject.)

The question is—how could golf survive and flourish through the centuries as it was passed down from generation to generation? The answer is—tradition. And what a rich and wonderful tradition it is!

# Golf: The Sport of Honor

Perhaps golf's finest tradition is honor. Playing by the rules and observing proper golfing etiquette are two examples. Golfers usually are the first to find their own ball and honor requires not cheating by moving it—unless permitted by the rules. In some cases, when a golfer inadvertently moves a ball while in the act of addressing it, honor dictates calling a penalty on yourself. I can't think of any other sport where there is such a reliance on the honor of the participants. Maybe that's why the game has endured over centuries.

**HISTORICAL HIGHLIGHT**

Scottish officers fighting in the Revolutionary War brought golf to America. The first organized club is believed to have been the South Carolina Golf Club, formed in 1786. However, the popularity of American golf began with the 1892 formation of the St. Andrews Club at Yonkers, set in an apple orchard overlooking the Hudson River and the Palisades of New Jersey. It took only a day to lay the course out between the apple trees.

Golfing immortal Bobby Jones once penalized himself a stroke that cost him the tournament. His comment was: "You might as well praise a man for not robbing a bank."

Keeping your own score is a necessity of the game and honestly writing it down validates the honor and trust of the sport. Etiquette, or our behavior, on the course is also an important part of golf's tradition. We all must be careful not to have a detrimental effect on any other golfer's game. We'll look at rules and etiquette in depth later in this chapter.

# Golf's Special Language

Just as it's advisable to learn the relevant computer jargon before you navigate around with software, the same is true with golf. Many of the terms and phrases first used by the caddies walking the links of The Royal and Ancient St. Andrews in Scotland are still used today. Others have been added as the sport evolved.

Can you match the following definitions with their golf terms? Beginning golfers should find this a lot of fun.

| Definitions | Terms |
|---|---|
| 1. A ball that was struck above its center causing it to skid along the ground | a. scramble |
| 2. Hitting the ground before hitting the ball | b. pin |
| 3. Taking an additional shot from the same location | c. skull |
| 4. A ball partially buried in a sand hazard | d. dance floor |
| 5. The part of the club that rests on the ground | e. sole |
| 6. A type of competition where all members of the team hit a ball from the same location for every shot | f. chili-dip |
| 7. The flag and pole that you see on the green and in the hole | g. mulligan |
| 8. The green | h. fried egg |
| 9. A short but high golf shot that is used around the green | i. lob |

*Answers:*  1.c 2.f 3.g 4.h 5.e 6.a 7.b 8.d 9.i

Some golfing terms have colorful stories behind them. The term bogey, which means one stroke over par, can be traced to Major Charles Wellman who played in the early 1880s in Norfolk, England. He referred to a then-current music hall song, "Hush, hush, hush. Here comes the Bogey man, he'll catch you if he can."

From that time on "Colonel Bogey" became an imaginary player held to play every hole on the course in standard stroke score. In 1895 the term was amended to mean that bogey "is not meant to be an impossible score. Rather a bogey would be a score that could be made by an ordinary player, not playing ideally well but without a single big mistake."

To really be able to understand the game of golf and its rules, it's important to have a pretty good knowledge of the language. For definitions of most of the golfing terms you should know, please consult the Glossary at the end of this book.

# Rules All Golfers Follow

Earlier in this chapter we touched on the importance of golf rules. The original rules came from the Scots and, in retrospect, what incredible foresight they had. The rules ensured that wherever golf was played, it would be played the same way. The Royal and Ancient Golf Club in Scotland and the United States Golf Association are partners in making sure the game and its great traditions continue to be upheld. The focus of both organizations is to ensure the rules do not waver. Can you imagine the chaos that would exist if the rules were subject to arbitrary interpretation? Unfortunately, many golfers think of rules as referring only to penalties, when actually using a rule may end up saving you a stroke.

# The United States Golf Association (USGA)

Dedicated to the promotion and conservation of the best interests of golf, the USGA is guided by its 16-member Executive Committee, which is the organization's policy-making board. The USGA represents more than 8,400 member clubs and courses. Thirty committees, made up of over 1,000 volunteer men and women, augment the executive committee. All of the volunteers donate their time and pay their own expenses.

Over the years the USGA slowly refines *The Rules of Golf*, which are strictly adhered to by both amateurs and professionals. The Rules are a balanced code that carefully guards the traditions of the game. Every four years, the USGA and Royal and Ancient (R&A) have a rules conference during the Walker Cup Match when it is played in Great Britain. By agreement between both organizations, this is the only time rules may be amended.

The USGA always attempts to respond to inquiries regarding the rules. Problems and situations encountered by golfers around the country are collected and published in the *Decisions on the Rules of Golf*. This annually updated book is printed and distributed by the USGA and the R&A worldwide.

 **Role in Handicapping**

The USGA Handicap System was established to allow golfers of different abilities to enjoy competing against each other on relatively equal terms. The system assigns a numerical handicap to a golfer based on a submitted number of scorecards. After being assigned a handicap, golfers consult their scorecard's handicap line and are allowed to deduct strokes that represent their handicap number or below. We'll look at handicaps in the next chapter.

## Why You Should Join the USGA

I hope you're beginning to understand the importance of the USGA to all of us who play golf. The USGA is also responsible for holding U.S. Open Competitions for both amateur and combined amateur and professional players. In addition, the USGA is on the forefront of improving the playing conditions for all of us. As a result of grants to various colleges and universities, new types of grass and management techniques have been developed. In all, the USGA has spent $23 million dollars on research to improve turf for golf.

You will enjoy *Golf Journal,* the USGA Publication. Golf House, located in Far Hills, New Jersey, is a must-see if you're in the New York–New Jersey area. The museum contains artifacts and memorabilia tracing the history of the game from its origins to the present. Over 8,000 books dedicated to golf comprise the library.

More than 740,000 people are members of the USGA. Arnold Palmer has served as National Chairman since the program's inception. You can contact the USGA for more information on becoming a member by calling them at 800-223-0041 or by contacting their Web site: http://www.usga/index.html.

# Golf Etiquette for
## 2000 and Beyond

In the new millennium, golf will face incredible opportunities and challenges. The sport is booming: More and more people are taking up the game. As a result, the traditions of the sport may be tested as never before. How we dress, behave, and play the game will be the determining factors if we are to take our place in golf's history in a positive way.

How we dress is a very important part of golf etiquette. It's a courtesy to others that we dress comfortably—but not in a sloppy manner. Most golf facilities request (and some require) that a collared shirt be worn. The length of shorts, if that's your preference, also has certain required measurements. You'll encounter dress codes like this at most private clubs.

Look at dress codes in a positive light. They help preserve important elements of the ambiance of the game. Just as the USGA staunchly maintains *The Rules of Golf,* all of us should do our very best to keep the game on the highest level possible. Relax a rule here and there and, before you know it, the sport will never be the same.

## Let's All Help Eliminate Slow Play

If you watch the pros on TV, you may pick up the impression that you have an unlimited amount of time to hit a shot or play the round. You watch them walk back and forth on the green, reading the putt from every conceivable angle. It seems they take countless practice strokes before finally making the putt. Realizing the wrong impression this slow play is fostering in the mind of the golfer/viewer, the PGA Tour is confronting the problem head-on. Pros who are playing slowly are warned by the PGA and penalized for slow play.

Why can't you just take as much time as you want? Think of it in these terms: Slow play means fewer people will have an opportunity to play each day. With so many new players looking for tee times, slow play creates a bottleneck of frustration. I'm not saying you should rush, but strive for a round that takes no more than four and a half hours maximum. I wish you could cut it to four, but players in front of you play a big role.  All of us can, and must, do our best to eliminate slow play. Here's a couple of ways you can speed up the game without affecting your concentration.

## Brad's R$_X$ for Curing Slow Play

1. Always play Ready Golf. Be prepared to hit your shot when it's your turn. As soon as you reach your ball, start gathering all the information you need such as the yardage to the hole and wind direction. Decide on a club, take your practice swings, and be ready to hit when it's your turn.

2. If you're walking, go directly to your ball or get as close to it as you can without affecting any golfer who is behind you. A common cause of slow play is a group of golfers walking en masse to each ball instead of each player walking toward his or her own. You can talk to each other between holes or at other convenient times.

3. If you're riding in a cart, the golfer who is the farthest away from the hole should be dropped off with several clubs. It doesn't make a difference who the designated driver is.

4. If you were riding in a cart and were the first to play your shot, start walking toward your partners so they won't have to drive all the way back to pick you up.

5. Limit the amount of time you search for a lost ball. If a partner has to return to the tee to hit another ball, it's okay to hit your shot rather than wait for him or her to re-hit and then come back to the second ball.

6. Don't play a second ball just because you may have hit a bad shot.

7. If the group behind you is playing faster and you have an open hole ahead of your group, please invite them to play through.

8. Let's all become guardians of the game as we work with each other to ensure golf's future. Remember, I'm not suggesting you rush— just be ready to hit your ball when it's your turn.

## Let's All Leave the Course in Better Shape Than We Found It

My friend and co-writer Steve Hosid learned to play golf in a very special way. His teacher, golf pro Augie Nordone, believed junior players should learn about etiquette and how to take care of the course before he would teach them how to hit the ball.

For the first several lessons, Steve was taught correctly how to repair ball marks on the greens, how to replace divots on the fairways, and how to behave on the course. Only when Augie was satisfied that Steve could be a golfer who would leave the course in better shape than he found it did he actually teach him how to play.

## If Arnold Palmer Can Do It—So Can I

While growing up in Latrobe, Pennsylvania, Arnold Palmer's father, Deacon Palmer, did an excellent job of teaching young Arnie how to take care of the golf course. I've played with him many times and also watched him play hundreds of rounds. To this day, he still goes out of his way to pick up a piece of paper, a blowing paper cup, or even someone's carelessly left cigarette butt. Many times, in fact, after 18 holes of golf his caddie's golf cart looks as if it could use two large plastic bags to unload all the things Arnold picked up off the course during the round.

Leaving the course in better shape than you found it should be a goal for all serious golfers. You may not financially own the course but, spiritually, all of us do. If we all treated the course in this way, think of the positive effect it would have. Nothing is worse than walking onto a green and seeing a fresh ball mark that someone selfishly didn't take the time to fix. All too often you will find unrepaired ball marks on every green. Why not be a guardian of the game and fix a few while you're waiting to putt?

# Correctly Repairing Divots and Ball Marks

Here's how to repair a fairway divot and fix a ball mark on the green. Opportunities for both always happen during the normal course of play.

## Fairway Divots

Sometimes a player removes a section of turf while making the shot. This is normal.

To correctly replace a fairway divot, locate the piece of turf that flew away as you hit your ball.

Place the divot back in the area it came from, just like fitting a puzzle piece. The grass is still alive and will continue to grow.

On some golf courses, a sand and seed mixture is provided on your golf cart. Use the mixture to fill in the still bare section of the divot area.

## Ball Marks

Walk on any green and you will see ball marks that have been thoughtlessly left unrepaired. Some marks are also the result of golfers trying to repair the green but not knowing how to correctly do it.

This is a ball mark. Properly fixed, it will heal itself in a very short time.

Insert a pronged divot repair tool around the outside of the ball mark, gently pushing the damaged portion of the green toward the center of the mark.

After you gently push the high area down and level it with your putter, the indentation caused by the ball is gone. The green will repair itself in a short time thanks to your help.

# Brad's Tips for All Golfers

1. We're all part of golf's history.

2. Let's all work together to eliminate slow play.

3. Leave the golf course in better shape than you found it.

# Enjoying the Game of Golf

*"Never bet with anyone you meet on the first tee who has a deep suntan, a 1-iron in the bag, and squinty eyes."*

### Dave Marr

*"I believe Golf's handicap system has been the driving force behind the game's growth and popularity. Quite simply, it levels the playing field allowing golfers with diverse abilities the opportunity of competing evenly. In what other recreational activity can you do that?"*

### Brad Brewer

**V**ery few sports offer the opportunity for diversity of competition like golf. While you may be familiar with the professional side of the sport through weekly televised tournaments, golfers of all skill levels participate in various competitive formats. In fact, if you're a high handicap golfer, golf is about the only sport that allows you to compete against the most skilled players in the game on approximately even terms. How is that possible?

# What's a Handicap?

Some people think of a handicap only in terms of horse racing. They read the Daily Racing Form to handicap the winner of a horse race. In golf, a *handicap* is a number that will vary depending on your level of play. Golfers use a handicap to compete with others on a level playing field.

## Using Your Handicap in Match Play

As Steve's handicap is 12, he can deduct a stroke for each hole that has a number of 12 or less in the handicap row of the golf score card pictured below. Steve shot a bogey 5 on the first hole (a bogey means one stroke over par), so he deducted a stroke and nets a par 4. A more skilled golfer with a lower handicap would not be able to deduct as many strokes. I shot a par 4 and can't deduct a shot, so we tied or halved the hole.

---

### HISTORICAL HIGHLIGHT

Golf historians believe the term *handicap* was taken from horse racing. Matches were handicapped (arranged) to compete for prizes.

## Using Your Handicap in Stroke Play

Still another way to play competitively is to deduct each golfer's handicap from his or her gross score (actual total number of strokes for the round). Your *gross score*, the actual number of your strokes for 18 holes, may not be competitive until you subtract your handicap to find your competitive net score.

|  | Steve | Brad |
|---|---|---|
| Gross score | 81 | 70 |
| Handicap | -12 | +2 |
| Net Score | 69 | 72 |

Steve had a good round, shooting below the average score his handicap was based on. (He must have glanced ahead and read a few chapters.) Because I'm a plus 2 handicap, I can't deduct any strokes but I have to *give Steve two additional strokes,* adding them to my own score—so he beat me, shooting a net 69. Although my golf ability level is much higher than Steve's, the handicap system allowed us to compete against each other in a friendly competition.

## How Do I Get a USGA Handicap, Brad?

If you want to establish a USGA handicap, you begin by submitting five score cards to your local pro shop (if it offers the handicap service). If the cards are from different courses, be sure to include the Slope and Index rating for each course played. The lowest score shot will be the basis for your handicap. The number of strokes you were above par will be factored together with the Slope and Index number for the course and a handicap number assigned. From that point on, the lowest scores from half the cards you submit will be used to keep your handicap current.

What happens if you travel and want to use your handicap on a different course? The USGA has developed the Slope system to assign golf courses a rating based on their degree of difficulty. Golfers can adjust their handicaps for the course they're playing. For example, if you want to play a course that is rated more difficult than the course used to establish your handicap, you will be able to delete more strokes. If the course is rated easier, you won't be able to deduct as many. For more information on Slope ratings and the handicap system, contact the USGA at 800-223-0041.

Once you've established your handicap, it's important that you keep submitting your scorecards so your handicap can be correctly adjusted and will reflect your game's current skill level. That's how it's supposed to work, since golf is a sport of honor. Unfortunately, some individuals sometimes turn in score cards with higher scores in order to receive a higher handicap than the true level of their game warrants. These golfers are commonly called *sandbaggers*. When they play and shoot their normal scores, the fraudulent handicap allows them to deduct extra strokes. These individuals are usually quickly discovered and chastised. Remember, while golf is supposed to be fun, its future depends on everyone's integrity. Let's all do our part and play by the rules.

As another example of handicapping, let's say we play the full 18 holes together sometime and decide we want to compete on a stroke play basis. I'm a plus 2 handicap golfer and you may be an 18 handicap. As an 18, on average you bogey or shoot 1 stroke over par on each hole. Using the handicap system, I have to give you 20 strokes off the score you shoot. This means I would have to shoot par or better on every hole to have a chance for a win. That's a very challenging match for both of us.

This level of competetion could never happen in tennis. If one player's skill level is much better than the other's, you can't have a match that's fun for both players. In reality, what unfortunately happens is that you tend to play with the same group of people all the time. Thanks to golf's handicap system, golfers can play with anyone and still have fun. The more people you play with, the more new friends and experiences you'll have.

# Playing a
## Scramble Format

If you've never played a Scramble format, I guarantee you will love it. Instead of each player in your foursome playing his or her own shot, the group's best shot is selected and all players play from that position to hit their next shot. This fun format is usually played in charity tournaments, business outings, and other events. Here's a shot-by-shot example of how a Scramble format works on a par 5 hole.

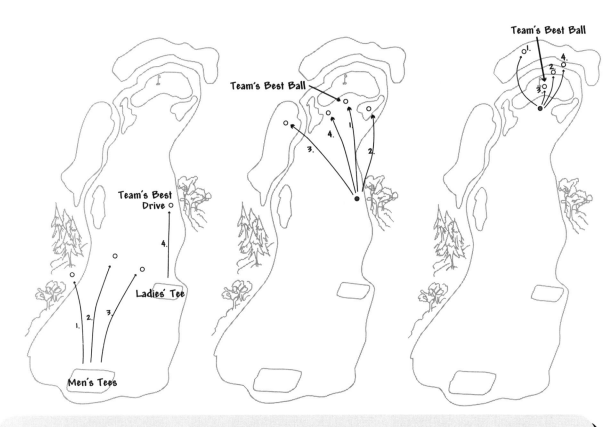

All players in the foursome or team hit their drives. If it's a mixed foursome, men hit from their tees, ladies from their tees. Then the team's best drive is selected.

All players hit their second shot from the team's best shot. The best second shot of the foursome (Golfer 1) is selected.

All players in the foursome hit their third shots from the team's best shot. Golfer 3 chipped near the pin setting up a birdie (1 stroke under par) opportunity for the team. All members of the group will putt from that spot.

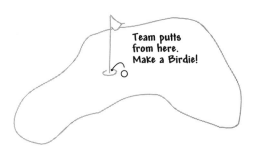

When you're on the green, the best ball position is chosen and all players putt from that position. A player from the team made the putt for a team birdie. If all team members had missed, the best position would have been chosen and they would putt for a par.

## FEEL FEEDBACK

*Remember the feeling of putting in a Scramble format and try to feel the same way when playing for your own score. This **putt to make attitude** will result in more holed putts and lower scores.*

Scrambles give all players a chance to help their team and maybe even face different types of shots and course positions than normally experienced. Higher handicappers will be playing from positions they only dream of. This can serve as a way for them to learn how important it is to have a good-quality golf swing, giving them more distance and allowing them to play the game from a different level. The whole Scramble format is one of fun and should be free from pressure. If you hit a bad shot, just pick it up and hit your next shot from the team's best position.

This is also a great format for beginning golfers. You can make a good chip or make a nice putt—your good shots will reward your entire team.

All golfers can benefit from this format as it helps teach players to be more aggressive as they play. Since you don't have the pressure of "If I make a mistake I'm going to be penalized," you can just go for it. Having the freedom to be aggressive in all phases of the game is a wonderful learning tool. For example, take an aggressive line off the tee—don't just play it safe. Use the un-pressured freedom to become aggressive. Your risk may be rewarded with a good shot and will give you confidence to play with newfound freedom. So unleash it and go with the flow!

In some cases, women may have the driving advantage and really help their team get off to a good start. Since the ladies' tees are closer to the hole, hitting a good solid drive gives the team an outstanding position to play the second shot.

You'll find your putting always seems to improve when you're playing in a Scramble format. Since you know a teammate will putt next if you don't make it, tension seems to disappear and you putt in a relaxed manner, intent on making it.

Once on the green, you can help your team by holing your putt. The team scores are usually birdies or pars. So when the results are posted, you'll see some incredible team scores way under par. If you see a team with way over par scores, this book would be a very worthwhile gift!

# What's a Shotgun for?
## To Shoot Birdies?

Not exactly! Tournament or outing organizers use a shotgun to begin an event so that everyone can finish at about the same time. No, the rangers don't use a shotgun to eliminate slow-playing golfers, at least not at our club.

Just as pellets from a shotgun scatter, golfers go to different assigned holes to begin the tournament. Since it would take far too long for all players and teams to tee off from the first hole, this way 18 foursomes (72 players) can tee off at the same time, each foursome starting at a different hole. In some cases, you may even play a double shotgun where two teams begin at each of the 18 holes.

If you are assigned to start on the 5th hole, for example, you play all the way through to the 18th hole and then continue on and play holes 1 to 4. You mark down the appropriate score for each hole, but just play them in a different order. Remember to begin scoring your card on the appropriate hole and avoid a common mistake. This format allows all golfers to finish within the same time period.

## Skins Game

Each year you see stars from the various tours play a Skins format on television. They play for incredible amounts of money with each hole being worth a certain amount. Should no participant win the hole, the amount is added to the value of the next hole. For instance, if a hole pays $10,000 to the winner and each golfer in the group shoots the same score, the hole is tied (halved) and the $10,000 is added to the next hole. If that hole is also worth $10,000, the winner of the next hole collects $20,000.

Back to reality for the rest of us. I'm not advocating wagering when you play golf, but sometimes it's a friendly part of the game. You could play for matchsticks, cocktail napkins, fifty cents or a dollar a hole, or whatever. Here's what the USGA says about wagering as published in *The Rules of Golf*:

> *"The United States Golf Association does not object to the wagering*
> *among individuals or teams of golfers when wagering is limited*
> *to the players. The sole source of all money won by the players*
> *is advanced by the players and the primary purpose is the playing*
> *of the game for enjoyment."*

A Skins format, in a friendly foursome, is a lot of fun and gives you a real sense of competition. Combine that by factoring in handicaps for your group and you're in for a lot of competitive play. *Remember, don't ever risk more matchsticks than you can afford to lose.*

## What about Nassau?

It's a lovely Caribbean island with white sandy beaches. Seriously, golfers also use the term Nassau for making the round more interesting. It's actually a three-part wager. An equal amount is wagered on the first nine holes, the second nine holes, and on the complete round.

## Stableford Scoring System

Stableford is a very popular and really unique scoring system that features a twist on the *low score wins in golf* rule. It's commonly used in Europe and Australia. In the Stableford scoring format, points are awarded for scores below par with points deducted for those scores above par, according to the following table.

| Score | Points awarded or subtracted |
|---|---|
| Double Bogeys or more | 0 |
| Bogey | +1 |
| Par | +2 |
| Birdie | +3 |
| Eagle | +4 |
| Double Eagle | +5 |

The winner accumulates the most points at the end of the round. The PGA Tour's International Tournament uses a modified version of this format every year and the pros enjoy the change from the regular tournament scoring system. You might occasionally enjoy using a Stableford scoring system in your weekly game too.

## Snake

If you tend to 3-putt a lot (which means it takes you three putts to put the ball in the hole when you're on the green), you will be a real snake charmer in this game. The first player to 3-putt gets the snake (a rubber one or an imaginary snake, depending on how realistic you want to get) until another player 3-putts. This goes on until the end of the round. The player with the snake at the end of the round loses to the other players.

Some of the other games you can play are Wolf, Bingle, Bangle, Bungle, and Trash—or you can make up some of your own. The intent of all of these games is to have fun. I've included some books you may want to consult on a variety of golf games in the Resources section of the book.

## Let's Talk about Competitive Events

If you want to get more involved in competitive golf, I suggest starting at the local golf course or at the local club level. It doesn't have to be a country club—many public golfing facilities conduct competitive events open to golfers of all skill levels. Go to the municipal golf course in your area and ask for their calendar of competitive events. Some facilities have a notice board, usually around the pro shop area, with upcoming tournament information posted.

**BRAD EXPLAINS**

*Here's a quick primer on the language of golf:*

*Par*
*The number of strokes a skilled player takes on a given hole.*

*Birdie*
*1 stroke under par*

*Eagle*
*2 strokes under par*

*Double Eagle*
*3 strokes under par*

*Bogey*
*1 stroke over par*

*Double Bogey*
*2 strokes over par*

Most of these events are set up in different handicap flights. This is like having tournaments within tournaments and means you'll be competing against similarly skilled golfers. Handicaps are not deducted from your score—they're just utilized to place you into the correct flight. Once the event begins, it's a stroke format. The score you shoot is the score that is counted. The lowest total score in each category wins the flight championship.

**BRAD EXPLAINS**

*Here's a list of flights by handicap. This is the usual range but it can vary.*

| Flight | Handicap Range |
|---|---|
| *A Flight* | *8 handicap or lower* |
| *B Flight* | *9 handicap to 14 handicap* |
| *C Flight* | *15 handicap to 20 handicap* |
| *D Flight* | *above 20 handicap* |

# Starting a Competitive Career

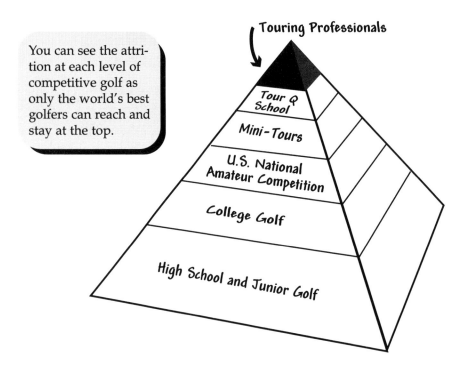

You can see the attrition at each level of competitive golf as only the world's best golfers can reach and stay at the top.

Touring Professionals

Tour Q School

Mini-Tours

U.S. National Amateur Competition

College Golf

High School and Junior Golf

If you were to ask some of today's pros how they progressed through the ranks of competitions to reach the PGA (Professional Golf Association) or LPGA (Ladies' Professional Golf Association) Tours, chances are their answers would all be pretty similar. They all probably started by playing competitively against a friend. Maybe it was for just a soda or a sleeve of golf balls, or even just bragging rights—but they began to learn how to compete against another golfer.

Social competition was followed by club-level competitions that offered junior events, a good chance to compare their abilities against others. They started to develop the disciplined tournament mentality, learning how to play by the rules, honestly mark their score cards, and compete against the very best golfers at their age level.

Chances are they also competed on their high school golf teams and in the USGA Junior Amateur golf programs. Local matches against other schools are followed by regional matches. The very best teams compete at the state level. Here they got to play on wonderful golf courses against the very best competition in their states. Today's pros learned that it takes more than a perfect golf swing to be a good golfer as they adjusted themselves to the new environment.

The very best high school golfers are offered college scholarships. Wonderful scholarships are available for boys and girls who show they have the ability to win or place high in their high school competitions and reach the national level in the USJA (United States Junior Amateur) events. Collegiate coaches seek out young golfers who show they have what it takes to successfully compete.

While in college, today's pros faced some of their future Tour competitors in conference and national team competitions. Some of the great college players like Arizona State's Phil Mickelson, Stanford's Tiger Woods, and Texas's Justin Leonard also entered, played, and won the U.S. Open Amateur Championship while in college. Tiger Woods also won several U.S. Junior Amateur Open Championships along the way. The coveted U.S. Open Championships are open to all through various regional and national qualification events.

A look at both the players on the PGA and LPGA Tours shows the important role college golf played in their careers. The very best players from all parts of the globe come to America to play college golf. Along with a superb education in the classroom, they also learned what it takes to play golf and be successful at the highest levels of competition. After graduation comes the real world and the decision: "Am I good enough to make the Tour?" At this step there are thousands of good competitive golfers all with the same dream—making the Tour. Some players qualify and play in *Golf's minor leagues,* the mini-tour events.

The mini-tours pretty much resemble the PGA Tour of yesterday. Golfers get together and share rides from tournament to tournament and cope with meager hotel accommodations. They learn how to live on the road fending for themselves without a college coach to smooth the way. They're trying to survive in a very competitive arena for small purses (the amount of money paid to the winners and top finishers). It's a big change and a huge learning experience. The goal is to enter the Tour's qualifying tournaments, sometimes called *Q School*. This pressure-filled series of tournaments are the gates to Valhalla for all serious competitive golfers, a coveted card allowing you to play on the PGA or LPGA Tours. With only forty slots open for PGA Tour cards, the competition is fierce. Every driving range in America is littered with the broken dreams of those whose games aren't quite good enough to handle the demands and pressures of golf played at the top professional level.

Mike Schmit, the Baseball Hall of Fame third baseman, is an outstanding golfer. Naturally, some writers have speculated that he might try to seek a card for the Senior PGA Tour when he turns 50. Asked what he has to do to get his card, Schmit jokingly but honestly replied: "First, I have to shoot par, and then I have to shoot in the 60s for any chance." Being a good golfer doesn't necessarily qualify you to be a tour professional. There are lots of good golfers, but the touring pros are the very best—and they proved it to get to the Tour.

Once players have qualified and fulfilled their dream of making the Tour, staying there and keeping their card is the primary concern. Robert Damron joined the tour after the 1997 Tour school. When friends congratulated him, he replied: "Thanks, what it means to me is, I now have a chance to fight the lions."

Keeping the level of competition at its highest levels, the PGA Tour only allows the top 125 money-winning players an automatic Tour Card for the next season. Some exemptions are granted for victories or special circumstances. But if a touring pro does not earn enough money to make the top 125, back to Tour school they go to face the thousands of other golfers with the same dream of earning one of the forty new Tour Cards for the next season.

# Using Golf to Improve Your Odds at Business

*"Playing golf helped me relax and concentrate. And the irony is, I made lots of money on the golf course—making deals and coming up with ideas."*

from **Donald Trump's**
Top Ten comeback tips: Play Golf was tip #1

*If you are involved in business and play golf, you may be surprised at how beneficial the sport can be to you on a personal level.*

**Brad Brewer**

**G**olf is the corporate sport of America. Just look at the professional tournament schedule: Businesses not only sponsor the event but company names are part of the event title—sometimes the only identification of the event itself. "I'm going to watch the Honda, the Office Depot, or the Sara Lee" are common references to well-known events on the PGA and LPGA tours. Here's a partial listing of the events that take place during the opening months of the tours. Can you match the event with where it's played?

---

### Match the Tournament with the Location

| EVENT | CITY |
|---|---|
| 1. Mercedes Championships (PGA) | a. Orlando, Florida |
| 2. Health South Inaugural (LPGA) | b. La Jolla, California |
| 3. Mastercard Championship (Senior PGA) | c. Key Biscayne, Florida |
| 4. The Office Depot (LPGA) | d. Palm Beach Gardens, Florida |
| 5. Buick Invitational (PGA) | e. Carlsbad, California |
| 6. Royal Caribbean Classic (Senior PGA) | f. Big Island of Hawaii |

*Answers:*    1.e  2.a  3.f  4.d  5.b  6.c

---

Tournaments are the obvious and visible signs of the synergy between golf and business. Furthermore, this synergy goes way beyond commercials and name recognition. If you are a businessperson and play golf, you may be surprised at how beneficial the sport can be to you on a personal level.

# Learn about Your Customers

Golf is a great tool for learning about the people you do business with. If you're interviewing a candidate for a job, buying products from a vendor, considering entering into a business partnership with an acquaintance, or thinking about lending money to someone, golf strips away the polished veneer and gives you an insight into the person's true character.

Playing 18 holes takes four-plus hours. During the time you spend together on the golf course, it's difficult to hide one's true self. Golf draws out an individual's real personality and any traits that may not show up when you read a resume or sit at the boardroom table with your "game face" on. On the other hand, if you're the one sending an embellished resume to a prospective employer, beware! Out

on the golf course, you too will be identified by your actions, your demeanor, the way you act under pressure, and by how you work within the etiquette and traditions of the game.

Numerous qualities are revealed on the golf course—both your own and other people's! I'm not talking about how anyone plays the game. Golfing ability and talent have nothing to do with it! In a business situation, skill is not even relevant. All golfers have different skill levels as far as their ability to hit the golf ball. I'm referring to how people handle adversity when a shot lands behind a tree or out of bounds. How do they respond? How do they rebound from that situation?

You can see how competitive people are or you may identify self-destructive tendencies. We hope to see constructive tendencies in someone's ability to solve problems in response to specific situations on the golf course. A sense of humor, or lack of it, can be observed under many circumstances. The game of golf will definitely communicate these personality traits during the four hours it takes to play. That's one of the beautiful things and one of the advantages about playing golf with people. It reduces their inhibitions, allowing them to be free and natural.

# Build Business Relationships

There is no better way to build a relationship with a potential client (or with someone in your company you professionally need to bond with) than by playing golf together. The business world is full of seminars and retreats led by motivational experts whose main purpose is to help people learn about relationship building and problem solving. The beauty of business-related golf is that, during the four-plus hours you spend on a golf course together, you are sharing a common experience in a relaxing setting.

Take a corporate CEO, for example, who may appear "dry" as far as personality is concerned, due to talking mostly about facts and figures. Corporate executives focus on business aspects, so it's difficult to get to know their true personalities. Normally, you can't get inside an executive's head or get a handle on what makes him or her "tick." Take that same individual out of the business arena and onto a golf course and you will discover the real personality inside the suit. He or she will be in "recovery mode," relaxing and enjoying themselves. Quite often, setting this casual tone allows you to build the relationship you're looking for. People usually let down their guard on the golf course. If your customer does this, it can be a real benefit—you'll be able to build a friendship that can enhance your business relationship.

# Golf: A Tension Release Valve

Golf is a perfect opportunity to leave the stress and frustrations of your job behind as you go out and do the recovery you need in order to perform better at your job. Often we are frustrated to the point where the ability to focus and flow in our business is hindered and we waste time trying to regenerate and refocus.

Even if you don't have four hours to play a full round, you can go to the driving range for half an hour and hit some golf balls, then grab a healthy turkey sandwich and head back to the office for your one o'clock appointment. Now that's a lunch break! Sometimes you can play nine holes during a two-hour extended lunch period. The main thing is to get away from your office environment, recover, and rejuvenate.

A wonderful way to get rid of built-up tension is to play at the end of the day, even for a few holes. It's great exercise out in the fresh air and a positive way to release accumulated tension. I'll guarantee it will help you recharge and refocus. And, back in your business arena, you'll have gained a competitive edge from the time you spent away from the office environment relaxing with golf.

## Scramble Your Way to Team Building

Even when you play with your customary partners in a weekend foursome, golf is mostly played as an individual activity. It comes down to playing your own ball for your own score. In business, too much of a maverick environment can result in a lack of common direction for a company. Team building—building activities and teams to solve problems—is a consistent theme in corporate America.

In the speeches I give around the country to corporations, I offer an alternative to retreats and seminars as a way to build the team mentality. I recommend one of the most enjoyable team-building activities I know—playing the Scramble format described in Chapter 3. Playing with your company associates in this format promotes a completely different outlook: No longer are individual players only concerned with individual effort.

Regardless of your ability, you're going to participate in helping your team. Each member of your group has a skill level, even if it's just the ability to convey enthusiastic moral support—a trait, I might add, that is very important to the team's success potential. Because "attitude" is everything! It helps the team focus on the goal together. While having fun, all the participants play for the best team score in order to beat the other teams.

Team members often find themselves in new situations compared to when they play for their own score. Most likely, they'll find themselves in different positions and playing different shots.  Scramble is an activity that draws everyone together and makes each individual feel part of the team. And perhaps it just might provide that extra little spark for an associate who is not presently playing golf to decide to take up the game. Golf can help anyone become better at developing the customer relation skills that are so necessary today. People in business can learn about their customers' personality traits or bond with associates they're working with.

# How Some Companies
## Use Golf

You don't have to be associated with a Fortune 500 company to use golf to your advantage. Instead of sponsoring professional tournaments, you can entertain clients or reward associates for outstanding performance with a special round of golf or with a trip to a golf school. Many companies understand the benefit of taking some of their top clients or prospects on a golf outing to a local club or an out-of-town golf resort. It's an outstanding way to build relationships and customer loyalty. Putting the right mix of individuals together helps everyone make new business contacts and, as a result, everyone benefits.

## Golf Schools

The Arnold Palmer Academies around the country are seeing a huge increase in the number of corporate groups booking executive retreats. We're able to tailor golf instruction around meetings and play time on the course. Everyone comes away from the event relaxed, committed to the company's goals, and better golfers.

Usually it's a group consisting of both men and women. In the last few years, our records show that more and more women have become part of executive golf school retreats. Some may have never played golf before and are trying to learn. If a woman is struggling with lessons, their male colleagues lend encouragement, empathy, and respect. This supportive attitude is a result of the same experiences that the men went through while taking up the game, and they admire the new golfer's commitment to learning how to play. An interesting fact is that we usually see quicker learning acceleration from our women clients—for the most part, women are better lesson takers. Let's save that discussion for another time!

## Women Are Vitally Important to Corporate Golf

More and more women are climbing the corporate ladder and becoming involved in golf outings. The Executive Woman's Golf League is growing quickly around the country. Check the Resources section for their national address and phone number. Many national advertisers (like Cadillac) targeting executive women with their products reach them through golf-related advertising and promotions as well as through executive women's golf outings. This is an affirmation as to how important and valuable this segment of the market has become.

Women executives are realizing how beneficial golf is as a business tool. It provides a common interest with their male counterparts—the "ice-breaking" experience that begins to build a stronger business relationship. I've been told by some of America's top women executives that golf gatherings allow them to network while at the same time recover from their stressful lifestyles.

Arnold Palmer presents a $550,000 check from Champions for Children that will be used to build a pediatric heart center at Orlando's Arnold Palmer Hospital for Children and Women.

# Business and Charities Benefit from Golf

Charities are the primary beneficiaries for the proceeds from Professional Tour events. You can organize or play in a charitable golf event in your city. In Orlando, Florida, the home of more professional golfers than anywhere else in the country, *The Bert Martin's Champions for Children* annual golf tournament is a shining example of how a community comes together to help a children's hospital. Golfers pay to play in the annual event with the touring professionals from the PGA, LPGA, and Senior PGA tours. Golfers get to play with Arnold Palmer, Scott Hock, Mark O'Meara, Payne Stuart, Dawn Coe Jones, Dow Finsterwald, Steve Lowery, Robert Damron, Bart and Brad Bryant, Kelly Leadbetter, and many other pros residing in the area.

Here Arnold Palmer congratulates and thanks his teammates during Champions for Children.

Executive Director Sherrie Sitaric is interviewed by the Golf Channel during the event.

The proceeds fund specific projects in the hospital that Arnold and Winnie Palmer helped build in Orlando. As a result of the yearly tournament, the Arnold Palmer Hospital for Children and Women has been able to build a pediatric cardiac unit and a cystic fibrosis center, along with other projects, all funded by proceeds from the annual charitable event. I'm honored to have been asked to play as a professional ever since its inception. And, our Academy is becoming more and more involved with the tournament.

While Champions for Children is one of the premier charity events in the country, every event provides an invaluable service to its community. All the golfers who come together to play in the events have their love of golf coupled with a desire to help their communities in common. You'll enjoy playing in them and your company's efforts, through golf, can make a difference in your community!

# PART 2

# Selecting Golf Equipment to Enhance Your Game

*Everything you ever wanted to know about selecting the right equipment just for you is in this section. You'll be an informed consumer next time you're in the market for woods, irons, balls, and the other game-improving necessities. Did you know that the grips that came with your clubs may be too small and could be partly responsible for some faults in your swing?*

*Without changing anything in your swing, using equipment that can help your game is bound to cut some strokes and provide some added distance. Expensive high-tech equipment is not necessarily right for your present game.*

*Low handicappers will find valuable information on club selection too. Degrees of loft are recommended for certain types of play along with some help in deciphering the shaft selection process and clubface inserts.*

*Many golfers think customized equipment is only available for Touring Pros. You probably have expert clubmakers and repair people right in your community. You'll learn how they can help you as you customize your present set of clubs.*

# Let's Start with Your Golf Bag

*"An Ordinary golf bag will cost from two dollars and a half up."*
**Alexander Revell**
in *The Pro and Con of Golf, 1915*

*"Pack your golf bag as you would a suitcase containing everything you might need for your 18-hole golf journey."*
**Brad Brewer**

**M**ost people tend to think of their golf bag as simply a receptacle for carrying clubs and balls. Improving your game, however, requires a new thinking about something even as simple as a golf bag. Just as you prepare and pack for a trip—considering the various weather and temperature conditions you may encounter, I suggest thinking of your golf bag as a case containing everything you might need during your 18-hole golf journey.

The golf bag can carry everything you need.

Golf bag circa 1930. Just enough room to carry clubs and balls.

Today's golf bag construction features plenty of storage space to carry virtually everything you'll need during your round.

Try to anticipate any contingency you may encounter during the four-plus hours of the round. Today's bags provide plenty of pockets with ample space to take care of your needs.  It's true the bag can get heavy, but since most golfers either walk while pulling a cart or ride around the course in a golf cart, the weight should not be a problem. If you like to walk and carry your own bag, obviously weight needs to be a consideration. You can find golf bags that feature lightweight construction and a well-padded shoulder strap. Some even have built-in stands that keep the bag upright when you put it down. Even these smaller bags have enough space to carry whatever you need.

# Wet Weather Gear

Staying dry on the course is extremely important during your round. A big colorful golf umbrella is ideally suited for that purpose. Your golf bag has loops at the top for the handle and a flap at the bottom for the pointed end of the umbrella to fit into so it's always easy to get to.

If you're pulling a cart or walking, use a heavy-duty golf umbrella large enough to keep you and your clubs dry.

Playing in the rain is something most golfers unfortunately shy away from. I'm not talking about a driving rain with thunder and lightning, but the type of light rain that keeps many golfers indoors. However, if you're a competitive golfer who enters tournaments or if you have traveled to Scotland and played where "Old Tom Morris" walked the links, you will play through a heavier shower too. The long pocket of your golf bag that runs from top to bottom is an ideal place to carry a rain suit. The water-resistant pants and jacket will keep you warm and dry. Your golf pro shop or golf specialty store carries rain suits in various price ranges.

Think of playing in the rain as a great opportunity to really improve your game by learning to play within yourself. An added benefit is that you probably won't have to wait for a tee time. So think about preparing for rain as you set up your bag.

# The Large Pocket

Running along the side of your bag is a big pocket. Sometimes the only thing golfers carry in this big space is the travel cover that came with the bag. Here's a diagram with my suggestions of items you should consider taking along on the round.

I've already mentioned the value of including a rain suit in your bag. An extra towel is another item that helps keep both you and your equipment dry in wet weather.

Staying warm is just as important as staying dry. In some climates, it's not unusual to experience a change of temperature during the round. A lightweight wind shirt is made of material that keeps the warmth of your body in but won't inhibit the nice free-flowing swing you're going to develop.

If the day starts out warm but you anticipate that the temperature might drop, consider taking along a sweater or a sweater vest. Don't let colder temperatures negatively affect your positive mental attitude. If you are prepared, it might be just the advantage you need over your competitor.

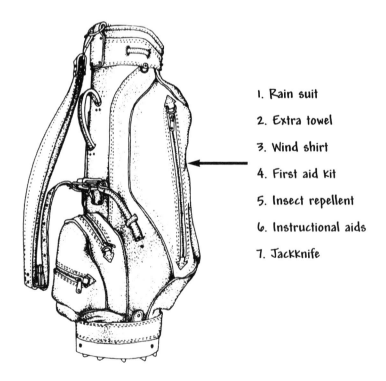

1. Rain suit

2. Extra towel

3. Wind shirt

4. First aid kit

5. Insect repellent

6. Instructional aids

7. Jackknife

## Pack a First Aid Kit

Here's a good idea you might not have thought of. A small utility bag is an ideal way to carry a first aid kit and other items you can find immediately when you need them. How many times have you rummaged through your bag looking for a Band-Aid? If you include them in a small bag that fits nicely in the large pocket, they'll always be easy to get to. Golf doesn't have to be frustrating—just think ahead and be prepared. Here are some additional items you should carry in the small utility bag.

Sunscreen, insect repellent, and lip balm should always be carried in your bag.

## Pack Instructional Aids

Sometimes golfers have found some instructional aids help them when they practice. Depending on the device, the large pocket provides a good place to store them so you know they'll always be with you for a session on the range.

Keep a pocket-size journal in your bag to write down and keep practice notes, lesson tips, and miscellaneous reminders about your golf game. It's good to keep records, so jot down swing thoughts that are working for you.

## The Jackknife

Golfers need to be prepared for any contingency that arises on the course. Purchase a jackknife that has a built in "tool kit" to handle problems that might arise with your equipment. When something needs to be tightened or cut, the small built-in screwdriver or scissors can be enormously beneficial.

# Where Should I Keep My Gloves and Balls?

The pocket that's located right above the vertical pocket is the place to keep the items you'll need the most during the round. Some items you'll carry with you as you play. After the round, transfer the items back to this pocket and you won't have to go searching for them next time.

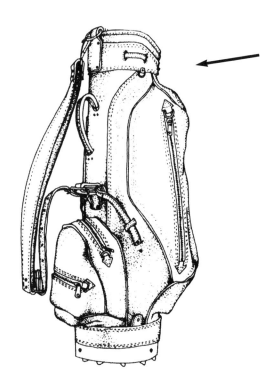

- Extra tees, a ball marker (used when you want to mark the position of your ball on the green) along with a ball mark repair tool should be carried in the top pocket of your golf bag.
- A few golf balls
- Tees
- Coin pouch with ball markers and pennies
- Ball mark repair tool
- Yardage book
- Extra glove
- Two extra pencils and one extra score card
- A "Sharpie Marker"-type pen, in case you run into Arnold Palmer and want his autograph, or if you want to identify your golf balls by putting a special mark on them.

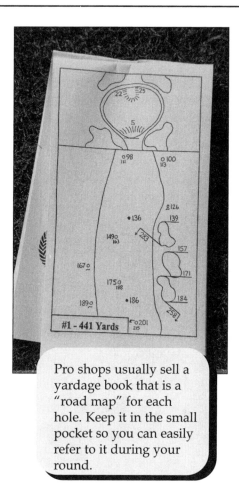

Extra tees, a ball marker (used when you want to mark the position of your ball on the green) along with a ball mark repair tool should be carried in the top pocket of your golf bag.

Pro shops usually sell a yardage book that is a "road map" for each hole. Keep it in the small pocket so you can easily refer to it during your round.

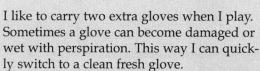

I like to carry two extra gloves when I play. Sometimes a glove can become damaged or wet with perspiration. This way I can quickly switch to a clean fresh glove.

# Brad's Guide to the Lower Pockets

Most bags have two lower pockets. I suggest carrying your balls and any other back-up item you think you might need during the round in these.

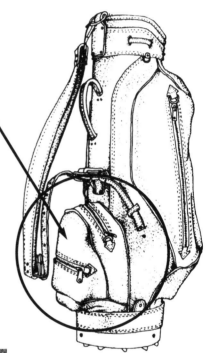

Extra loose golf balls

Extra sleeves of golf balls

High energy snacks (avoid sugar-based snacks)

The Rules of Golf

Any other item you might need during the round

Extra loose balls should be kept in one pocket with a few sleeves stored in the other.

## How Many Golf Balls Do I Need?

The number of golf balls you will need depends on your handicap. My preference is to take at least six new golf balls with me when I play. Added to that are two or three balls that I've used in a previous round.

If you're a higher handicap golfer, you may want to bring a dozen balls with you. The course you're playing on should also play a role in your decision. If it's a course with a lot of water, it's better to take a few extra balls to ensure you have enough to finish the round. At Pebble Beach, the traveling hospitality cart sells golf balls!

Speaking of losing balls in the water reminds me of what Bob Hope said when someone gave him 90 balls as a gift with "Happy Birthday Bob" printed on them. His reply: "Now when I hit one in the water, the fish will know who to send it back to."

## Always Carry The Rules of Golf

All golfers should carry a current copy of *The USGA Rules of Golf* book with them. You will be surprised at how using the *Rules* may help you save some shots. Later in this book, I'll show you some examples.

*The Rules of Golf* easily fits into your golf bag. Keep a copy in your golf bag to consult during the round.

# The Subject of
## Snacks

You can purchase a wide variety of high-energy snacks that help keep your energy levels up during the round. Look on the label to make sure they are high in carbohydrates but low in fat and sugar. Some snacks can even help keep you hydrated in very hot or humid weather.

Natural items are worthwhile additions to your bag. Certain fresh fruits should also be considered. Bananas put potassium back in your system. Don't wait too long and let your energy levels drop before eating. It takes a while for food to be converted into energy. I suggest nibbling as you go to maintain consistent energy levels.

Stay away from products with a lot of sugar. Sugar gives you a big energy spike followed by a sharp drop in energy. If you are striving for consistency, neither are beneficial to your game. A heavy sugar buzz may send that 3-footer sailing right off the green as a result of a quick jerky motion.

# Choosing the Right Woods for Beginners to Low Handicappers

*"I'm the best furniture maker in the world. No one hits the wood clubs like I do."*

### Lee Travino

*"If Tiger Woods or Laura Davies, two of the longest drivers on their tours, loaned you their driver, your driving might actually get worse. You need clubs that are right for your game."*

### Brad Brewer

**G**olf may be an Old World sport but its present and future are melded together by technology. Even though the last 10 years have seen metal and graphite replace wood as the primary material used for constructing the head of this long game club, we still refer to them as woods. Woods are the clubs you need to give you distance from the tee and on the fairway. Woods used off the tee are called drivers and fairway woods are used on the ____?

If you answered fairways, you're partially right. Woods are also very effective when hitting from certain lies (where the ball is resting) in the rough. The mass of the clubhead makes it less likely to get wrapped up in the grass that can sometimes cause off-target iron shots.

Tom Lehman and Fuzzy Zoeller, woods in hand.

It's important to have the right equipment in order to play good golf. When I refer to right equipment, I'm not suggesting that the most expensive or highly technical advanced driver is going to turn your game around. What I mean is that what's right for a pro is not necessarily right for you.

# Customizing Your Clubs

Regardless of the equipment you buy, the clubs can be customized just for you. Chapter 8 will explain all of this. Don't ever let anyone tell you, for example, that the grips that come with

**HISTORICAL HIGHLIGHT**

In 1502 King James IV of Scotland commissioned a bow maker to make him some "golf clubbies." Even back then, technology was playing an important role in the quest for longer hits. By selecting a bow maker instead of a shipwright or a carpenter, His Royal Highness was trying to find someone who understood the elasticity of wood. His goal, of course, was a flexible, whippy club that would provide more clubhead speed and longer distances.

the clubs are always perfect for you. Most people need to have their grips tailored to fit the size of their hands. For instance, if you're a woman, you may find ladies' clubs have grips that are too small for the length of your fingers. Your finger length may be longer than some men's. When you grip a club that's too small, you have to make some sort of compensation that would destroy your swing even before you make it.

Before buying any club, check the way your hands grip it. The fingers of your left hand (if you play right-handed) or right hand (if you are a lefty) should touch but not dig into your palm. If they can't just touch, the grip is too thick in diameter. If they squash into your palm, the grip is too thin. The club is not defective; the grip can be customized to fit you properly. It's not a big job—so try to negotiate with the salesperson before purchasing the equipment.

# Your Driver: Length and Accuracy Off the Tee

If Tiger Woods or Laura Davies, two of the longest drivers of the ball on their respective Tours, loaned you their drivers, your driving might actually get worse.

Grip

Shaft

Clubhead

Clubface

The reason is that their clubs are specifically set up for their games. You need clubs that are right for your game. On the subject of long-driving Touring Pros, my friend and past British Open Champion Ian Baker-Finch had an amusing comment on the length of John Daly's drives: "His driving is unbelievable. I don't drive that far on my holidays."

I'm going to help you become a knowledgeable consumer. So forget all the advertising and hype you've read. When you go into your pro shop or golf specialty store, you'll have an understanding as to what type of equipment and which loft angles can best help your game. In the photos on these two pages, I've labeled the important parts that go into the construction of the driver.

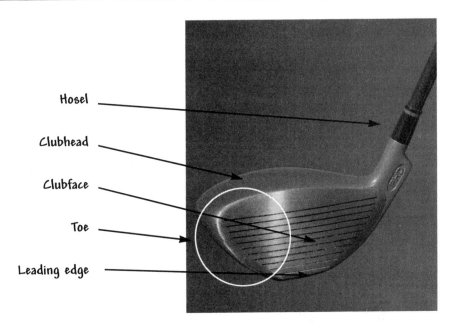

Hosel

Clubhead

Clubface

Toe

Leading edge

# Beginner or High Handicapper? You Need Help in Developing Clubhead Speed

Clubhead speed is one of the keys to distance, so it's important to find equipment that improves your game. If you're someone who is just beginning the game or a high handicapper, you need a club that's going to help you develop maximum clubhead speed for your ability level. It should also be forgiving of some of your mis-hits; in other words, the club will help the ball stay on target even if you don't hit the ball in the center of the clubface (what golfers call the "sweet spot"). If you currently (before we work together) hit your ball more off the toe of the club, you'll find this type of club a bit more forgiving. Look for a slightly over-sized club that's designed to have a low center of gravity and a wide forgiving hitting area. This is accomplished by the way and where the club manufacturer weights the club (distributes the weight in the clubhead).

I recommend that your driver have a graphite shaft to match the oversized head so that your swing stays balanced. The total weight of the entire club should be lighter than a standard club. This helps you swing the driver quicker than with a standard golf club. You'll find a variety of good clubs on the market designed just for you. Most professional shops should have demonstration drivers you can try; specialty stores usually have an indoor net or will let you try the club for a day or two.

It's extremely important to hit a club before purchasing it. You wouldn't buy a new car before taking it for a test drive, would you? If you already own a driver, evaluate whether the new club has increased your distance and accuracy. It's also good to know fitting specifications for your club, such as club length, loft, and lie. I also suggest consulting your local PGA professional for advice.

## Correct Clubface Loft Can Increase Your Distance

The loft of the club, or the angle of the clubface to the ground, is also important. Your ability level and the type of swing you currently have must be considered. Later in this book, we'll work together on helping you understand what your current swing looks like, but for now—take my word for it—some higher handicap golf swings tend to shut the clubface when it contacts the ball. This angle of attack decreases the amount of loft built into your clubface, making it difficult to get the ball up into the air. Do you hit lots of drives that never seem to get airborne? (See Figure 6-1.)

I suggest you try a 12-degree or 13-degree driver. This is almost the amount of loft of a 2-wood. However, when you impact the ball, your type of swing will de-loft the driver to about 9 degrees, which is the average loft for a driver. This should help launch your ball into the air.

If, on the other hand, you tend to hit very high drives (sky them) that don't go very far, your need for built-in loft is different from someone who has trouble getting the ball airborne. Your clubface, as it contacts the ball, is causing the ball to go high but not far. (See Figure 6-2.)

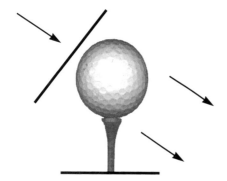

Figure 6-1. Closed clubface contacting ball prevents it from getting into the air.

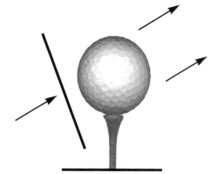

Figure 6-2. Too open a clubface causes a skyed drive.

So what do you think we can do, equipment-wise, to give you more length? That's right, select a less lofted driver. I suggest, in your case, finding a driver with a built-in 7 degrees to 8 degrees of loft. Even if you make the same poor swing, the face of the club, when it impacts the ball, will open a few degrees and impact the ball with less loft than the driver you're currently using. This should lower the trajectory of your drive, increasing your distance.

## BACK TO BASICS

Choosing a driver to compensate for some swing problems is only a Band Aid, a quick fix at best. If that's all you're looking for at this stage, that's fine. You probably will see some additional distance and begin to have more fun. However, I know you can really improve your swing and your game if you allow me to help you become your own best golf coach in Part 3 of this book. I'm here ready to help any time you want to start.

## Brad, Can You Show Me the Difference Between an 11-degree and a 9-degree Driver?

Compare the angle of the faces of the drivers in both photos. You can easily see the 11-degree driver has more loft built into it.

11-degree driver.

9-degree driver.

# Low Handicap
## Golfers

As a low handicap golfer, you already have a very good idea about the type of driver that works best for you. Most good golfers, however, are always looking for that special club that will give them the edge over their buddies or competitors. Sometimes the edge may come from the loft of the driver and the stiffness of the shaft. I'll explain more about different shafts later in this chapter, but I would suggest a 9-degree lofted driver if you honestly feel you can repeatedly make a good golf swing.

However, the type and location of the course you're playing should also be a factor in your decision. If you're playing a course with softer fairways that will not let the ball roll after it lands, try a 9-degree to 10-degree driver to keep your launch angle correct. If you're playing in windy conditions or on courses that are hard, allowing the landing ball to roll for extra distance, try a 7-degree or 8-degree driver to keep the ball lower. A lower ball will bore into the wind, rolling for extra yardage when it lands. Launch it too high and the wind takes over.

## Special Technologies

Club makers are always coming up with new technologies or materials to make the ball respond in different ways to the clubface. If you need extra spin ratio or want the ball to come off the clubface quicker, there are clubs for each preference.

Sometimes there is a trade-off. When you gain one advantage, you can lose another characteristic. If the insert on the driver face causes the ball to spin more, it's going to cause you to lose distance. Better players will sometimes opt for this type of clubface because it allows them to have some additional control over the direction the ball flies. If you like to work the ball left to right or right to left, a better player would traditionally like that. A good combination that works best features a wood head with fiber or resin inserts.

If, on the other hand, you're a low handicapper looking for a straighter and longer shot, certain clubfaces are built for your game. They have inserts made of materials that encourage the ball to come off the face as fast as possible, because it retards ball spin. Titanium is currently the "hot stuff" on the market.

# Fairway Woods

This may surprise you, but touring pros do not use a driver off the tee on every hole. Sometimes they use a fairway wood or a long iron. Their strategy is to target the location that provides the best approach to the hole. This requires accuracy and the longest drivers of the ball are rarely the most accurate. Tiger Woods was the second longest driver on the PGA Tour in his first year (294.8 yards per drive) but ranked 96th in fairways hit. Tiger's ability to recover enabled him to rank 4th in greens in regulation, putting him in position to putt for birdie.

**BRAD EXPLAINS**

*Being on a green in regulation means you reached a par 3 hole with your first stroke, a par 4 was reached in 2 strokes, and you were on a par 5 green in 3 strokes. In all cases, you were putting to make a 1 under par birdie for the hole.*

Do you honestly have Tiger's golfing ability at this stage in your game? That means accuracy should be a very important consideration for you. I think the average high handicap golfer tries to hit it too far, too often. That's one of the reasons they hit it off-line. They're attempting to add too much power to the shot going for the extra 10 yards. They also can't work the ball from left to right or right to left like the low handicap golfers, so they should be trying to reach a target position on the fairway that better suits their game.

**BACK TO BASICS**

The next time you play, write down the number of fairways you hit with your drive. Don't count the four par 3 holes most courses have. Instead, divide the number of fairways hit on your drives by 14 (the holes that required a long shot off the tee) to get your percentage of fairways hit. Of course, since that doesn't factor in reaching your target, you may want to consider the above equation for finding your percentage of targets reached. How many fairways do you think the pros hit on average per round? The average is 9.5 fairways for a percentage of 59.

What I'm suggesting is that you should sometimes consider using a fairway wood or even a long iron off the tee in order to increase your accuracy. If I recommended using a less lofted driver to cure skying the ball as a club selection quick fix, don't hit a fairway wood off the tee until we have a chance to work on your swing.

When you're choosing the 14 clubs the USGA allows you to carry in your bag, including the putter, consider your game and the course you're playing. Some golfers may carry two woods while others choose four or more. The higher the number, the more lofted the club. For example, a 9-wood is more lofted than a 3-wood.

## Try These in Your Bag If You're a Beginner or High Handicapper

If you're just getting into the sport, I suggest choosing a couple of additional woods instead of some of the longer irons. (We'll select irons in the next chapter.) Higher-lofted fairway woods are easier to hit than long irons.

My suggestion: driver, 3-wood, 5-wood, 7-wood. If you follow this suggestion, you'll have to eliminate carrying the 2- and 3-irons to follow the USGA 14-club rule. The built-in loft of the woods, with the exception of the driver, is pretty standardized.

## Low Handicappers: Have You Considered a Utility Wood?

Many of the Touring Pros are starting to carry a specialized utility wood in their bags. I don't recommend specific brand names, but these clubs are readily available in pro shops and golf specialty stores and you may have even seen them in infomercials.

One thing to consider, however, is that pros have access to specifically customized clubs and lofts for their game and for the specific course they're playing. So if they choose one of these specialized utility woods, they know they're not giving up distance with the lofts of the other wood or woods in their bags.

Left to right:
5-wood,
3-wood,
driver.

This is something you need to think about unless you have a club room at home stocked with shelves of drivers and fairway woods or have access to the manufacturing tour vans that follow the tournament trail. These utility-type woods are great out of divots, cart paths, fairway bunkers, and tight lies. They are very easy to hit and land the ball softly. I suggest trying a demo club to see if it helps your game.

# Head Covers: The Choice Is Yours

Head covers should protect all your woods when they are in your bag. This is one area where you can be really creative. Head covers come in all shapes and forms and can reflect your other interests or affiliations. I've even seen head covers depicting the Three Stooges—perhaps not the most positive role models for our friendly woods!

Steve Hosid's USC Trojan head cover. Some golf courses sell their own covers.

The "Tiger" head cover is readily available. His distance off the tee is not included. Other animals, not related to golfers, are also available, like the elephant. I've seen an entire zoo collection covering one bag of clubs.

# Let Me Tell You about Long Shafts

One question I'm often asked is: "Brad, should I buy a long-shafted driver?" Here's the key to using a long-shafted driver: Do you have good fundamentals when you swing a golf club? Will your swing tempo allow you to swing a golf club of that length and still keep the club in a position to attack the golf ball consistently? If you can honestly answer "yes" to both questions, I believe a long-shafted driver can add extra distance to your drives.

The longer shaft creates more clubhead speed. The downside is that it's much harder to control. The longer the shaft, the more a mistake is multiplied. If you're presently having trouble with accuracy and direction, this club is not suited for you. You will only compound your accuracy problem. While you may get another 10 yards, it could be another 10 yards farther into the woods. So don't gain distance at the expense of accuracy.

Shafts bend and flex during your golf swing.

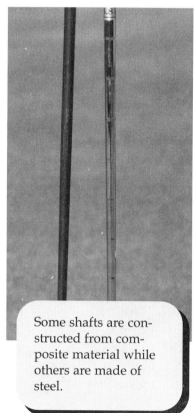

Some shafts are constructed from composite material while others are made of steel.

Rocky Thompson plays a long-shafted driver on the Senior PGA Tour. He's mastered the club now but, in the beginning, it took a little getting used to. A member of the media asked Rocky how he knew that he was the only player using the 54-inch driver. Thompson answered: "Nobody else is that stupid."

Each year the PGA of America puts on a worldwide golf merchandising and trade show in Orlando, Florida, that encompasses 1.2 million square feet filled with golf vendors, open only to the members of their organization. Everyone who manufactures anything for or about golf takes a booth in hopes of selling their products to the club pros.

One entrepreneur had a unique idea for golf shafts. He wanted to sell shafts as a receptacle for keeping the ashes of a dearly departed golfer. His marketing approach: "It only takes a few seconds to realize this is more appropriate than keeping the remains in an urn on the mantel or in a shoe box in the closet."

Somehow I think he double bogeyed with that idea. But, if he could have proved it added 10 extra yards, many golfers would have considerd it!

## Shafts Are Crucial to Your Game

Shafts are very important to your game and are particularly important as your game improves. As you fine-tune your game, you can select shafts that can help you maximize clubhead speed. How the shaft flexes and where it flexes will increase the snap at impact.

Your golf pro, local club maker, or golf specialty store can help you select the right shaft for your game. Stronger players will tend to use stiffer shafts, while others may find a softer shaft is better suited for extra distance and control.

Are you price-conscious and purchasing clubs on a budget? You'll find today's steel shafts are very close to the overall weight of the more expensive graphite shafts. Make sure you get the correct flex in the shaft for your game. There are literally thousands of shafts available to choose from, so making the choice by yourself could drive you nuts. Your local PGA professional can assist you after seeing your swing. It doesn't mean that you have to go into the pro shop to buy the shafts, but pros are very knowledgeable and understand what's right for your game. Your pro may either have exactly what you need or can order it.

A properly selected shaft can also improve your accuracy as well as length. The clubface has to be squared to the target line as it impacts the ball. You may currently be using a shaft that is too stiff or too flexible, causing the clubface to torque open or shut, depending on your game. A PGA professional will help you determine if that's the case.

# Brad's Suggestions for Purchasing Woods

1. Drivers are available with different built-in clubface lofts.

2. Don't just buy a driver off the rack—test and select one that can improve your game.

3. Woods are easier to hit, so consider carrying additional woods instead of long irons in your bag.

4. The flexibility of your shaft should match your game. Let your local PGA pro help you decide what's right for you.

# Choosing Irons, Wedges, and a Surefire Putter

*"'Give me the iron!' either party cries,*
*As in the quarry, track or sand he lies."*

**George Fullerton Carnegie**,
in *The Golfiad*, poems on golf, 1833

*"You've heard the old saying 'You need the right tools for*
*the job.' Your clubs are your tools, so select irons that can*
*help you get the job done in the fewest number of strokes."*

**Brad Brewer**

**I**n the 1930s, when steel shafts came into play, a new marketing term was introduced: *matched sets of clubs*. Golfers and manufacturers rejoiced. No longer would shafts have to be made from wood with its natural variances of flex and feel. Clubs could now be mass manufactured with precise specifications as to weight, size, and flex. Excited golfers rushed to buy clubs made for every contingency they might encounter. It was not unusual to find 20 or more clubs in their bags.

To conform to the USGA 14-club rule, some players may choose to use additional woods and replace a 2- or 3-iron. Others may choose to carry a 60-degree lob wedge and eliminate a wood or an iron. As you can see, you have the freedom to choose clubs that can best help you. You might also decide to substitute and change clubs if you play longer or shorter courses or as your skill level increases. It's your choice. Now, let's look at an iron's various parts.

While all irons share similar characteristics, they can vary in appearance and construction. Your selection will be based on a number of considerations: personal preference, budget, and feel. Do you like looking down at the iron and seeing a thick top edge or a thin one? Do you want offset or non-offset clubheads?

## HISTORICAL HIGHLIGHT

On January 1, 1938, the USGA imposed a new rule limiting the number of clubs a golfer could carry. The limit was decreed to be 14. The following year, the Royal and Ancient followed with a similar ruling. The purpose of the new rule was "to restore the making of individual shots, and increase the skill of the player." This rule has been observed faithfully since that time.

## Beginners and High Handicappers

If you've never played the game before, you may not know the difference among the various types of clubs. Whichever irons you decide to buy, I suggest buying the complete matched set rather than mixing irons. Your wedges are the only individual irons you can consider purchasing separately. It's important to have a uniform set because you want to get used to the same feel. Irons in the same set will have a unification of weight distribution and flexes.

With most irons, you'll be making the same swing and allowing the change in loft of the clubface and length of the shaft determine how far the ball goes. That's why it's much better to have the club respond the same way each time. It's very difficult to get accustomed to different clubs with different feels.

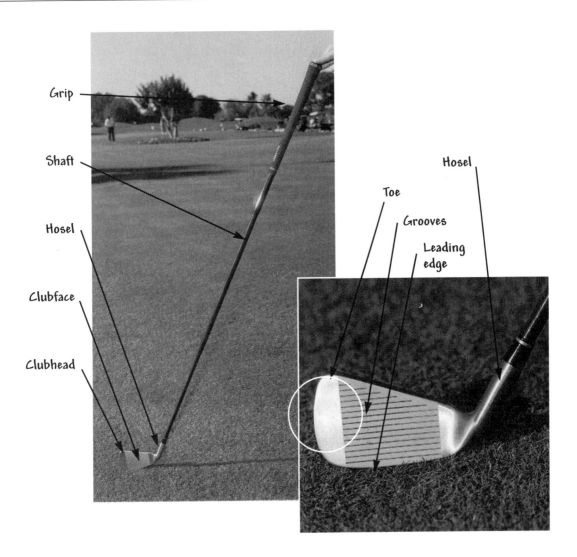

Grip

Shaft

Hosel

Clubface

Clubhead

Hosel

Toe

Grooves

Leading edge

## Low Handicap Golfers

Your skill level allows you to fine-tune your game by *dialing in* the right equipment. Your golf swing is undoubtedly constructed on solid fundamentals and you consistently can make a good repeatable swing. If this is the case, you may have found you want different feels from your long, middle, and short irons. This can also be accomplished by customizing your individual clubs. We'll deal more with that in Chapter 8.

## Forged Irons

Forged blades, or *muscle back* irons, are still used by some golfers today. The nature of their construction requires intensive and highly skilled labor to turn out a consistent clubhead. Golfers who have used forged irons may find it difficult to get used to some of the modern-day golf equipment. Some golfers feel that forged irons make it easier to *work the ball* and that they have a softer feel. These clubs are usually heavier in overall weight; I don't recommend using the new lightweight modern shafts with them.

Forged blade iron.

## Cavity Back Irons

Notice how the back of the iron looks open in places, like a cavity? This type of club is popular today. The casting of the metal into molds is cost effective and produces a golf club with a consistent feeling. Manufacturers have designed the clubs so that the weight distributes to the perimeters of the club for a forgiving performance. If you mis-hit the ball either on the toe or heel, counterweighting allows the club to compensate somewhat. The result is that you will end up with a better shot than you would have made with a forged club. The clubface is usually slightly offset, which I'll explain next.

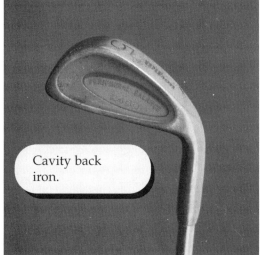

Cavity back iron.

## Offset Irons

Club designers have found that placing the hosel in front of the leading edge of the golf club helps many golfers keep the blade more square through impact, which helps you hit the ball straighter. When we get to Part 3 of this book, you'll learn that on-target shots are a result of the clubface being square to the target as it impacts with the ball. (See Figure 7-1.)

Offset iron.

Offsetting provides a little additional time for allowing the clubhead to square itself since it's behind the hosel and shaft of your iron. It's designed to be very user friendly. If you've had a problem with your shots going to the right (left for left-handed golfers), the problem may be that the clubface is open to the target line when it impacts the ball. (See Figure 7-2.) An offset club provides a little more time for the clubface to square itself and you are less likely to be off target.

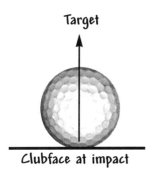

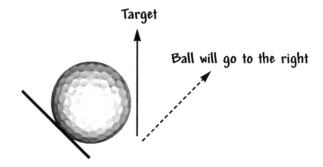

Figure 7.1. The clubhead is square to the target line as it impacts the ball.

Figure 7-2. Open clubface at impact causes off-line shots. The more open the clubface, the more off-line you'll be.

# Brad, Do I Need All the Irons?

Earlier in the chapter you learned about the USGA 14-club rule. While the rule limits the number of clubs you are allowed in your bag for a round, it doesn't eliminate your freedom to choose the clubs best suited for your game. Here is a list of 14 clubs many golfers choose to carry.

| Woods | (3) |
|---|---|
| Driver | |
| 3-wood | |
| 5-wood | |
| **Long Irons** | **(3)** |
| 2-iron | |
| 3-iron | |
| 4-iron | |
| **Medium Irons** | **(3)** |
| 5-iron | |
| 6-iron | |
| 7-iron | |
| **Short Irons** | **(2)** |
| 8-iron | |
| 9-iron | |
| **Wedges** | **(2)** |
| Pitching wedge | |
| Sand wedge | |
| **Putter** | **(1)** |

A matched set of clubs: 2-iron through 9-iron.

# Situations Where You Might Want to Change Your Clubs

Just as you included certain gear in your bag to prepare for what you may need on your 18-hole golf journey, consider giving as much thought to the 14 clubs you'll carry. Here are a few examples of different situations.

You've just been given the opportunity to play a links-style golf course like St. Andrews. This means that playing in the wind is almost a certainty. The same scenario holds true if you're playing your home municipal course on a blustery day or taking a vacation to Hawaii with its 25-mph trade winds. You normally like to carry a 7-wood in your bag, because it's easy to hit. Keep in mind, however, that the ball's trajectory is pretty high. In the wind that high launch angle is going to cause a loss of distance and strokes. Consider substituting some long irons that can stay lower and bore through the wind. Your high flying lob wedge probably won't give you too much help either. This frees up a space for another longer iron.

On the other hand, if you're playing a hilly golf course with lots of elevated greens encircled by deep bunkers, you'll want your 60-degree lob wedge to carry you over the trouble, landing the ball softly on the green. I'll show you how to hit it later in the book, but it's a great club to help get you out of some difficult situations. In this case, you will want to pull a long iron from your bag and put in the lob wedge. You've heard the old saying: "You always need the right tools for the job." Your clubs are your tools, so select the ones that can get the job done in the fewest number of strokes.

# What Causes the Ball to Go Different Distances?

Which iron, the 9 or the 5, do you think will hit the ball farther?

If you took physics in high school, you remember the term *lever.* In golf, as in physics, a longer lever increases the swing arc and increases distance. Good golfers know that choking down on a club shortens the lever and decreases the distance. This comes in handy for shots lying in-between your normal club yardage range.

The 9-iron on the left has more loft, so the ball will go higher but not as far as a ball hit with the less lofted 5-iron on the right. The loft of the club, along with the length of the club, plays a significant role in the distance the ball travels.

| Average Distances Golfers Hit their Clubs | | | |
|---|---|---|---|
| *Club* | *Beginner* | *Average Golfer* | *Good Golfer* |
| Driver | 190 | 220 | 250 |
| 2-wood | 180 | 215 | 235 |
| 3-wood | 170 | 210 | 225 |
| 4-wood | 165 | 205 | 215 |
| 5-wood | 150 | 195 | 205 |
| 2-iron | 145 | 180 | 190 |
| 3-iron | 135 | 170 | 180 |
| 4-iron | 125 | 160 | 170 |
| 5-iron | 120 | 155 | 165 |
| 6-iron | 115 | 145 | 160 |
| 7-iron | 105 | 140 | 150 |
| 8-iron | 95 | 130 | 140 |
| 9-iron | 80 | 115 | 125 |
| Pitching wedge | 70 | 100 | 110 |
| Sand wedge | 55 | 80 | 95 |
| Lob wedge | Short distance club with high trajectory | | |

(Note: These yardage figures are approximate.)

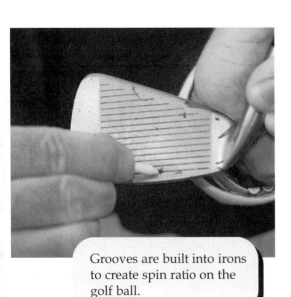

Grooves are built into irons to create spin ratio on the golf ball.

# Keep Your Grooves Clean

The grooves on your irons actually grip the ball at impact and start the spinning motion that aerodynamically affects the trajectory. Because the clubhead contacts the ground, the grooves can fill up with dirt, sand, and grass. If the grooves are dirty and not allowed to grip the ball at impact, you could *hit a flier* coming off the face of the club. I just used golf language to indicate what the flight characteristic of the shot might be. It would be *hot* (here I go again) and *tough to stop or work.* Perhaps this might be a good time to turn to the Glossary and start picking up the language of golf.

To hit the shot you're committed to, it's vital to keep the grooves clean. If you're playing on a sand-based course, wiping them with a wet towel should do the trick. For dirt or clay, use a groove cleaning tool or a tee and run it through the grooves. Most of the material will come out. It's a good idea to carry a damp towel on your bag for cleaning your clubs off after every shot.

# Why Do the Pros Use Three Wedges?

To make birdies! While most spectators love to watch and whistle at a Touring Pro's rocket drives, the real secret to a pro's success is his or her short game. They've found that having three wedges in their bag gives them a chance to get the ball *close to the pin* from various distances. Close to the pin means a makeable putt.

If you're a high handicap golfer, my suggestion is to stick with two wedges: a 56-degree sand wedge and maybe a 49-degree pitching wedge. At this stage of your game, it's important to put the lofted woods in your bag.

These are 1993 U.S. Open Champion Lee Janzen's three wedges. Left to right: 48-degree pitching wedge for shots between 105 and 125 yards, a 55-degree sand wedge for shots between 70 and 105 yards, and a 62-degree lob wedge for shots 60 yards or closer. Don't copy his distances, instead determine your own distances through practice.

# Choosing a Surefire Putter

Your scoring partner comes literally in all shapes and sizes. The putter is the most artistic club in your bag. When you shop for your putter, you'll see the wide variety available. Just like a painting, every artist's style and technique are different. Putters are like that too—they're designed differently to appeal to the various needs of golfers.

It's not unusual to change putters frequently. However, you probably won't ever collect the 3,500-plus putters that Arnold Palmer has collected during his playing days. At one time, each of those putters looked very good to him and worked well for a while. He's the type of individual who chooses the putter he feels will work best for him for that particular round.

I recommend the same philosophy for you, to a certain extent. Choose a putter that has a personal look and feel that you like. The weight of the putter, like the weight of any club, is very important. To have a feel of the *instrument* as it swings is conducive to rolling the ball toward your target.

If you have hard grip pressure, you should look for a putter that is a little heavier so that you can feel the head as you swing. A mallet or thick brass-headed putter might be ideal. The shafts are also important. They should contribute to your feeling and be long enough so you are comfortable at the address position.

When you're putter shopping, also consider the grip. Putters come with rounded grips, paddle grips, or all the variations in between.

## Do You Putt like Phil Mickelson?

If you swing the putter open and shut like a door, like Phil Mickelson or Ben Crenshaw, you should look for a putter that allows you to feel the toe as it opens and closes. That's a toe-weighted putter. A blade putter is a good example.

## Face-Balanced Putters Help Most Average Golfers

When you look at an instrument designed to help the average golfer, the face-balanced putter is a recent and wonderful addition to the market. The balanced face helps keep the putter square to the target as it goes back and through.

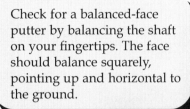

Check for a balanced-face putter by balancing the shaft on your fingertips. The face should balance squarely, pointing up and horizontal to the ground.

You can test for the weight of a toe-weighted putter by balancing the shaft on two fingers. If the weight is at the toe, the putter points down.

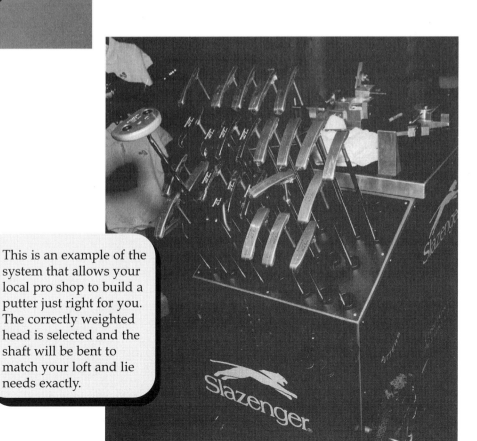

This is an example of the system that allows your local pro shop to build a putter just right for you. The correctly weighted head is selected and the shaft will be bent to match your loft and lie needs exactly.

## Most Golfers Never Consider Putter Loft and Lie

Too many people neglect to get a putter that's designed specifically just for them. They'll just pick it right off the shelf and adjust their putting technique to the instrument.

In today's market, some companies have designed a system that will allow your local shop to build the putter just for you. Just like the pros, you can have a customized putter that will work together with your technique to hole more putts. It's going to help more people putt better. You will not have to compensate for the putter.

## What about a Long Putter?

This is a hot item. I see a lot of players trying to bring back the feel they've lost over the years. The long putter teaches you to swing the putter back and through in a pendulum motion, minimizing the movement and keeping it simple.

A rhythmic pendulum stroke, back and through, is easy to create with a long putter.

The single most important feeling you get from a long putter is the feeling of the instrument swinging back and through. It's much easier to coordinate. What's interesting is that some golfers who practice with the long putter for a while and then go back to the traditional length find that their putting has greatly improved.

# Brad's Tips for Selecting Irons, Wedges, and Putters

1. Choose a set of irons that look and feel good to you.

2. Cavity back irons with offset are user friendly and can improve your game.

3. While the pros carry three wedges in their bag, another wood or iron may be a better choice for your game.

4. Choose a putter that appeals to your eye and your technique.

5. Long putters give you the feeling of a simple one-piece, back and through pendulum swing.

CHAPTER 8

# Customizing Your Equipment

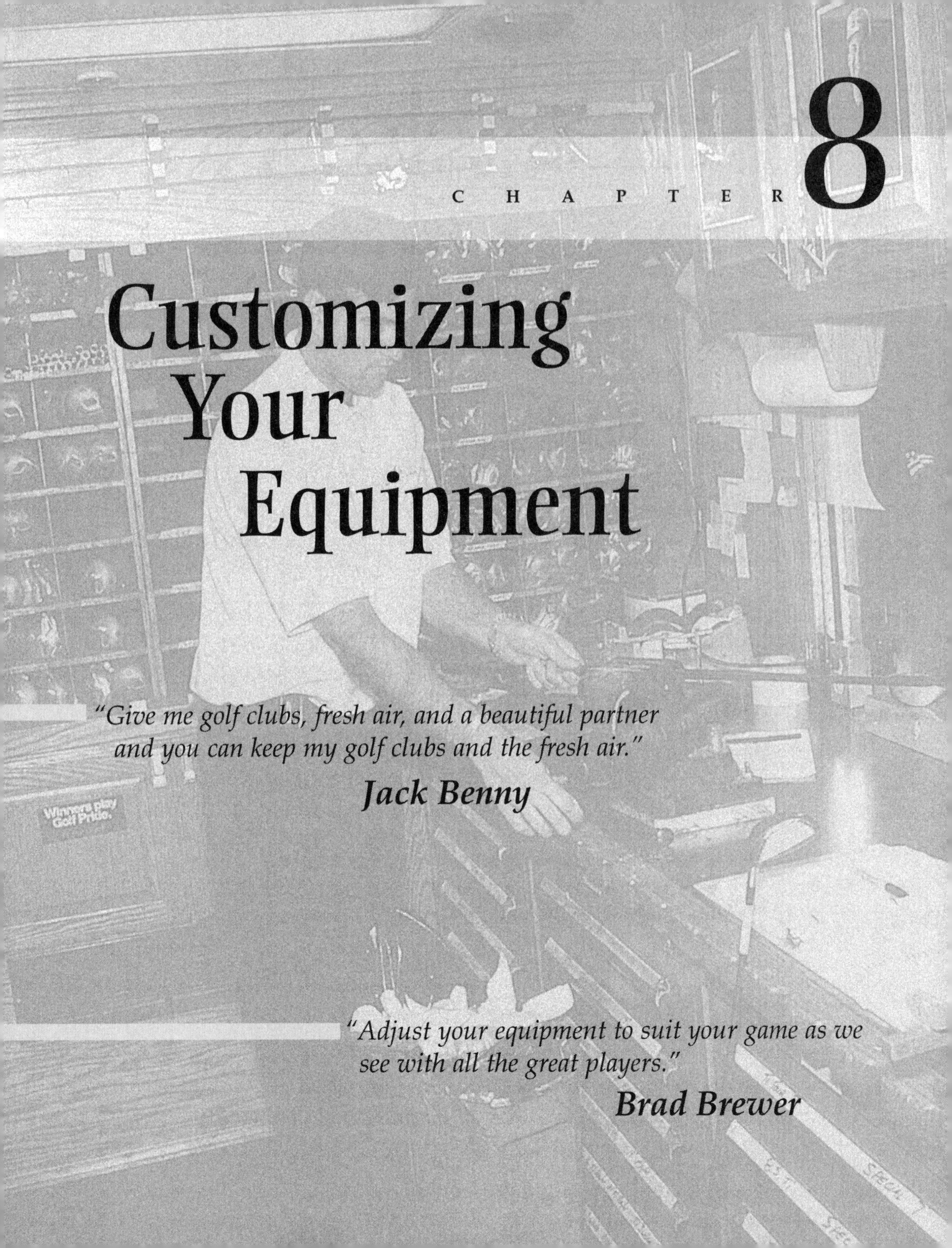


*"Give me golf clubs, fresh air, and a beautiful partner and you can keep my golf clubs and the fresh air."*

***Jack Benny***

*"Adjust your equipment to suit your game as we see with all the great players."*

***Brad Brewer***

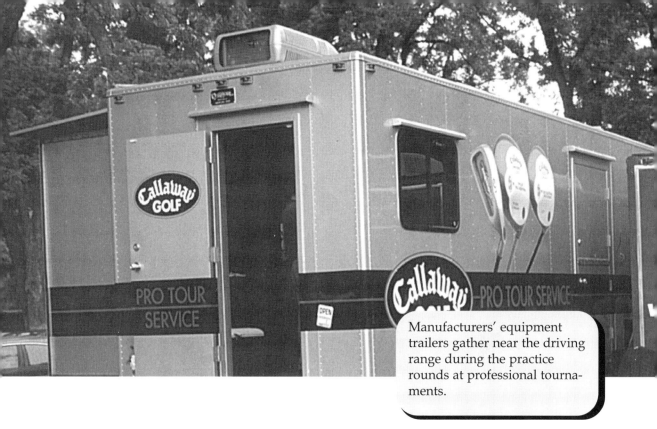

Manufacturers' equipment trailers gather near the driving range during the practice rounds at professional tournaments.

**G**reat players are always tinkering with their equipment, trying to get the clubs to be exactly right for them. It has a lot to do with that subjective term: *feeling*—how they are feeling at that particular moment as far as their golf swing is concerned. Everyone goes through cycles with their bodies as feelings change and, consequently, the club has to be adjusted.

If you have a chance to attend a PGA or LPGA Tournament, try going to some of the practice rounds on Monday, Tuesday or Wednesday, if you really want a behind- the-scenes insight into tournament golf. You'll see equipment vans from the major club manufacturers, along with shaft technicians, set up close to the driving range.

This *club village* is a bustle of activity as pros and caddies have equipment adjusted, parts replaced, or take something new to the range to try out. Mostly only small changes are made, as they tweak the equipment until it feels just right.

Even with their consistent swings, pros can't always make the ball do just what they want. If a player is hanging his drives a little bit to the right (the face is not square to the target line at impact), for example, they may add some lead tape to the toe of the club to help compensate. This helps give them the feeling of the toe

How would you like to have all these clubs at your disposal every time you play? The manufacturers' trailers are stocked with a wide selection of clubheads, shafts, and grips.

Technicians help make necessary adjustments or build something customized for the tournament pros. All clubs must conform to the USGA standards.

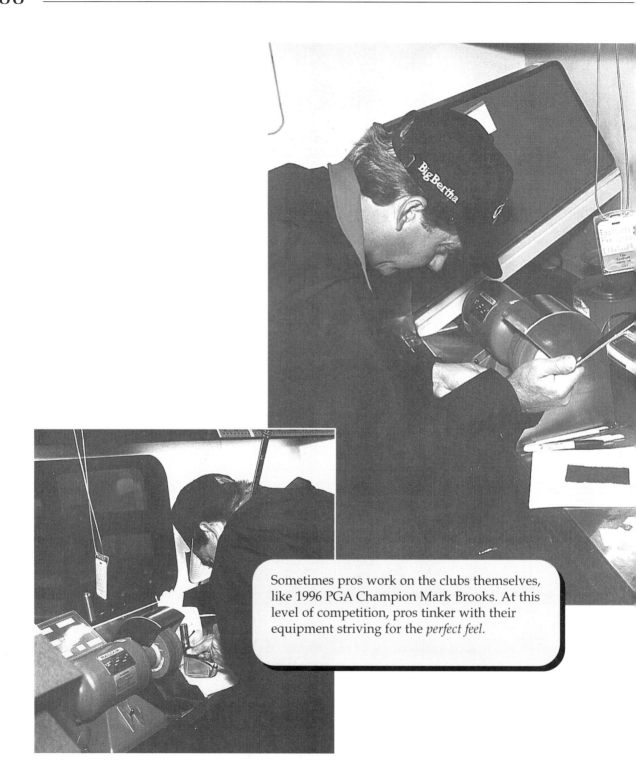

Sometimes pros work on the clubs themselves, like 1996 PGA Champion Mark Brooks. At this level of competition, pros tinker with their equipment striving for the *perfect feel*.

turning over a little bit coming through impact.

Early in the week, pros are relaxed, joke around, and are receptive to talking to the galleries. It's a good time to ask some questions about their equipment or their games. Once the tournament begins, however, they still may be friendly but become more focused on their work. Some fans don't understand that while golf is a game, for a pro it also represents their livelihood.

# Brad, Who Can Customize My Equipment?

Only the pros have the luxury of having a manufacturer's equipment trailer following them around from tournament to tournament. However, your local golf professional may have some of the same equipment, or, each city usually has several individuals who specialize in equipment repair. Look for them in the yellow pages heading for golf club makers or golf club repair.

As in any specialized business, they have the right equipment to do the job effectively and hopefully help your game. I've found many of these individuals have an incredible knowledge about the history of club making. They may even have built some re-creations of the old-time clubs.

Club design and repair books are available if you want to really learn more and make it a hobby. I've listed some in the Resources.

# Let's Start with Your Grips

Most new golf clubs come with a standard 58 round grip. Unfortunately, one size does not fit all. Have your pro or club maker look at how your hands grip the club. If the grip is too big or small, several methods are available to customize the size to conform to your requirements.

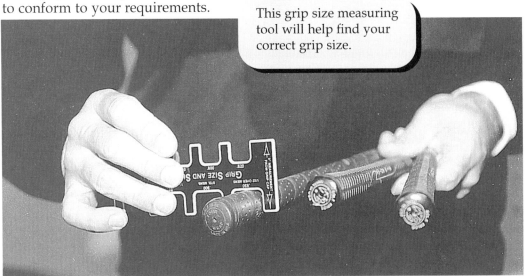

This grip size measuring tool will help find your correct grip size.

## HISTORICAL HIGHLIGHT

The earliest clubmakers specialized in bows and carpentry. As the demand for clubs increased, certain family club making businesses affiliated themselves with individual courses such as St. Andrews. Some of the club makers were also the best golfers of their era. The legendary "Old Tom Morris" was the professional and also repaired and built members' clubs at the Royal and Ancient St. Andrews, in Scotland.

# Brad, What Is the Ideal Fit for Me?

To check if the size of your grip is correct:

1. The middle and ring finger of your left hand (right hand if you play left-handed) should touch just fractionally the palm of your hand as it's wrapped around the grip.

2. It's too thin if your nails dig into your palm.

3. It's too thick if your fingers can't touch the palm at all.

# How Will They Customize My Grip?

Customizing your grip requires extracting or cutting the old one off, so you're going to have the opportunity of selecting a new grip. Choose one that feels good to you from the many styles and materials available. Look at the selection on the next two pages.

Grips come in different widths, so finding a size close to what you need is easy. For customization, masking tape is wrapped around the shaft to build it up to the proper proportions before the grip is slipped over. I suggest mentioning to the club maker that you really want this customized. It may be necessary to additionally build up various sections of the grip with masking tape for an ideal fit.

## BACK TO BASICS

I can't emphasize enough how important a good grip is if you want to develop the free-flowing, consistent golf swing that will lower your scores. All good swings begin with good grips—it's a fundamental.

Hold the club with a minimum amount of pressure, with your hands positioned in a neutral grip. A grip that is too large or small will require a compensation of some sort that could incorrectly change your hand positions and grip pressure, adversely affecting your swing. I really suggest checking the size and condition of your grips if you want to improve.

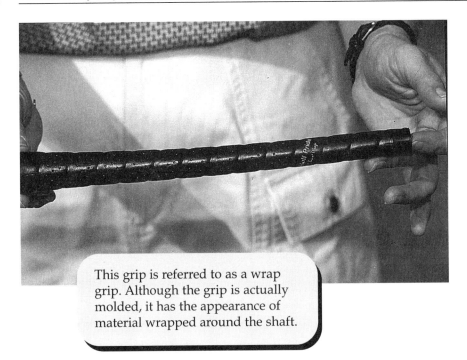

This grip is referred to as a wrap grip. Although the grip is actually molded, it has the appearance of material wrapped around the shaft.

This cord-type grip is very popular with some golfers.

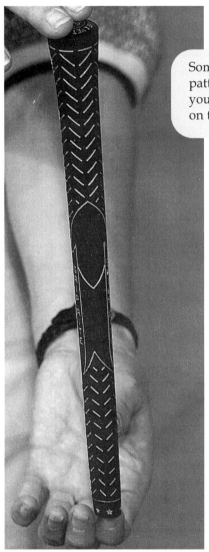

Some grips feature a pattern outlining where your hands should go on the club.

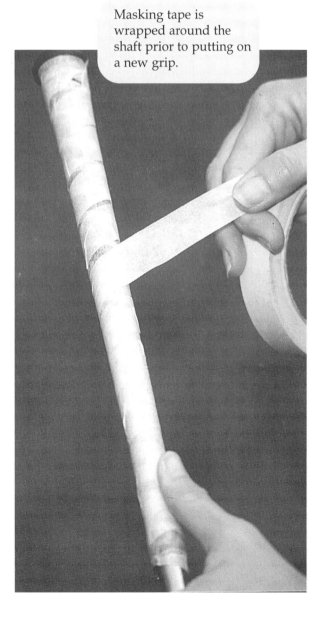

Masking tape is wrapped around the shaft prior to putting on a new grip.

# One Last Word about
## Your Grips

Because your grip is your only physical link to the club, it's very important to be sure your grips are kept clean at all times. They should feel a little tacky but not slippery. Grips can be cleaned with a wet towel and then towel dried. Replace them at the first signs of wear. It's well worth the price.

# Ladies, You May Need the
## Same Size Grip as a Man

As I mentioned earlier in the book, ladies' clubs traditionally come with thinner grips on them. The problem is that women can have longer fingers than men. You need wider grips to hit consistent high-quality golf shots.

# What Can You Do with
## Your Shafts?

Most golfers will never have the need to replace the shafts that came with their clubs. If you're in the market for new equipment, it's rare that a manufacturer does not offer sets of clubs with different shafts already installed. One thing you may want to check is to be sure the club is the correct length for you and is balanced properly for your needs.

However, if you have clubs that you really love and want to keep, replacing the shafts is an option. Be a wise consumer and make sure that someone doesn't charge you more to replace the shafts than it would cost to buy new clubs. As I mentioned earlier, you really should have a PGA Professional help you decide if a "shaft transplant" is needed.

A professional's trained eye observing your ball flight will determine if you need a softer or firmer shaft. Choosing the correct shaft will help you develop more clubhead speed and longer distance. A shaft that's not right for you can also cause some direction problems because it won't allow you to consistently square the clubface at impact.

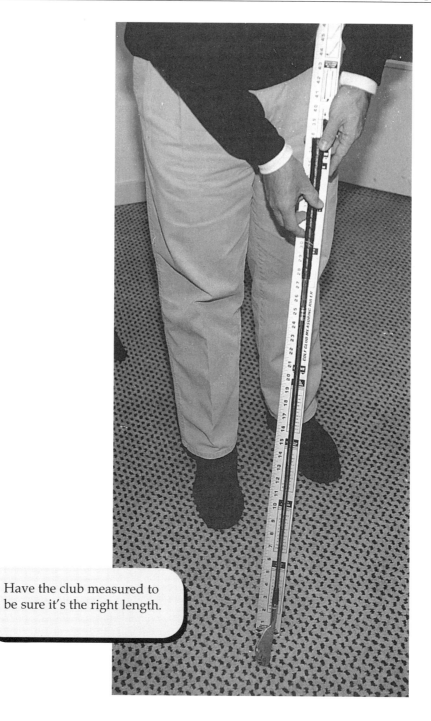

Have the club measured to be sure it's the right length.

# Brad, Can I Adjust My Shafts for Loft and Lie?

You can have the angle formed by your shafts and clubhead adjusted to give you a better *lie*. Changing the *loft* is also possible but I would suggest you have your pro look at your swing and ball flight before asking for that adjustment.

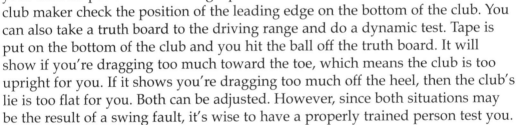

Correct lie. See how the club's leading edge rests correctly on the ground.

## How Do I Check My Lie?

You can test your lie statistically by taking your address position and having a pro or club maker check the position of the leading edge on the bottom of the club. You can also take a truth board to the driving range and do a dynamic test. Tape is put on the bottom of the club and you hit the ball off the truth board. It will show if you're dragging too much toward the toe, which means the club is too upright for you. If it shows you're dragging too much off the heel, then the club's lie is too flat for you. Both can be adjusted. However, since both situations may be the result of a swing fault, it's wise to have a properly trained person test you.

If the lie is too flat for you, the toe is going to stick too far up in the air. When you swing down and through, the toe is going to curl over the golf ball causing a pull-hook.

If the lie is too upright for you, the heel is up in the air and when you swing down and through, the toe digs into the ground. This causes your clubface to stay open and you hit shots that go to the right (left for left-handers).

Adjusting the lie of the club is extremely beneficial to most amateur golfers, since everybody's lie is marginally different. If the leading edge can naturally rest correctly on the ground, you won't have to manipulate the club, putting yourself out of position as you address the ball.

## Adjusting the Club's Lie

With the right equipment, adjusting the lie is a simple procedure.

At our Academies, we're beginning to see more people coming for lessons with better fitting equipment—clubs that are marginally closer to where they should be. It's a result of manufacturers starting to design different systems for fitting clubs that are fairly simple, yet accurate.

**BRAD EXPLAINS**

*Loft is the angle the clubhead is set to get the ball lofted up into the air. The lie of a golf club is the way that the bottom of the club rests on the ground. You want the leading edge to rest correctly on the ground so you have the most hitting face coming square into the golf ball.*

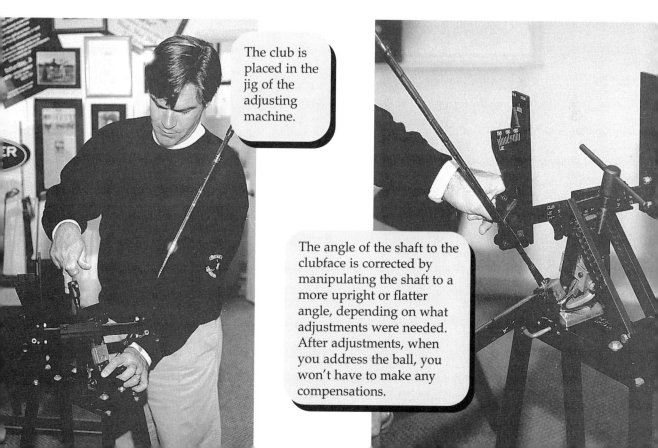

The club is placed in the jig of the adjusting machine.

The angle of the shaft to the clubface is corrected by manipulating the shaft to a more upright or flatter angle, depending on what adjustments were needed. After adjustments, when you address the ball, you won't have to make any compensations.

However, we also see golfers who have spent a lot of money on their clubs and they're either too upright or too flat for them. While the adjusting equipment can help, today's clubs are cast rather than forged and can be bent only so far before the tensile strength of the club causes it to break away or crack. Small adjustments can be made but major ones are a problem. That's why it's important to get the right loft and lie to start with when you purchase the clubs.

When you're shopping for new equipment, it's important to look for a manufacturer who has designed specific club-fitting systems into their clubs. This makes your purchase easier.

# Brad, What Is Weight or Lead Tape Used for?

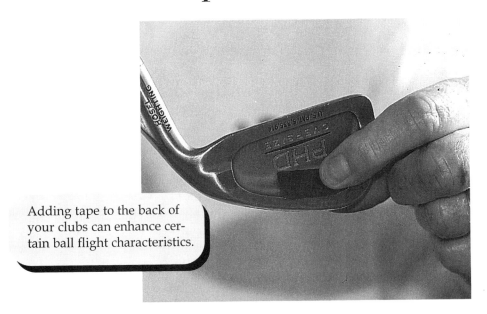

Adding tape to the back of your clubs can enhance certain ball flight characteristics.

If you do go to a tournament, you'll be able to get close enough at times to see the top of the pro's irons. The first thing that comes to mind is: "What is all that tape on the clubheads?"

As you start getting to be a better golfer, you'll develop a preference for how the club should feel. This is usually a result of how the club is weighted. It would be nice to say that all clubs come out of production exactly the same. Unfortunately, that's not the case. Lead tape, available in pro shops, golf specialty stores, or catalogs is applied around the back of the clubhead to balance the club correctly.

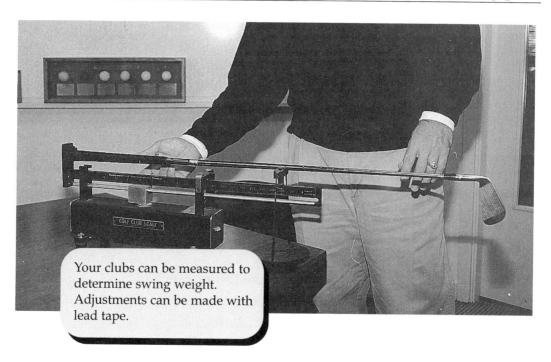

Your clubs can be measured to determine swing weight. Adjustments can be made with lead tape.

You can also customize the clubhead to the characteristics you're looking for. As an example, if you want to hit lower shots with the club, raise the center of gravity by putting some tape on the back of the top of the club. If higher shots are your preference, lower the center of gravity by placing the tape on the back of the clubhead's lower edge. You can also toe or heel weight the club by placing lead tape on those areas and dialing in the feel you're looking for. Some golfers want to add weight to the club's overall weight. That is accomplished by counterbalancing the club. Put some lead tape under the grip. Jack Nicklaus did that for most of his career. MacGregor made the equipment for "Golden Bear" many years. Nicklaus wanted a D3 swing weight. The clubs came out and were heavier than that. To counterbalance the heavier weighting in the clubhead, they stuck lead tape under his grip. He changed his grip from time to time but never knew that the grips were counterbalancing the club with the lead tape. He played this way for years.

When he eventually found out about the lead tape, he made MacGregor mill the clubs to his specifications. When he played with the new clubs, he found that wasn't the feel that he was used to, so he went back to the original feel and played with counterbalanced clubs for most of his career.

The best players in the world can tell you exactly how they want their club to feel or if something is off. I was in Arnold Palmer's workshop one day as he was going over a new set of irons. We were weighing the clubs for the particular swing weight he wanted; in this case it was a D4. The scale indicated they were ranging between D2 and D5.

We would hand him a golf club, he would take a couple of swings to get the feel of the club, then put on or take off some lead tape, swing it again, and give it back to us to weigh. When we weighed the club he had worked on, it turned out to be exactly D4. He could be chatting with us while getting the feel of the next club, add or move some tape, hand it back, and it would be D4. He was that precise with the feel.

Would you like to know the difference in feel for a swing weight? It's like putting a dollar bill on the clubhead, and yet he could tell the difference.

## Put Your Name on Your Clubs

Once you get your equipment just the way you want it, be sure to identify the clubs as yours. Every so often, all of us forget to pick up a club we leave on a hole. We may have taken a wedge along with a putter and laid the wedge down after using it.

By placing an identification label on the shaft, just under the grip, you stand a good chance of getting your club back if someone else brings it to the pro shop. Many golf professionals or specialty stores have computer programs that can print out a label with your name and phone number. It's a simple way to help protect your investment. One more tip: Never leave your clubs in an unlocked car.

# Gloves, Balls, and Shoes

*"I could only hit balls thrown down at my feet."*
**Tom Watson**

*"A free-flowing, powerful golf swing is encouraged if you're comfortable: comfortable holding the club with the help of a glove that won't slip; comfortable hitting the correct trajectory ball for your game; comfortable as you walk the extra distance to your next shot because the previous two helped you make a good quality swing."*

**Brad Brewer**

The three items we'll be discussing in this chapter have one characteristic in common: You can choose what feels best to you. I'm sure that makes sense when you consider gloves and shoes, but what on earth does "feel" have to do with a golf ball? I'll explain shortly, but first, let's begin with golf gloves.

# How a Glove Helps Your Golf Swing

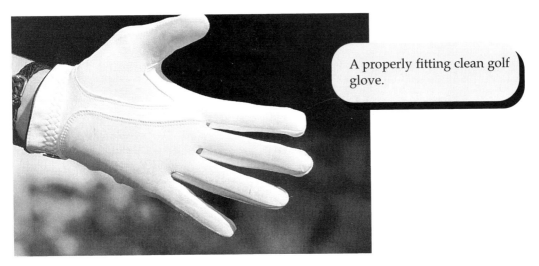

A properly fitting clean golf glove.

The next time you play, take a look around at the other golfers waiting to tee off. Specifically, take a look at their gloves. If you see a worn-out, sweat-stained, wrinkly glove, that glove belongs to someone who is overlooking one of the easiest ways to improve his or her game—a fresh glove.

Most people think a glove's main purpose is to protect them from developing calluses caused by friction between the grip and their skin. That's true to a certain extent, but a glove's more correctly defined reason for existence should be *to help you hold onto the club, reducing slippage and twisting through impact.*

Since we know that a good grip is important to the swing, your ability to hold the club correctly is vital. If you have the tendency to develop calluses, a glove will help protect the sensitive areas of your hand. *Hands that are not painful have an easier time gripping the club.*

If you're about to begin playing golf, calluses and blisters will be a common occurrence as you'll mis-hit the ball quite a bit at the start. A glove will help although you can still pick up a blister along the way. An older wrinkled glove will probably cause more blisters than it prevents. The bunched material gets caught between your skin and the club and, as you swing, friction causes the skin to blister. *Blisters are not conducive to holding the club with less tension in the hands.*

I believe a glove also helps build your confidence to be able to hold the club with relaxed pressure. Gripping the club tighter doesn't help you hit harder; on the contrary, clubhead speed and distance are a product of a swing that develops maximum centrifugal force that can only develop when the body allows it to happen naturally. You can't control it. Just swinging fast is not the answer—you could never generate the clubhead speed you'll need. *Relaxed grip pressure encourages the consistent free-flowing swing you're capable of making.*

Combine a clean properly fitting glove with clean tacky-to-the-touch new grips and you'll be amazed at how little pressure you have to exert to hold onto the club during a swing. The slight tackiness of the grip is the perfect compliment to the leather or synthetic material of the glove. Why put unnecessary obstacles in your path to improving your game? Have several new or like-new gloves available throughout your practice and during the round.

## Choosing the Right Fit

Just as with the grip on your club, one size of glove does not fit all. They are available in men and women's sizes. Each category has the traditional small, medium, large, and extra large and *cadet sizes.*

Your glove should be snug but not tight. Material should not bunch up in the palm, under the fingers, or at the tips. The back of the glove

**BACK TO BASICS**

I've emphasized the importance of a good grip several times throughout the early part of this book. I know I'm repeating myself but, in doing so, I hope to help you understand how a good grip will help you become a much better golfer.

Once you develop a comfortable neutral grip, you will be able to let your body take over and make a repeatable, free-flowing golf swing. As simple as a golf glove sounds, a worn-out glove is slippery, ill-fitting, and, as a result, you'll have the tendency to grip your club with increased tension, immediately changing the dynamics of your swing. Don't skimp on a glove—it's part of your vital link to the club.

**BRAD EXPLAINS**

*Golf glove cadet sizes are available in the traditional size ranges. The difference between regular and cadet sizes is finger length. Cadets are constructed for hands with shorter fingers. Glove manufacturers try to help you get the correct fit, so take the time to try on as many gloves as you think necessary until you find the right comfort and fit.*

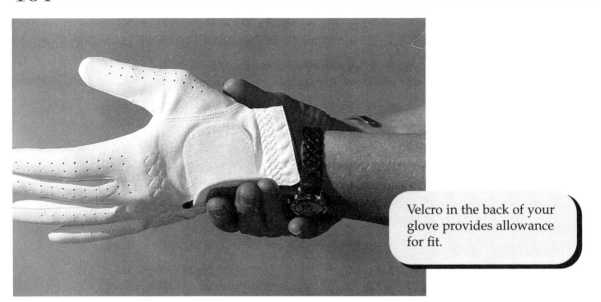

Velcro in the back of your glove provides allowance for fit.

should fasten easily. Velcro is predominately used for this purpose, providing some allowance for a custom fit.

## Most Gloves Have Attached Ball Markers

The next time you're on the green and looking for a way to mark your ball (so you can clean it or remove it from someone's path to the hole), don't fumble through your pockets, just look on your glove.

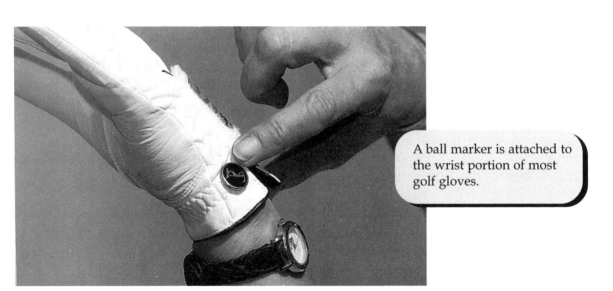

A ball marker is attached to the wrist portion of most golf gloves.

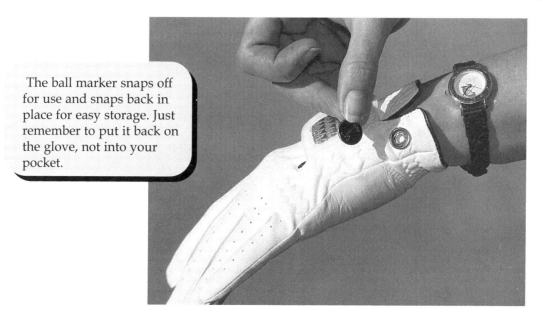

The ball marker snaps off for use and snaps back in place for easy storage. Just remember to put it back on the glove, not into your pocket.

## Using a Weather Glove Can Help Even If It's Not Raining

Some glove manufacturers also offer a glove that helps increase "gripability" in inclement weather. Different materials are used that have waterproofing attributes that keep the glove drier. It's not uncommon to see the pros wearing gloves like this when it's hot and humid too.

Manufacturers use various marketing terms to describe gloves that are designed for inclement weather. Let your pro or golf specialty store show you the different types available.

# Taking Care of Your Gloves

If you notice your glove is wearing out in the palm, the best way to take care of the problem is to correct your grip and make center clubface impacts. Palm "wear-out" is a telltale sign of a grip that is incorrectly held more in your palm than your fingers. Possibly the grip that's on your club is too thick for the size of your hands. Make sure to grip down on the club so that about one-half inch of the grip is above your hands. Did you notice that I slipped in a subtle plug for gripping your club correctly?

## Really Taking Care of Your Glove

Aside from gripping your club correctly, there are several things you can do to prolong the life of your new golf glove.

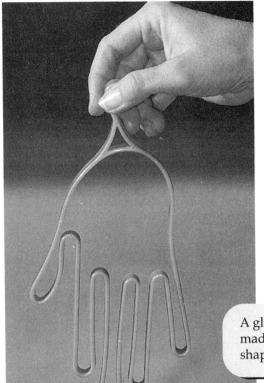

1. Follow the manufacturer's recommendations printed on the packaging.

2. Hang the glove to dry from the steering wheel of your golf cart and make sure it's dry before returning it to your golf bag.

3. Never ball up the glove and jam it into a bag pocket. Keep the packaging it came in for storage. Fold it as neatly as if you were going to return it to the store shelf.

4. Consider using a glove tree.

A glove tree is usually made from plastic and is shaped into fingers.

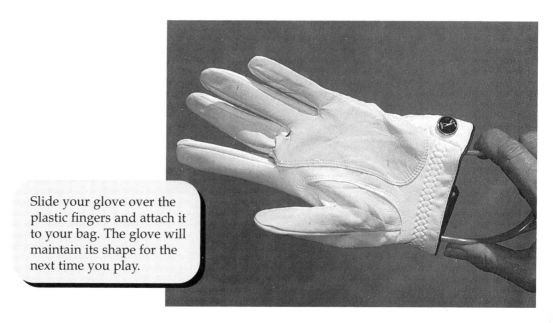

Slide your glove over the plastic fingers and attach it to your bag. The glove will maintain its shape for the next time you play.

# Balls, Balls, Balls

So many types of balls to choose from!

I've heard Arnold Palmer and other top touring pros say that the biggest difference in the game over the past 20 years is the way the golf ball has changed. The pros used to get golf balls that weren't always round. During the manufacturing and shipping processes, the rubber bands that were an integral part of their inner construction shifted, causing the balls to be a little bit off-round. Sometimes they looked more like hardboiled eggs than the desired 1.68 inches in diameter sphere.

Balls used to be hand-tested before making it into the pro's bag. It was a pretty simple test that required spinning the balls in a salt solution to check the buoyancy. The top of the ball would be marked and then the ball would be spun in the solution again. If the mark came up to the top, the ball was in round. On average, four to six balls out of a dozen were rejected for being out of round.

Today's golf balls come to you with a great deal more assurance that they are the way they should be. Nowadays the design and manufacture of golf balls is much higher in quality and the materials used are much more durable and consistent.

What an incredible selection we have to choose from. High spin, low spin, high trajectory, medium trajectory, low trajectory, extra spin, soft feel, hot extra distance—these marketing terms describe the vast selection of balls available to golfers. There are almost as many different balls as there are head covers!

## Brad, Should I Use the Balls the Pros Use?

Just as you need to match your clubs to your game, the same is true of the type of ball you should select. A pro uses a balata-covered two- or three-piece ball and is willing to give up some distance for control.

You want to use a ball that is going to feel good and contribute to the consistency of your game. Up until now, you may never have given any thought to how important choosing the right ball is. I'm not telling you not to rejoice when you stumble upon another golfer's lost ball and put it in your bag! For some golfers, finding a ball instead of losing one is like discovering all the gold in the lost city of Atlantis—it's a priceless find.

However, certain aerodynamic characteristics and how the ball is constructed can be selected to help contribute toward improving your distance. The reason the published *Rules of Golf* state that a ball must be no less than 1.68 inches in diameter is because the smaller the ball, the less drag it has and the farther it can go. Oversize balls are perfectly legal and some players use them to reduce their hooks and slices. The larger golf balls don't spin as much.

## The Dimples

The dimples on a golf ball are more than just cute decoration. Their pattern and how they are arranged contribute to the way the ball flies through the air. Dimples don't create spin—that's a function of the ball interacting with the clubface at impact—instead they provide the lift that keeps the ball in the air longer.

Aerodynamically, the dimples interact with the air causing the ball to follow a high trajectory or a low one, depending on their pattern. If you have a tendency to hit higher shots, selecting a high-trajectory ball might not be what you need. I recommend that you talk to a golf professional who has seen your normal ball flight. A pro can steer you to a selection of golf balls to compliment your game.

> ### HISTORICAL HIGHLIGHT
>
> Modern manufacturing techniques that improved the consistency of golf balls led to the adoption of rules by the USGA and R&A. In 1921, both associations specified 1.62 inches in diameter as the approved size. Ten years later, the USGA increased the size to no less than 1.68 inches in diameter. The R&A adopted the same standard in 1987.
>
> The USGA tests brands of balls for distance regulations and rejects those exceeding them. They want a standard to be maintained and have the survival of the sport to think about as well. Without USGA standards, it wouldn't be long before today's golf courses would be rendered obsolete by farther-flying golf balls.

Figure 9-1. A dimpled golf ball.

## Not All Golf Balls Are Constructed Alike

Golf balls may look similar on the outside, but they can be constructed differently on the inside. Here again, choose the construction characteristics that are right for your game. To better understand ball construction, let's consider the following examples.

## One-Piece Golf Ball

Figure 9-2. One-piece ball.

You'll rarely use a one-piece ball to play with but most likely you will be hitting them on some practice ranges. It's the least expensive ball and its long life makes sense for the economics of the range. This ball is usually made out of a material called Suryln and the dimples are molded in during the construction process. It has a softer feel when it meets your clubface and will not go as far as balls you may use on the course. *Keep this in mind when practicing how far you can hit certain clubs on the range.*

## Two-Piece Golf Ball

Figure 9-3. Two-piece ball.

This is the most popular ball among most average golfers today. It's an extremely durable ball and its construction provides more length than any other golf ball. This ball has a high roll distance after landing, depending on the course. Its core is made from resin or high-energy acrylate. The blended cover is virtually indestructible and resistant to cutting from contact with the irons. The trade-off is that its distance-enhancing characteristics require a low spin rate to keep the ball from climbing too high. This also makes it somewhat more difficult to control, especially when you want it to stop quickly on the green.

### Three-Piece Golf Ball

This ball is a solid core version of three-piece construction. Rubber yarn is wound around the solid core, made of rubber. The yarn aids control of the ball. Usually the cover will be made from Suryln or synthetic balata, which is durable yet softer in feel.

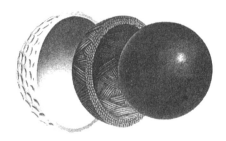

Figure 9-4. Three-piece ball.

### Three-Piece Ball with a Liquid Center

This ball provides a softer feel at impact and has a design characteristic that allows it to spin more after impact. Some distance is given up with this ball but the advantage gained is higher spin and softer feel. The softer feel is a result of a cover that actually mashes up against the clubface at impact. This flattening causes the ball to stay on the clubface a little longer than a harder distance-type ball. This allows good golfers to work the ball left or right or high or low, depending on the type of shot they need to hit. (I'll show you the basics of working the ball in Part 5.)

Figure 9-5. Three-piece liquid-center ball.

The cover of this ball used to be made out of balata, a liquid that was milked from the balata tree. Today a synthetic balata is used for the cover. It still provides softness and feel but durability is greatly improved. What do you think is in the liquid center? Usually Karo corn syrup and water!

# Brad, Which Ball Is Right for Me?

As I suggested earlier in the chapter, your local PGA professional can steer you in the right direction. As a guide, the following chart matches some of your needs to the type of ball and uses the industry's marketing terminology.

| How You Play | Type of Ball |
|---|---|
| *Beginners and high handicap players* | |
| Want the most distance possible<br>Want the ball to roll<br>Don't usually work your shots | Two-piece, low trajectory |
| *Preferred PGA Tour ball and single digit handicap golfers* | |
| Prefer the softest feel around greens<br>Working your shots is important<br>Want to spin the ball<br>Not as concerned with distance, but<br>　　want feel and ability to control the ball | Three-piece balata, high trajectory |
| *Preferred ball, medium to single digit handicaps* | |
| Like to work the ball but distance is<br>　　also important<br>Want roll but also a softer feel | Three-piece Suryln cover, high trajectory |

# One More Thing about Balls

Keep your golf balls clean. Should the dimples get filled up with material, it can alter the flight or rolling characteristics of the ball. Once your ball is on the green, mark it with your ball marker, clean it, then replace it on the green at the spot you marked. Before teeing off, wipe the ball with a wet towel if it's dirty or use the ball washer that some courses put up by some tees.

Check your ball before teeing it up. If you notice scrapes or abrasions, it's time to retire it. Defects can have an adverse effect on the ball's aerodynamics. Technically, you may have hit a high-quality shot, so why let a bad ball ruin it.

Use those older balls as practice balls for your short game. They'll give you the same sort of feel your normal ball does. Collect them in a *shag bag*, a golfing term for a small bag with handles.

# Shoes

Golf shoes come in a variety of styles, colors, and spikes. They can be made out of very soft materials or look similar to dress shoes—the choice is yours. You will even find shoes that repel water for wet days or dewy mornings. Prices vary considerably but a less expensive pair does not mean that it's inferior. Shop wisely and be sure you try them on later in the day. As the day progresses, fluids accumulate in your feet, and shoes that fit comfortably in the morning may feel tight in the afternoon. Blisters are no fun and hardly conducive to creating a positive feeling about your game. Also, be sure your socks are not worn out at the heels.

The main purpose of golf shoes is to give you traction when hitting the ball. The spikes, unlike a plain sole, make contact and even penetrate the ground (depending on which spike you wear).

Golf shoes are available in many styles and colors.

Women's golf shoes can be very stylish. Shop wisely and select shoes that are comfortable.

# Brad, Please Explain the Soft Spike Revolution

The revolution has to do with spikes. Unlike the metal variety, soft spikes are easier on the greens. Earlier in the book, we addressed the courtesy aspects of the game. As more golfers take up the sport, greens are being subjected to more wear and tear by metal spikes that penetrate into the ground, killing the roots of the grass. If you accidentally scuff the green, the spikes leave abrasions. Putting requires rolling the ball along a target line to the hole. If spike marks get in the way, the ball can be jostled off course. The more people playing, the more spike marks.

Metal spikes viewed from the side.

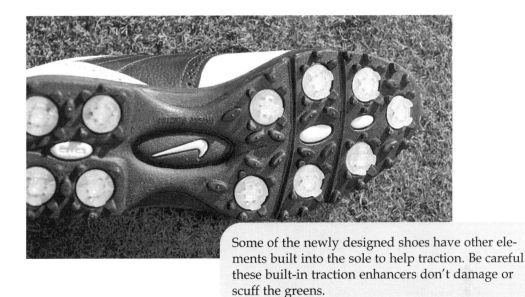

Some of the newly designed shoes have other elements built into the sole to help traction. Be careful these built-in traction enhancers don't damage or scuff the greens.

Soft spikes don't penetrate the ground. Instead, plastic spikes are arranged to provide traction without destroying the grass roots. The greens are not damaged and all of us have truer greens to putt on. From my experience at our club, I can see the difference that more players wearing soft spikes has made. I wear them myself and don't feel I'm at a disadvantage from the player who wears metal spikes. However, you will have to replace them more frequently than you do metal spikes, as they wear out a little faster.

## Do I Have to Buy a New Pair of Shoes to Get Soft Spikes?

The answer to that question is usually no. You can unscrew your metal spikes and replace them with soft spikes. Because so many courses are making soft spikes mandatory, it may be a good idea to convert your shoes. Only a few manufacturers make shoes with permanent metal spikes. In that case, a new pair of golf shoes is the only way to get the soft spikes. If you plan on buying new golf shoes, you probably should buy a soft spike version or ask the store to convert the metal spikes that come with the shoe to soft spikes. Let's all show courtesy to each other by keeping the putting surface of the green in the best condition possible.

## One Last Word about Soft Spikes

Here's a word about safety. Soft spikes can sometimes fill up with material you pick up on the course, such as grass clippings and leaves. If the spikes fill up, they won't provide traction and you could slip when walking up or down a small hill. Check the bottom of your shoes frequently during a round and clean out the soft spikes with a brush or a tee.

# PART 3

# Becoming Your Own Golf Coach

*This unique section will help you understand your own golf swing like never before. You'll find out how to use your home video camera just like the pros. Learn by videotaping your own swing. Perhaps you're happy with your swing the way it is. That's okay! This section will be ready to help you anytime you wish. It's your lifetime guide.*

*Once you know the correct angles for videotaping your swing, photo examples will help you understand your faults. After reading this part of the book, you'll look at all golf swings through the eyes of a coach. Once you develop an understanding of your swing, you'll learn how mastering five simple fundamentals will help you create your own free-flowing golf swing. If problems creep back in, this section will be your lifetime reference for diagnosing swing faults.*

# CHAPTER 10

# Who Can Spend More Time with You than You?

*"The more I practice, the luckier I get."*
**Jerry Barber**

*"Can anyone else offer a continual and ongoing analysis of your game as you can yourself, once you have the proper knowledge of what to look for and how to interpret what you see?"*
**Brad Brewer**

**B**efore you begin reading this chapter, I would like to be sure you understand my intentions for writing it. *Golf for Everybody*—the title of this book—doesn't mean to imply that everybody has the same approach to the sport. In this chapter, you'll find lots of information about how you can improve your game with methods like videotaping, goal setting, and scheduling. I don't want you to think, however, that you have to do every single thing I mention in order to improve your game. Golf does not have to be time-consuming. Pick and choose areas from this chapter that appeal to you now. Later on you can always add other elements. If you want to play competitive golf, you'll find some proven and tested methods to spur your progress along.

# Your Coaching Qualifications

I believe most golfers possess the qualifications for becoming their own coach. I'm not suggesting that it's not a good idea to get professional help from a golf school or your local PGA teaching pro, but you can't have teachers with you all the time. In fact, it's against the rules to ask for advice while playing in a tournament competition. If you really want to improve your game, developing the ability to coach yourself is an important consideration. Here are a few reasons why:

1. Is there anyone more motivated than you are in improving your game?

2. Does anyone really know more about you as a person?

3. Can anyone else offer an ongoing analysis of your game as you can yourself, once you have the proper knowledge of what to look for and how to interpret what you see?

4. Is there anyone better suited to establish practice times than you are?

5. Can you think of anyone else better suited than you are to set the attainable goals that will help your progress toward improvement?

6. Is anyone else available to work closely with you each and every time you want to go out and practice like a pro?

Regardless of your current level of play, I'm convinced that you can be your own number one coaching asset. Now that you are going to become your own coach, let me suggest some other very important items that in effect become your assistant coaches.

# "Golf for Everybody"

There are many good golf instruction books available—my mentor Arnold Palmer has written some that I've listed in the Resources—but one of the purposes of this book is to help you see and better understand your own golf swing. Have you ever actually seen your own swing or has it only been described to you through the comments of friends or instructors?

I suggest that you begin by videotaping your swing. Chapter 11 provides valuable information about recording the swing properly using the correct set-up angles with your home video camera. Chapters 12 through 15 have photo examples you may recognize as similar to your own swing and include explanations about any problems.

Once you gain an understanding of what your swing problems are, you are well on your way toward improvement. I truly believe that improvement begins with understanding, and this also holds true for whatever you do in life. I hope this book will help develop a "coach's eye" in helping you determine which areas need working on and in evaluating your overall progress. Most golfers go though a time when they may develop a different problem or slowly regress to their natural tendencies. Hopefully *Golf for Everybody* will be your continual reference for evaluation, diagnosis, and suggested cures.

# Videotaping Your Swing and Watching It for the First Time

Many instructors and touring professionals regard the video camera as a major advance in coaching. Used properly, you will find it to be an asset in your game improvement strategy. What you thought and felt you were doing in your swing may not be the case. Here are some suggestions to help you get started:

- Use Chapter 11 as a guide to setting your camera up correctly for the two most important views.

- The first time you see the video of your swing, view it at home several times at regular speed, then watch it in slow motion or frame by frame—even before looking in this book for identifying problems.

- Look through the "eyes of an instructor" as you're viewing your swing. Closely observe your overall motion and weight balance throughout. Is your swing smooth with a full backswing or is it rushed and jerky? Look at club positions going back and coming through, not to diagnose problems, but to start training your eye to look at the nuances of the golf swing you'll be working on improving.

- Mentally compare your swing to professional swings you've seen during tournament coverage on television.

- Compare your swing to the feelings you have when you make it. How do they compare to what you're actually seeing?

- Once you get an overall feeling for your current swing, look at your grip, address position, posture, alignment, ball position, and whether or not you maintained a steady head throughout the swing.

- Beginning with Chapter 12, let me help you understand what you're seeing in your own video.

# How Do You Currently Play?

All coaches have to fairly assess the individuals they're working with to be able to plot an improvement strategy, so take some time to analyze your current game.

1. Begin keeping statistics of your fairways hit, greens in regulation, number of putts, sand saves, and number of penalty shots per round.

2. Are you long off the tee or short?

3. What side of the fairway or rough is your usual lie?

4. Does every shot you hit have a similar pattern to it?

5. Do you tense up when you have to hit over a bunker or water?

6. Honestly evaluate each phase of your game: driving, fairway woods, long and short irons, wedge play, and putting.

7. Honestly pinpoint your exact feelings about specific clubs and certain situations.

8. Are you afraid of hitting out of the sand or unable to hit a high soft wedge?

9. How do you feel about putting? Are you confident or nervous?

10. List your top two strengths and weaknesses.

Be honest with your self-evaluations, just as a coach would be. The purpose is not to tear yourself down but rather to allow you to honestly evaluate every facet of your game and how you feel about each. Write these appraisals down for future reference and goal setting.

# The Golf Journal

I know this has been mentioned several times in this book, but keeping a golf journal is imperative to improving your game. As we analyze your swing together using Chapters 12 through 15, it's a good idea to jot down your current swing problems along with your personal evaluation of various facets of your game. If you decided to go for expert help to a qualified golf school or golf instructor, it's valuable to write down areas to work on in your own words. Along with your video, the journal provides a baseline reference illustrating your starting point to improvement. Improvement can be measured only by knowing how far you've come from where you've started.

Use the journal to document how you went about correcting any problems. Should similar problems arise, you'll have a written record of how to correct them. Record drills and attainable goals. Any information that played a role in improving your game is priceless information and your golf journal provides a permanent record.

# The Sense of Feel

Some of the greatest players in the game are considered "feel players" rather than "technical players." This means they are not overly concerned with the mechanics of the swing, preferring instead to rely on their feelings. These feelings were developed and linked to mastering the fundamentals of the golf swing.

1. Grip
2. Address
3. One-piece take-away
4. Steady head
5. Acceleration

As you're working on improving your game, sweep out the cobwebs of old swing thoughts and develop new feelings for the correct aspects of your improved golf swing. It's much easier and more fun to play using your sense of feel rather than having to recall the mechanical aspects of the game. It also frees your mind to focus on the target and just do it. Write those feelings down in your golf journal or talk to your video camera when practicing.

# The Game Improvement Plan

After you've seen your swing and had a chance to compare it with the photos that show similar swing problems, it's time to start working on a plan to help yourself improve. Every successful business has a written plan that serves as its road map to success. Although business plans may be revised from time to time, they are carefully thought out with specified objectives and how to reach them. Companies then go though due diligence to make sure their goals and the means to achieving them are realistic. Whether you are involved in business or are the executive in charge of running your home, you need to plan. Use this same strategy in writing a master plan for improving your game.

1. List your long-term goals.

2. List your short-term attainable goals.

3. List the days you can practice on the range and make them part of your schedule.

4. Organize a practice routine that takes advantage of the allotted time. This is practicing like a pro.

5. Schedule some time at home to practice. You can do it while watching television or in front of your mirror.

6. Does your schedule permit a visit to a golf school or some local instruction with a PGA teaching pro?

7. Write your game improvement plan in your golf journal.

## Long-Term Goals

Lowering your handicap by a certain number of strokes within a year or lowering your score within a certain time frame are long-term goals. Please be realistic in determining your goals and remember that they can best be reached by adhering to some short-term goals along with faithfully following the game improvement plan.

## Short-Term Goals

A short-term goal is a reasonable improvement in a specific fundamental or area of your game that you honestly feel is attainable in a specified amount of time. Here's my definition of an attainable goal: goals that are easily reached. Your progress must be easily seen and tracked. Depending on the goal, it should be reachable today or within a 30-day period. Set your target on the tasks you are going to do on a daily basis in order to accomplish your attainable goal, and include these tasks in your schedule.

By meeting and even exceeding short-term attainable goals, you're providing yourself with a constant source of motivation. You won't be able to achieve your long-term goal in a short time. Although this can be frustrating, by meeting short-term goals you keep yourself fired up.

# Practice like a Pro

Time is a precious commodity for all of us. To maximize the time we have for practice, we should have a clear understanding of what we want to work on and accomplish. If you're working on mastering a basic fundamental, for example, your practice session needs to be organized with some drills and exercises. I've included those in Part 7 of this book. As it's important to create new feelings associated with the improvements, time has to be properly allotted.

It's also important to balance working on your mechanics with the real objective—getting the ball to the target. If you have an hour a week to practice, break that hour up into specific time periods that will allow you to focus on one thing at a time. Don't try to work on every fundamental at the same time—you will end up tying yourself into knots. Improvement kicks in when the fundamental becomes part of your swing. Like the pros, establish good practice schedules and habits.

I've included two examples on the next page of scheduling and evaluation charts to help anyone dedicated to improving his or her game to competitive levels. Even if you don't have plans for competition, these examples provide an insight into the dedication it takes to reach that highly competitive level.

# Brad's Coaching Tips

1. Become your own coach along with taking some professional lessons.
2. Videotape your swing.
3. Develop a "coach's eye" as you learn about your swing.
4. Develop your own unique Game Improvement plan.
5. Sweep out the cobwebs and develop a new sense of feel.
6. Document your progress in your golf journal.
7. Maximize your time and practice like a pro.

## ARNOLD PALMER GOLF ACADEMY

DATE: _____

CLIENT'S NAME: _____

### PRACTICE LIKE-A-PRO!

Cycle: __Competitive Development__
Theme: _____
Summary: _____

| ATTAINABLE GOALS | GOALS | MON | TUE | WED | THR | FRI | SAT | SUN |
|---|---|---|---|---|---|---|---|---|
| Time to Bed/Time Up | 11-6 | | | | | | | |
| **Hours of Sleep** | 7 | | | | | | | |
| Quality of Sleep (A-F) | A | | | | | | | |
| Exercise: Aerobic/Weights/jog… | 20 min | | | | | | | |
| **Stretching Routine** | Yes | | | | | | | |
| Golf competition | 18 holes | | | | | | | |
| Fundamental practice | 0 hrs | | | | | | | |
| *Swinging Practice* (Time) | 60 min | | | | | | | |
| Scoring Zone Practice | 2 hrs | | | | | | | |
| Suppliments (Vitamins A,C,E,Beta car) | ACE | | | | | | | |
| **Diet (fat grams)** | Act | | | | | | | |
| Body Weight | Ac | | | | | | | |
| Visualization Practice! | 1 h | | | | | | | |
| IPS Trainning Tape | 30 | | | | | | | |
| Motivational or recreational Reading | 3 | | | | | | | |

| | | |
|---|---|---|
| *Attitude (positive and fun)* | | |
| Resilience (flexible, adapt) | | |
| **New Adventures** | | |
| **Organized (time management)** | | |
| *Leader (inspires others)* | | |
| Desire (want, need, dream) | | |
| *Problem Solver* | | |
| Actor skills (ability to act IPS) | | |
| *Learning Ability* | | |
| *Modesty (grounded)* | | |
| Energy Level | | |
| Recovery (quality rest wave | | |

"The Differen

© *Bradly P. Brewer*

## ARNOLD PALMER GOLF ACADEMY

CLIENT'S NAME: _____

DATE: _____

### PRACTICE LIKE-A-PRO!

Cycle: __Fundamental Development__
Theme: _____
Summary: _____

| ATTAINABLE GOALS | GOALS | MON | TUE | WED | THR | FRI | SAT | SUN |
|---|---|---|---|---|---|---|---|---|
| Time to Bed/Time Up | | | | | | | | |
| **Hours of Sleep** | 11-6 | | | | | | | |
| Quality of Sleep (A-F) | 7 | | | | | | | |
| Exercise: Aerobic/Weights/jog… | A | | | | | | | |
| **Stretching Routine** | 40 min | | | | | | | |
| Golf competition | Yes | | | | | | | |
| Fundamental practice | 0 holes | | | | | | | |
| *Swinging Practice* (Time) | 2 hrs | | | | | | | |
| Scoring Zone Practice | 30 min | | | | | | | |
| Suppliments (Vitamins A,C,E,Beta car) | 1 hrs | | | | | | | |
| **Diet (fat grams)** | ACEBc | | | | | | | |
| Body Weight | Actual | | | | | | | |
| Visualization Practice! | Actual | | | | | | | |
| IPS Trainning Tape | .5 hr | | | | | | | |
| Motivational or recreational Reading | 15 min | | | | | | | |
| | 30 min | | | | | | | |

| | | | |
|---|---|---|---|
| *Attitude (positive and fun)* | | | |
| Resilience (flexible, adapt) | A | | |
| **New Adventures** | A | | |
| **Organized (time management)** | A | | |
| *Leader (inspires others)* | A | | |
| Desire (want, need, dream) | A | | |
| *Problem Solver* | A | | |
| Actor skills (ability to act IPS) | A | | |
| *Learning Ability* | A | | |
| *Modesty (grounded)* | A | | |
| Energy Level | A | | |
| Recovery (quality rest waves) | A | | |
| | A | | |

"The Difference between Ordinary & Extra-ordinary is that Little Extra"

© *Bradly P. Brewer*

# CHAPTER 11

# The Video Camera

*"Photographs of me on horseback, yes. Tennis, no.  And golf is fatal."*

**Teddy Roosevelt** warning President
William Taft to never be photographed playing golf

*"Video is used by the world's best golf instructors as a
teaching tool. Now it's your turn."*

*Brad Brewer*

I f you ever have the opportunity to visit a professional tournament, plan on spending some time on the practice range. You'll see many of the pros using video cameras to record their swings. Video is ideal for quickly showing them exactly what took place during their swing. They may be trying to correct a problem or trying to link a feeling to the swing they just made.

While the pros use video on a regular basis both on the practice range and working with their swing coaches, very few amateur golfers have ever seen their own swings. Have you? You may be very surprised when you see it. Often, what you feel you are doing is not what it looks like on tape.

# Your Assistant Coach

Your home video camera is an ideal candidate to be your new assistant golf coach. Once you learn how to set it up correctly, it will tirelessly be on the job assisting you—as long as you have a few charged batteries.

What you should look for in a video camera:

- Many cameras have controls that allow you to select a sports mode. This programs the camera for the faster shutter speeds that you'll need to capture important positions in your golf swing.

- Some cameras have remote controls that allow you to begin taping and stop taping without having to walk to the camera.

- Your camera should have a clean lens and several batteries that are at full charge.

- Some of the new digital cameras will allow you to input the swing into your PC or laptop and use some of the computer golf coaching programs that are commercially available.

## How to Set Up the Camera Properly

The video camera can help you only if you are correctly viewing what takes place in your golf swing. I'll show you how to position your camera correctly and also how to best take advantage of the available light.

## Lighting

You will be setting your camera at two different angles to view your golf swing: *face on* and *down the line.* The position of the sun plays a major role in how clear and bright your tape will be. If it's a bright sunny day, you do not want to have the camera shooting directly into the sun. The ideal sun position for down-the-line taping is with the sun behind the camera or within 180 degrees. For face-on shots, behind the camera is the best angle for the sun to be or slightly to either side. Once the sun creeps behind the person being taped and shines into the camera lens, the exposure will look dark. On evenly lit days with hazy sunshine, direct sunlight does not present problems.

# Setting Up the Video Camera for a Down-the-Line View

I believe it's important to build a practice station as we set up the video camera in order to help you practice correctly.

Put your video camera on a tripod. This is very important as you need a tripod to position the camera at the correct height and angle while providing a steady base. We'll position it later.

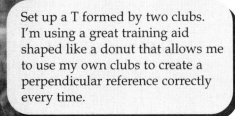

Set up a T formed by two clubs. I'm using a great training aid shaped like a donut that allows me to use my own clubs to create a perpendicular reference correctly every time.

Place a golf ball off the T at the distance you normally would tee it up in your stance. Remember, we are trying to see what you are presently doing now, not correcting anything yet.

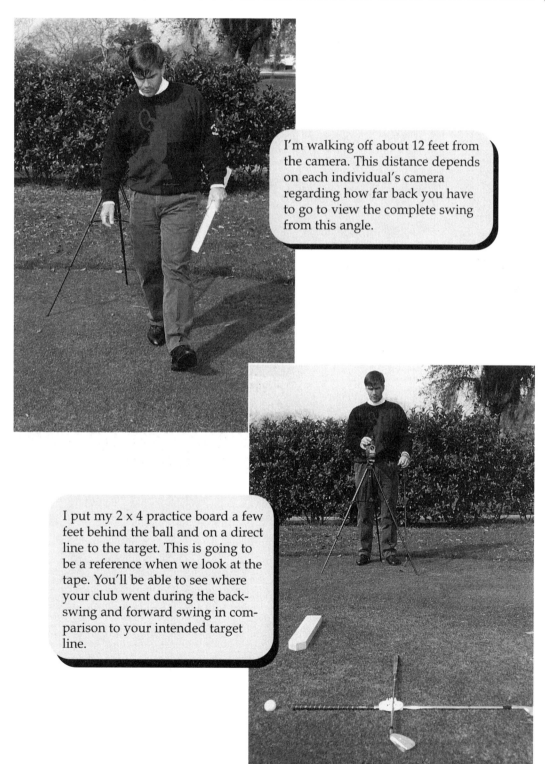

I'm walking off about 12 feet from the camera. This distance depends on each individual's camera regarding how far back you have to go to view the complete swing from this angle.

I put my 2 x 4 practice board a few feet behind the ball and on a direct line to the target. This is going to be a reference when we look at the tape. You'll be able to see where your club went during the backswing and forward swing in comparison to your intended target line.

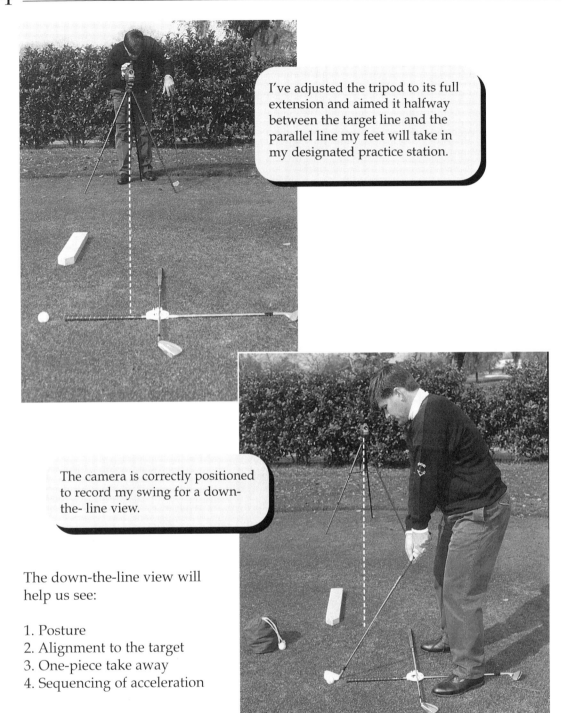

I've adjusted the tripod to its full extension and aimed it halfway between the target line and the parallel line my feet will take in my designated practice station.

The camera is correctly positioned to record my swing for a down-the- line view.

The down-the-line view will help us see:

1. Posture
2. Alignment to the target
3. One-piece take away
4. Sequencing of acceleration

# Setting Up the Camera for a Face-On View

To shoot a face-on view requires moving the camera so that it faces you and is directly lined up with the ball and the T. One club should be pointing directly at the camera and perpendicular to the other club when viewed through the viewfinder.

The camera records your golf swing with a face-on view.

Another view of how it should look showing the distance the camera is away from you. Make sure you allow ample room for your complete swing, including the clubhead at the top, to be recorded.

The face-on view will help us see:

1. Grip position
2. Width of stance
3. Your ball position
4. The steady head position
5. One-piece take-away
6. Sequence of acceleration

# Brad's Tips for
## Video Setup

1. Be sure your camera is set in the sports mode or fast shutter position.

2. Tape a swing when you set up your camera to be sure you've been able to record it correctly. Be sure you can see the clubhead throughout the entire swing.

3. Tape drills as well as your swings.

4. Compare the elements of your swing with those in Chapters 12-15 to learn more about what you are currently doing incorrectly.

5. Seeing your current swing coupled with an understanding of what's happening with it is an outstanding learning experience.

6. Use video for comparing your practice swing to playing on the course swinging motions. Sometimes they can be very different.

7. I also suggest taping your pre-shot routines to see exactly how you prepare for each shot.

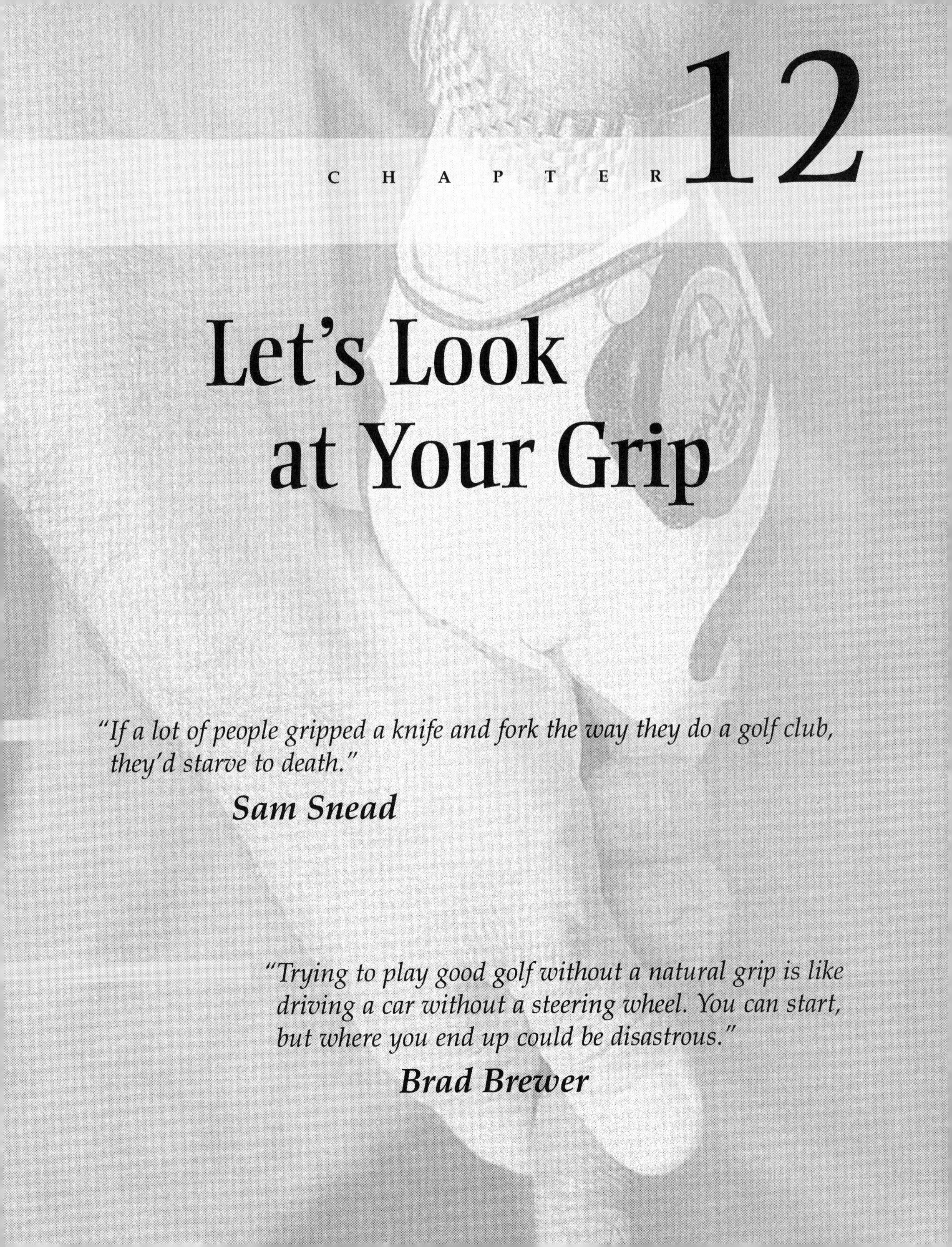

# CHAPTER 12

# Let's Look at Your Grip

"If a lot of people gripped a knife and fork the way they do a golf club, they'd starve to death."

**Sam Snead**

"Trying to play good golf without a natural grip is like driving a car without a steering wheel. You can start, but where you end up could be disastrous."

**Brad Brewer**

L et's begin our video assessment of your swing by looking at your grip, the starting point for good consistent golf swings. I've also included a photo of a neutral grip for you to compare your hand placement to. A neutral grip position is the starting point for ensuring that you can make a free-flowing motion, generating maximum swing speed with a natural squaring of the clubhead as it impacts the ball. If you're thinking "That's way too many things for me to think about and control," you're absolutely correct. But don't worry, you won't have to—it's going to happen naturally after you master the fundamentals.

## ATTAINABLE GOALS

*Learn a correct neutral grip position and you have established the core foundation that will allow you to make a good swinging motion. It's as simple as that.*

As we look at the various incorrect grips in this chapter, I'll explain why they contribute to a faulty swing. The more you understand about what causes a fault, the easier it is to understand the changes you need to make. I'll show you step by step how to grip the club in a neutral position in Chapter 24. I've also included some drills to help make your grip feel natural.

# Brad's Suggestions for Identifying Your Current Grip

1. Videotape a face-on (front view) close-up of your grip.

2. You can also check your grip by looking in the mirror at home, but a video will document your current grip before you start working on improving it.

3. Freeze the grip frame on your TV.

4. Place a ruler on the screen and over the V formed by your thumb and forefinger.

5. If the ruler points to the outside of your right shoulder or beyond, your grip is considered too strong (outside and beyond the left shoulder for left-handed golfers).

6. If the V points to the center or left shoulder, your grip is considered too weak (center or right shoulder for left-handers).

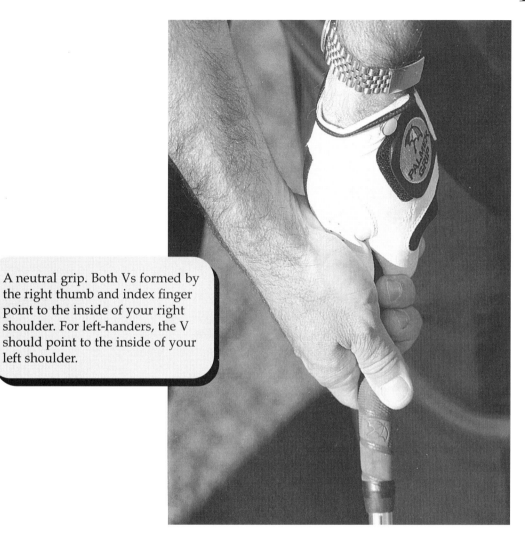

A neutral grip. Both Vs formed by the right thumb and index finger point to the inside of your right shoulder. For left-handers, the V should point to the inside of your left shoulder.

### Back to Basics

Whether your grip is too weak or too strong, I'll show you the correct neutral hand placement positions in Chapter 24. I'll include some drills to make your new grip feel natural.

# Can You Find Your Current Grip in These Examples?

Compare your grip to these examples. Even if you can't find it exactly, you'll probably see one that's similar.

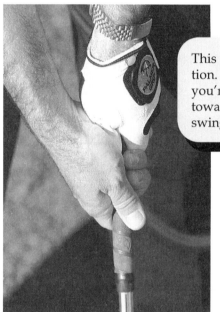

This is a good neutral grip position. If your grip looks like this, you're already well on your way toward improving your golf swing.

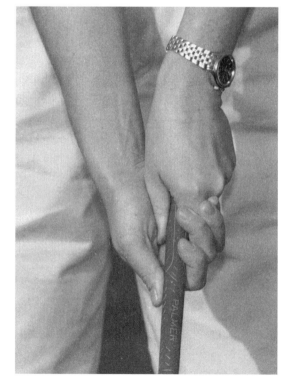

A typical beginner's grip. Weak left hand with a strong right hand. The thumb is incorrectly placed on top of the shaft. A natural tendency for most people is to pick things up with the thumb and index finger. This is a very common fault with beginners. The swing problem that develops is a picking up of the club rather than swinging it back in the take-away portion of the backswing. A lifting and chopping golf swing is the unfortunate result.

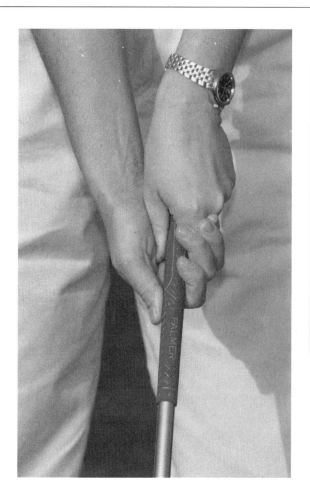

## Back to Basics

This incorrect grip may feel natural and comfortable. However, it will not allow you to make a good golf swing. It's an example of how, in the beginning, you may fight your natural desires and tendencies as you build new and correct feelings. Chapter 24 shows you step by step how to grip the club correctly. You'll find easy-to-work-on practice tips for improving your grip at home, even while watching TV.

This incorrect grip usually belongs to someone attempting to cure a wicked slice. Both hands are way too strong. The Vs are pointing to the outside of the right shoulder. To help control the club, the thumb and index finger are pinching the shaft. This grip position will make it very difficult for the clubhead to release naturally as it impacts the ball. If it does release, the clubface will be so closed down that it will be difficult to get the ball off the ground. A low "shrimp shot" (low and left) is usually the unfortunate result.

Golfers with the above grip are compromising their natural swinging motion by dragging the handle through impact to keep the clubface open a little bit. Unfortunately it also causes what I call "Army Golf." Left, right, left, and you won't know which will come first—the push or pull. The swing can't have much power because the grip does not allow a release of the club through impact with maximum power. The entire swing turns out to be an unfortunate compensation for this incorrect grip position.

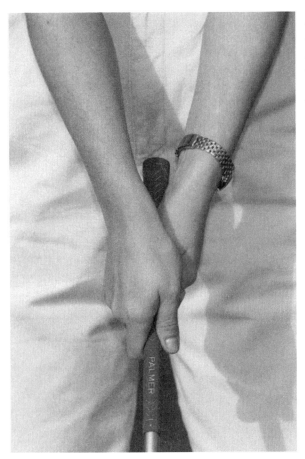

An incorrect weak grip. The Vs are pointing between the chin and left shoulder. This tends to be the usual grip position for a golfer who has played for a while but tends to hook the ball. They are trying to compensate with their hands to help them keep the clubhead more square coming through impact.

## Swing Killers

This photograph shows an especially bad grip position for women golfers. Unfortunately, it is one that we see very often in our Academies with beginning golfers. It can be detrimental to their entire swing. This incorrect grip will hinge the wrists into a shut position going back and usually causes a loss of power because the player has to cast out early from the top of the backswing.

Weak grips create a feeling of heaviness as the club is taken back. The club is going to feel heavy because the wrists are in a position where they are not able to hinge naturally during the backswing. The club will tend to swing inside and then has to be lifted, instead of the one-piece take-away and a natural wrist hinging that happens from a good grip.

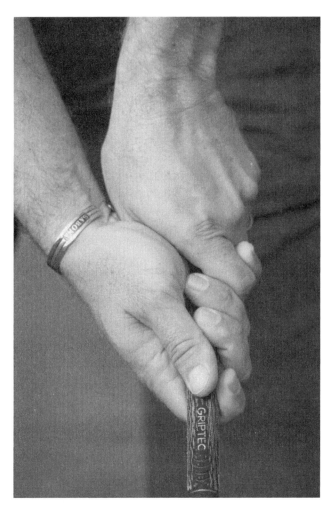

A very strong grip. Some very good professional players, like Paul Azinger, have played their entire careers with this grip and made a lot of money. Both Vs are pointing to the outside of the right shoulder in a very strong position. You can see almost four knuckles of the left hand.

To get the club square at impact, Azinger has to hold off his release of the clubhead and rotate hard with his hips and shoulders. Remember, he practices this for hours and hours. However, even with all of his talent, his shot making is limited by his grip position.

It's very difficult for an average golfer to consistently hit good shots with this grip. You would have to spend time working on the special moves Azinger makes to get back to the ball with a square clubface. Even he has problems occasionally. If his hip and shoulder movements become slower, the ball will go to the left; if he's too quick with his rotation, the ball will go to the right. A neutral grip is a better choice for most golfers.

# Brad's Coaching Tips
## for Correct Grips

I suggest that you commit to developing a good natural grip. I'll show you how, step by step in Chapter 24. Once you have mastered this most important of all the fundamentals, keep checking it. All golfers including Touring Pros have a tendency to slip back into old or incorrect positions. Check your grip on the range and use the drills I've included in Chapter 24 to help make it feel more natural.

# How Do You Address the Ball?

*"I think addressing the ball means you walk up to the ball, take your stance, waggle your club, look down at the ball, and say "Helloooooo ball."*

**Art Carney** as Ed Norton helping Jackie Gleason learn to play golf in an episode of "The Honeymooners"

*"Setting up in a good athletic position at address is another of golf's fundamentals. It's imperative to have a correct posture throughout the entire swing in order to create good consistent ball striking."*

**Brad Brewer**

**A**lmost every swing fault has its root in the way golfers set up at address. You might find a temporary Band-Aid swing tip that eliminates the bleeding but you can't correct the swing problems until you understand and master the basic fundamentals at address. In this chapter I'll concentrate on address problems.

This is how your address position posture should look when seen from the down-the-line view.
1. I'm in a good athletic position with my knees slightly flexed.
2. I've pushed my hips back creating the proper angle tilt.
3. My hands are relaxed from my shoulders and are under my chin.
4. The weight is on the balls of my feet.

Compare this photo to your address position.

Ball position is the second position of address imperative to making a good golf swing.

1. The ball should be positioned at the bottom of the swing arc.
2. This ensures maximum clubhead speed and the natural squaring of the clubface.
3. For driver through 7-iron, the ball should be positioned about two inches off your left heel.
4. Alignment, the third position of address, should have your feet, shoulders, and hips parallel to your target.

Compare this photo to your address position.

# Identifying Your Current Address Position

1. Videotape a down-the-line view of your address position.

2. Videotape a face-on (front) view of your address position.

3. Freeze a down the line view address frame on your TV. This will show your: a. posture, b. ball position, c. alignment

4. Find a similar position in this chapter to help you understand what your problems are.

5. Freeze a face-on view address position frame. Check your grip, ball position, width of stance, weight distribution, and head position.

6. Find a similar position in this chapter and I'll help explain the areas for you to focus on in your address position.

**BACK TO BASICS**
After you have compared the good and bad address positions and understand the problems, please turn to Chapter 25. I'll show you how to set up to the ball correctly and provide some drills that will help you work on mastering this basic fundamental.

# Can You Find Your Current Address Position Here?

If your address position closely resembles mine in the previous two photographs, you are starting off your swing with a good athletic position, proper posture, alignment, and excellent ball position. The rest of the examples are posed positions I've selected to illustrate the most common problems I see.

In this down-the-line view, John is demonstrating a typical slouched-over posture. As a result of being a little too far away from the ball, he's reaching for it with his arms and extended flex in the knees. If you're reaching too far, you also have a tendency to flex down with your knees to get your weight balanced. The arms should be hanging down from his shoulders but, as you can see, John's hands are almost outside of his head. This is a very restricted position to make a good one-piece take-away and maintain balance throughout the golf swing. He's so crouched over that it's almost impossible for him to get back to the ball consistently.

Denise has set up with the ball too close to her causing her arms to hang too close to her body. She won't have enough room to make a good one-piece take-away. She's also very upright with her chest and her spine angle is almost perpendicular to the ground. There isn't much tilt to the spine to create a nice natural angle. From this position it will be difficult to coordinate the moves to make a good golf swing. The tendency is to lift the club up high and way above your swing plane. To get back to the ball, she would likely have a descending angle of attack.

Denise is demonstrating a hyperextended reaching for the golf ball. She has no knee flex and, to try to get some weight distribution, she's pushed her derrière back too far, causing the weight to be on her heels. Because there is no balance in the lower body, the club will have the tendency to work really quick to the inside and around. From that position it will be very difficult for her to maintain her stability throughout the shot. She'll have a lot of movement causing lots of mis-hits.

This address position shows Denise has aimed to the right of the target line, illustrated by the marker. She's probably aimed 20 yards to the right of her target. In this position, the tendency is to take the club too quickly inside because there's lots of room, causing her to move off the ball slightly. Coming back, she would most likely come over the top to get back to the ball. This will result in a pull shot. A lot of golfers play this way because it's easy for them to make a big turn and it feels good to hit that hard pull. Unfortunately, that's a very difficult shot to control, and most golfers should work on fundamentals that will allow them to have a consistent swing.

Denise is in an incorrect address position where she is set up over the top with her right shoulder and forearms. It's a tendency I see with a lot of beginners who are very strongly right-side dominant. The left side is usually weak in the grip and you can see how the right shoulder and forearm are over the left side. When you set up in a position like this, it's very difficult to swing back into the ball. You'll be coming over the top all the way, because you set up over the top to begin with. You probably hit a lot of hard pulls and hold on cut shots with the famous "chicken wing finish."

You can easily see the wide stance Denise is demonstrating. See how her feet are extended beyond the width of her shoulders. From this position she will find it difficult to make a good body pivot away. The usual result is a reverse pivot where the weight never gets loaded up to the right side or a huge sway of the upper body to the right, causing extreme head movement off the ball.

This is a case where the stance is too narrow. Denise would have the tendency to sway with the lower body. The weight would be lost to the outside of the feet. There's just not enough of a width of stance to support a good swinging motion.

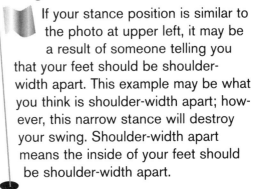

## Swing Killers

If your stance position is similar to the photo at upper left, it may be a result of someone telling you that your feet should be shoulder-width apart. This example may be what you think is shoulder-width apart; however, this narrow stance will destroy your swing. Shoulder-width apart means the inside of your feet should be shoulder-width apart.

Does your ball position look similar to this photo? Denise is demonstrating a ball position that is back of center towards the right foot. You can see how it creates a sharp angle between the left arm and the shaft. This position results in too much weight on your left side at address and causes the club to have a very sharp angle of attack working up and down. While this might be the stance you would adjust to in real heavy rough or one that requires a descending blow, for your normal iron shots this will only create a heavy divot, and a lot of hurt in your left wrist.

The ball is too far forward in this stance. It's off her left toe instead of two inches off the left heel. The hands are too far behind making it very difficult for her to take the club back in a one-piece motion. Denise's clubhead will drag behind the hands in the first part of the take-away, causing a cupped position. The tendency is to break down at impact with the club-head passing the hands, causing a variety of mis-shots.

# Brad's Coaching Tips for a Fundamentally Sound Address

Because the incorrect positions shown in this chapter are representative of the problems I usually see at address, I'm sure many of you found your position or one fairly close to it. Just as with the grip, you have to master the basic fundemental of a proper address position in order to improve your game.

In Chapter 25, you'll find a step-by-step approach designed to help you work on developing a good address. I've also included some drills to help you. Just as with the grip, you can work on your address at home in front of a mirror.

# Let's Look at Your Swing

*"My swing is so bad, I look like a caveman killing his lunch."*
*Lee Travino*

*"The golf swing itself is relatively simple, but so many people make it hard. If you can master the basic fundamentals, the rest of your golf swing will take care of itself."*

*Brad Brewer*

**A**fter you've had a chance to look at your videotape, this chapter will help you put it all in perspective. I would like to make something extremely clear before we start: The problems we'll see here are mostly caused by faults that occurred earlier when you gripped the club and addressed the ball.

I'm assuming that you are a good athlete. Like all good athletes, you instinctively know where your target is and will do whatever it takes physically to get your body to perform the task at hand. This is why we see such a variety of swinging motions on every golf course around the world. In fact, I would classify some of you as great athletes, due to your ability to coordinate the hand/eye skills required to compensate for your faulty swing mechanics! Now that we know what a great athlete you are, this chapter can do nothing but improve your understanding of the fundamentals you need to improve the ease with which you hit solid shots.

Most swing faults are really compensations you make to get back and hit the ball. Other swing faults are a result of misinterpreting information you have heard or read and tried to incorporate into your swing. The golf swing itself is relatively simple. If you can master the fundamentals, the rest of your golf swing will take care of itself. The five fundamentals are:

1. Grip
2. Address
3. One-piece take-away
4. Steady head
5. Acceleration

I'll help you with demonstrations and drills in Part 7. If you don't want to work on developing a new swing just yet, that's okay. You'll find plenty of other chapters that will help you cut some strokes off your game without having to make swing changes. The information for improvement is here anytime you want to use it. Now let's take a look at some common swing flaws.

# How to Begin

If you want to evaluate your swing faults, please videotape the swing from the face-on and down-the-line views. If you just want to see what you may be doing wrong without taping it, stand in front of a mirror or use a friend's eyes to look for some of the characteristics in the next sections.

Pre-check your video to see the faults you had in both your grip and address. They play major roles in the problems we'll see here. Compare the fault example photos in this chapter to the good swing photos of Brad to help you understand the problems with your swing. Once you've improved your grip and address fundamentals, the information and drills in Chapter 26 will help you put it together with the final three fundamentals: one-piece take-away, steady head, and acceleration.

## One More Thought Before We Begin

At our Academies, we teach that the golf swing is one flowing motion and not something that is put together with different positions. In this chapter, we are looking at various positions only to help you better understand the dynamics of the swing. Since we covered grip and address in Chapters 12 and 13, let's begin with take-away.

# Take-Away

The take-away is a unified movement away from the ball by the hands, arms, and shoulders. I've drawn a triangle to illustrate the desired movement. This is called a one-piece take-away. You can easily develop a good take-away using drills to help you develop the feeling. Here's how it should look as viewed face on and down the line.

## Back to Basics

I'll explain more about each of the correct positions and what you should be feeling in Chapter 26.

# Can You Find Your Take-Away in These Examples?

Kenna started her take-away with her hips and shoulders spinning the club to the inside.

Kyle, a left-hander, is taking the club back with his hands and wrists. Nothing else has moved. You don't see any shoulder motion and the lower body is not being naturally pulled into the take-away. Do you begin your take-away by picking up the club with the hands and wrists?

John is demonstrating another lift with a right-hand type of take-away. Not a lot of weight will naturally transfer over to the right side and he's beginning to have a reverse pivot. Notice how he's starting to lean away from the direction the club is traveling.

Thinking he is going to widen his swing arc, John is demonstrating the common fault of trying to hyperextend the arms away from the body. He's pushing the club out with his hands only instead of with the unified arm, hand, and shoulder one-piece take-away. Note how he's pulled his upper body and head too far to the right.

## BRAD EXPLAINS

*A reverse pivot is very common in higher handicap golfers. They have the weight on the wrong side of the body. During the backswing, when the weight should be transferred to the right side, they have the weight incorrectly shifting to the left. As they make their forward swing and impact the ball, the weight that should be moving to the left to create power is going backwards to the right side. I have some good drills to give you the correct weight transfer feeling in Chapter 26.*

This very strong right-side take-away, caused by pushing off with her left leg, has left Denise with a very weak left side. She started out with a bad grip that caused her to pick the club. It may look as if she's keeping it together, but she's not.

Denise is demonstrating a lift of the golf club, causing her to drop her left shoulder starting a reverse pivot. She just lifted the club up without any lower body natural movement.

Looking down the line with our reference board, Denise has an outside pick-up take-away instead of a low sweeping one-piece take-away. Note how the club is outside the line and the clubhead is closed.

See how Denise has straightened up in this lifting of the lower body take-away? Her knees have straightened as she turns her shoulders to the inside. The arms remain very close to the body without the ability to stay extended on her proper swing path.

This faulty take-away shows Denise turning her chest away too quickly. The arms have not extended and the position looks "around" because of going too quickly to the inside.

## Steady Head

As you continue on with your backswing, the steady head becomes a very important fundamental. Ideally, if you were to draw a circle around it at address, your head should stay pretty much within that circle during your entire swing.

### FEEL FEEDBACK

*If your head remains steady, your body will have a fairly constant axis, along with a good spine angle set at address, to rotate around. This makes it relatively simple to get back to the original starting point during impact. If you sway your head back, it's almost impossible to return it to the original position. All good strikers of the ball do move their heads slightly, but they will tell you they maintain the feeling that their head remains steady throughout the swing.*

## Can You Find Your Backswing Position Here?

Kenna is swaying off the ball. See how far she's moved away compared to the line? Her lower body got involved in the take-away instead of being natu-rally pulled into it with the one-piece motion back.

This is a classic reverse pivot. Her head is leaning to the left causing the weight to shift onto the left foot instead of shifting back to the right. The weight should be on the right.

This is what happens as Denise approaches impact with the ball. The weight is now on her right foot as she tries to get her head behind the ball by tilting it to the left. It's very impor-tant to incorporate a steady head into your swing.

This is a slight lean to the left caused by the arms and the hands picking the club up instead of sweeping it away in a one-piece take-away. It's small, but I wanted to show this because many golfers have a tendency to marginally reverse pivot due to improper take-away. You can see a slight left tilt to his head position.

# Acceleration

As you look at the tape of your swing, does it look smooth or jerky? Could it best be described as:

1. A finely tuned Ferrari, smoothly accelerating and reaching its maximum speed as it impacts the ball, or

2. A candidate for a new transmission—fast in the wrong places, shifts gears roughly, and loses vital acceleration as it impacts the ball.

## Smooth Acceleration Is the Key

1. Acceleration is defined as the increasing speed with which the clubhead moves through the ball.

2. Smoothness begins during the take-away.

3. The club continues back until it reaches the point where it must be forced to go any further.

Accelerate from the top of the backswing all the way through your follow-through.

4. The club is accelerated smoothly from the ground up and around a steady head.

5. If tension is present in the swing, or if any part of the body resists the flow of motion, smooth acceleration is impossible.

## Let's Look at Some Swings for Acceleration

Kyle, our left-hander, has lifted the club abruptly over his shoulder. As he approaches the impact zone, he's lost all the angle retention and the club is coming from outside to in. This will cause a glancing blow resulting in a slice or a chunky shot. He released the club way too early, losing all his power. As a result, he was not naturally pulled into a good follow-through. He's still hanging on his back foot because there was no acceleration through impact.

Denise is demonstrating how she won't be able to accelerate properly because she lifted the club instead of swinging it back with a one-piece take-away. Does she look coiled and ready to release? I'm afraid not. As she starts down, she's coming over the top from the outside. Losing all her angle retention is causing her to cut across the golf ball for a big slice. She has no acceleration in her swing to pull her off her back foot. As a result, she has a very abbreviated follow-through.

As Denise had excessive windup in her backswing, she took the club low and around. As she begins her downswing, the club will lay off from the inside, meaning it's still behind her. As she approaches the impact zone, her hands begin bowing out. With a bowed-out left wrist, she won't be able to release the club properly coming into impact. If your swing looks like this, you'll have a blocking sensation causing deceleration of your clubhead speed and shots that push out to the right.

John demonstrates a very high-flying right elbow and an across-the-line club. He had to compensate by working his body very hard to get the club back inside and, as a result, the club is laid behind him. You could put a drink on his clubhead at this point! He won't be able to get any good acceleration from this point, so he'll tend to hit blocked shots or big pulled hooks.

This is the classic sway. John has moved way off the ball with his upper body. As he starts down, he has to lunge forward with his upper body trying to get back to his original position. See how he's moved in front of the ball. This causes a throw-out of the club and he loses all of his angle retention. The lower body did not initiate this demonstrated swing from the ground up. Instead it was a throw-out and chest-over type of downswing. This swing ends up with a high right-side-and-around finish.

Denise is demonstrating how a reverse pivot robs you of power. At the top of her swing, her arms are lifted and she has swayed a little with her head to the left. She had to pull back on the start of her downswing to try to stay behind the ball. This caused her to block out with her hands and her left wrist is bowed. She has no acceleration because there is no natural swinging motion.

# Brad's Coaching Tips

1. Videotape your swing, or use a mirror or friend for reference feedback.

2. View your swing a few times, first at regular speed and then in slow motion.

3. Consult Brad's photos in this chapter to see how your swing should look.

4. Compare your swing with some of the examples in this chapter.

5. If you want to build a good swing, begin with the five fundamentals: grip, address, one-piece take-away, steady head, and acceleration.

6. Please don't get caught up with: "What did I do wrong?" practice habits. Identify your fault and then practice what you need to do correctly.

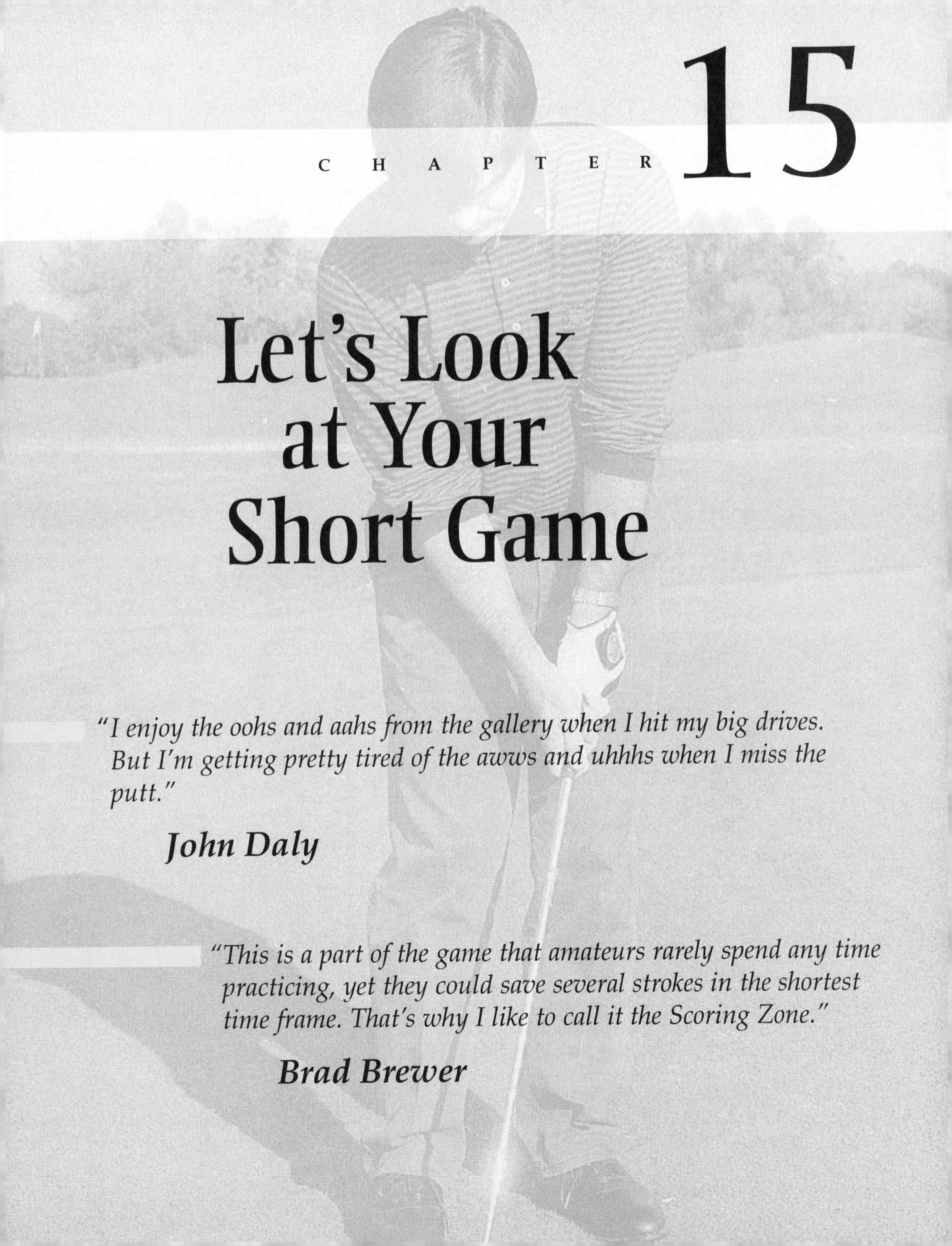

CHAPTER 15

# Let's Look at Your Short Game

*"I enjoy the oohs and aahs from the gallery when I hit my big drives. But I'm getting pretty tired of the awws and uhhhs when I miss the putt."*

***John Daly***

*"This is a part of the game that amateurs rarely spend any time practicing, yet they could save several strokes in the shortest time frame. That's why I like to call it the Scoring Zone."*

***Brad Brewer***

I like to call the area of the course where you hit pitch shots, chips, and putts the scoring zone. It's in this area that amateurs waste more strokes than anywhere else on the course. To make matters worse, my experience has been that they seldom practice the shots that can lower their scores in the quickest time frame. For the sake of evaluating your chipping and putting, we'll look at the same fundamental areas as we did for the full swing: grip, address, one-piece take-way, steady head, and acceleration.

Shoot a video of your short game using the same instructions we covered earlier in the book. Look at your video to see how it compares to the photos of how it should look. I've also included some examples of faults we commonly see.

Chapter 27 will help you work on this vital part of your game. I think you'll find the drills will help you create the feel you'll need out on the course.

# How Your Set-Up Position
## Should Look for a Chip Shot

Check to see that you have these elements:
- A good neutral grip.
- Choke down on the club for better control of the distance.
- Narrow stance with the ball approximately two inches off your left heel.
- Stance open to the target line, with feet, hips and shoulders parallel.
- Weight naturally set up more dominant on the left side with your hand slightly forward of the ball position.

## Bad Set-Up Position

This is a typical position for most people who are having trouble chipping. John's feet, hips, and shoulders are square and even a little closed to the target line when they should be open. He's not choking down on the club and will have a hard time controlling his distance and direction.

## Good One-Piece Take-Away

This shows the correct sweeping take-away position. My hands, arms, and shoulders have swung back in a good one-piece movement. I'm sweeping the club away from the ball. For the rest of my swing, I make the same one-piece movement in unison as I swing through, sweeping the club through the ball all the way to my follow-through with little or no wrist action at all.

This approach will make it easier for you to stay consistent with your tempo of acceleration and clubface staying square through impact. Make sure to keep a good steady head so you can maintain your original address positions throughout the swing.

## Bad Take-Away

John is taking the club back with his wrists very much to the inside. From here as he swings down, he'll have to try and manipulate his hands and roll over his wrists to square the club when it reaches the ball.

That didn't work and he dug the toe into the ground. This will result in a chunky shot or a ball that doesn't have any control when it reaches the green. This makes it very difficult to judge distance.

# Putting

This is an area where we see many variations and I want to stress that we have lots of room for personal preferences when it comes to putting. I believe Arnold Palmer has at some time in his life tried them all. I'm demonstrating what a good putting position and stroke look like based on what I see the greatest putters in the world do in common.

- Ball in the middle of my stance.
- Vs of both hands pointing to their respective shoulders in my grip.
- Dominant eye over the ball. (I explain that in Chapter 27.)
- Shoulders parallel to the ground at address.
- Feet, hips, and shoulders parallel to the target line.
- A pendulum stroke with the shoulders, arms, and hands moving in unison.
- Matching the length of the swing back and forth, with tempo and rhythm and smooth acceleration.

# Your Address Might Incorrectly Look like This

John is demonstrating a big cup in his left wrist. He's trying to control the entire club with the feel of his right hand. It's a big tendency for a lot of people to do that.

As he does that the clubface shuts down slightly. Coming through the ball, there is a tendency to break down with the wrists incorrectly, allowing the clubhead to pass the left side in a big way. This will cause pulled or topped putts.

John is demonstrating forward pressing his hands too far forward. He takes the club back with his wrists snapped up because it's the only way for him to take it back without scraping the grass. The take-away is an abrupt pick-up motion followed by a downward chopping motion. The only person I've ever seen putt effectively this way is Isao Aoki, but he has incredible hands.

John is demonstrating the common problem of setting your eyes outside of the ball and target line. When this happens, the tendency is to shove the club a little too much to the outside and cut across the shot coming in. Having an inside-to-out putting stroke is a definite problem causing mishits and pulled putts.

# Brad's Coaching Tips

1. You will be well on your way to improving your short game and cutting strokes, once you see what you're doing incorrectly.

2. Compare the examples and your swing to the pictures of my short game swings.

3. Chapter 27 will help you develop what you learned in this chapter so you become a much better "Scoring Zone" golfer.

# The Golf Course

*This part of the book offers help and suggestions for improving your game from the moment you decide to play through teeing off on the first hole. Ever go to a tournament and see how organized the pros are? Their minds are free to concentrate on the job at hand.*

*You'll find all sorts of helpful information here, including how to warm up properly so you can get the most enjoyment from your four and a half hours on the course. You'll end your warm-up session and head to the first tee mentally and physically prepared to challenge the course.*

# 16

# Preparing to Play

*"One of the most fascinating things about golf is how it reflects the cycle of life. No matter what you shoot, the next day you have to go back to the first tee and begin all over again and make yourself into something."*

## Peter Jacobsen

*"Your chances of having a good round are enhanced if you develop good routines on the course before striking the ball. I think a good routine, which so many people overlook, is how you prepare to play when you arrive at the golf course."*

## Brad Brewer

One of the keys to playing good golf is to be confident, prepared, and focused during the few wonderful hours you spend on the golf course. I assume your golf bag is packed with everything you might need (see Chapter 5), so off to the course you go.

# Before You Arrive

Actually, the preparation for your round began when you made your tee time. You did make your tee time, didn't you? The game of golf is booming and available tee times can be scarce, sometimes unavailable, unless you make prior arrangements—even at the most private of clubs.

## BRAD EXPLAINS

*A tee time is the starting time for a foursome on the first tee. Courses usually separate groups of golfers by eight minutes. When you're on the first tee, the group ahead of you must have hit their second shots before you can tee off to start your round. Unless a backup occurs along the way, you will play a well-paced 4- to 4 1/2 -hour round. That's why Ready Golf is so important (explained in Chapter 2).*

## Call to Make a Tee Time

The procedures for making *tee times* in advance vary considerably. In some areas, you have to register ahead of time with a state or local agency to receive a card entitling you to the privilege of calling by phone, several days in advance, to set up a tee time on a municipal or state golf course. This practice prevents people from calling and making blanket reservations and unfairly tying up lots of tee times. After asking for your card number, the agency can extend you the courtesy of making the advanced booking as they know you're a legitimate golfer. Some courses may accept tee time reservations several days or a week in advance. Private golf courses have their own member-only policies; the only way you can play is as an invited guest.

Other courses will not accept advanced tee time bookings: You have to go out to the course and tee off in the order you signed up. If you don't have your own foursome, the starter will usually add someone to your group. If you're a single golfer (someone who is not playing with anyone), you will have an easier time getting on than a foursome if the course is booked up. Sometimes a golfer doesn't arrive to play with his or her group and a spot opens for you. Many courses will not allow single golfers to book a tee time in advance. Instead, they fit you in when you arrive.

### Find Out about Tee Times before Booking a Golf Vacation

If you're planning a golfing vacation, inquire whether you can book your tee times when you make your hotel reservations. Some resorts have their own golf courses, while others may have affiliations with courses in their area. When you are investigating where to stay and play and see that golf is pictured in the brochure, don't assume that the hotel has its own course and prime tee times just waiting for your arrival.

# Once You Arrive

Your chances of having a good round are enhanced if you develop good routines on the course before striking the ball. A good routine for preparing to play is overlooked by many people. Rushing to the course and running out to the first tee just in time to tee off without warming up is hardly conducive to starting off the round at your mental and physical best. Take a moment to think about how, given unlimited time, you would construct the perfect schedule before you tee off. Here's my idea of what a good schedule might include.

1. Time to visit the pro shop and shop for some new clothes, try out a putter, or purchase any last-minute items.

2. Time to enjoy breakfast, lunch, or a snack.

3. Time to stretch so that you can be flexible enough to make your free-flowing golf swing.

4. Time to warm up on the driving range and get a feel for your short game.

5. Time to practice your putting.

6. A few extra moments to think about how you plan to attack the course today will send you to the first tee fully prepared.

Don't you agree that including at least some of these suggestions might help you become more relaxed and focused before playing?

# Photo Tour

Here's a photo tour of what it is like to prepare for a round at Arnold Palmer's Bay Hill Club and Lodge in Orlando, Florida. Bay Hill is the home of the annual Bay Hill Invitational PGA Tour Golf Tournament. It's a private club with a members- and members' guests-only policy. However, if you book a reservation and stay in the Lodge, the privileges of membership are extended to you during your stay— including the right to play this magnificent course.

Bay Hill is the Palmer's winter home and, if you stay in the Lodge, you may have the opportunity of seeing Arnold during the winter months. It's also the home of one of our Arnold Palmer Golf Academies. Even though this is a private club, Bay Hill's clubhouse area and sign-in procedures are similar to courses all over the country, both public and private. This photo guide will give you an idea of how to navigate around.

As you approach the clubhouse, look for the signs that direct you to the bag drop.

The bag drop is a drive-up location with an area where you can drop off your clubs so you won't have to carry them from your car in the parking lot.

Some courses have an attendant who will put your clubs on a golf cart for you. These are hardworking young men and women and it's appropriate to offer them a gratuity as a thank you for their help.

The golf cart carries two golfers and their clubs around the golf course. Normally the course has a charge for 9 holes or for 18 holes. If you choose to walk and didn't bring your own pull cart with you, you can rent one from most courses.

## BRAD EXPLAINS

*A gratuity, or tip, is a way of saying thank you. How much you should tip is up to you, depending on the help and courtesy of the outside attendant. At some golf courses, an attendant will clean your clubs and carry them to your car. If the club has a locker room and the attendant provides services to you, it's appropriate to offer a gratuity. Some golf courses do not allow their employees to accept gratuities—unless you are aware of this policy, it's appropriate to offer one. In the restaurant it's quite common for a gratuity of about 20 percent to be automatically added onto the bill. Check your bill before paying to see if this is the case.*

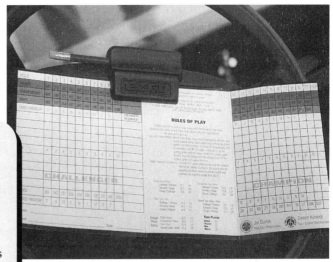

The score card for the course may already be on its holder located on the steering wheel. It's always a good idea to get at least one extra card, in case you lose this one. I have a collection from all the courses I've played around the world.

On courses with certain grasses, golf carts usually carry a mixture of sand and seed along with a scoop. This enables you to replace your divots and help heal the fairway by putting a small amount of this mixture into the scarred area.

## Can I Take a Caddie?

Some golf courses, usually private clubs, have caddies available to carry your bag if you decide to walk. Caddies are understanding and friendly, and, for the most part, possess local knowledge of the course. Their information can be extremely helpful if you've never played the course before.

Caddies are interesting individuals and are responsible for some of the language golfers still use today. They're also the subject of all sorts of stories.

*"I'm as worthless as a 2-iron."* Herman, Lee Travino's former caddie on what he's currently doing with his retirement time

*"He told me he caddied with me in the same group at the Hot Springs Open. That's why I voted for him, because he was a caddie."* Tommy Bolt, on why he cast his presidential ballot for Bill Clinton

*"If I needed advice from my caddie, I'd be carrying the bag and he would be hitting the shots."* Bobby Jones, on the subject of taking advice from a caddie

*"Never pick up a lost ball while it's still rolling."* Jack Nicklaus's advice to a caddie

*"Do I ever disagree with him on course strategy...never...unless he's wrong!"* Gary Nicklaus, on the subject of caddying for his father, Jack Nicklaus

## Check-In Time

Some courses have their check-in area in the pro shop, while at others you check in with the starter. This is when you pay for your round and for your pull or motorized cart. Caddies are usually paid separately.

## Navigating the Pro Shop

The pro shop carries many of the items golfers will need during their rounds and is usually the location of the pro's office. If you would like to talk to the pro or need to arrange lessons, either the pro or the assistant pros can help you. Follow the photo menu of some of the items available in the pro shop.

Golf balls. Pro shops carry a wide variety of golf balls. Ask for help if you're not sure which ball is best suited to your game. Pro shops will also have a display of golf gloves.

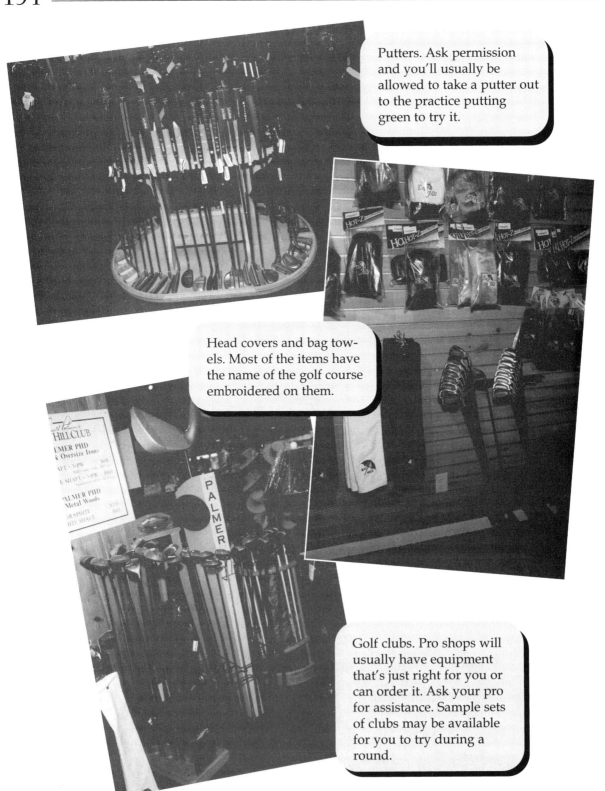

Putters. Ask permission and you'll usually be allowed to take a putter out to the practice putting green to try it.

Head covers and bag towels. Most of the items have the name of the golf course embroidered on them.

Golf clubs. Pro shops will usually have equipment that's just right for you or can order it. Ask your pro for assistance. Sample sets of clubs may be available for you to try during a round.

The Australian collection of unique hats from past British Open Champion Ian Baker-Finch.

LPGA golfer Michelle McGann is easy to spot at tournaments due to her distinctive hats.

Golf hats and caps. Some golfers wear hats for sun protection while others like to collect hats from the different courses they play.

Most pro shops have a sale rack where you can find some outstanding bargains.

Pro shops are a great source for purchasing memorabilia or artwork.

Men can also find golf clothing at the pro shop. Sometimes the name of the golf course will be embroidered prominently on the shirt. If you're wearing your home course shirt while on vacation, don't be surprised if someone asks you whether you know somebody from your hometown. You're part of an international organization and you'll often meet somebody who happens to know someone you know.

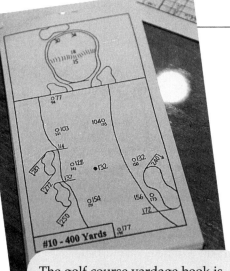

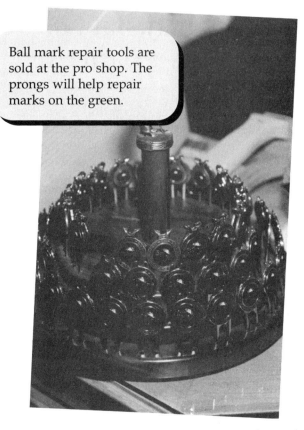

Ball mark repair tools are sold at the pro shop. The prongs will help repair marks on the green.

The golf course yardage book is your road map to the course. Distances to hazards and to the green from any location on the hole help you select the club and type of shot you want to hit. They are available for purchase in the pro shop at a nominal fee. I think a yardage book is invaluable as you work to improve your game. If you're playing a new course, purchase the book the night before and plan out how you are going to play each hole to best suit your game. I'll help you with that in Part 5.

Here are a few sample pages from "My Golf Journal," a book we use at our Academies. These journals are available in your pro shop or bookstore. They're perfect for keeping a written record of your game, lesson notes, swing thoughts, and strategies you used on the course. These journals are user friendly— all you have to do is fill in the information. I think a personal journal is a key ingredient to improving your game.

# It's Not Indy, But Golf
##    Needs a Starter Too!

At most golf courses, you'll find a "starter." This important job requires a friendly, intelligent person who calls the golfers to the tee when it's their time to tee off. This allows you to practice and not have to hang around the tee until your name or your group is called. Some starters will make an announcement that includes one additional group who will follow yours. The starter may say "The Paterson group to the tee, please, with the Henrichs group next." Sometimes, instead of saying "next," the starter will say "Henrichs group in the box," or "on deck."

One of the most knowledgeable and friendly Bay Hill starters is Frank Ramsdell. A retired businessman, he enjoys meeting and helping golfers get off to a good start.

The starter's booth may have important information posted. No information is more important to a golfer than how to avoid the deadly hazard of lightning while on the golf course.

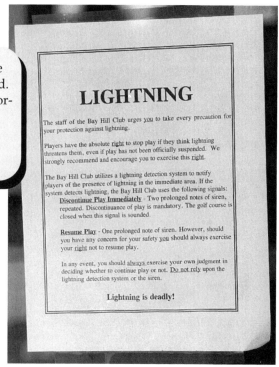

## LIGHTNING

The staff of the Bay Hill Club urges you to take every precaution for your protection against lightning.

Players have the absolute right to stop play if they think lightning threatens them, even if play has not been officially suspended. We strongly recommend and encourage you to exercise this right.

The Bay Hill Club utilizes a lightning detection system to notify players of the presence of lightning in the immediate area. If the system detects lightning, the Bay Hill Club uses the following signals:

**Discontinue Play Immediately** - Two prolonged notes of siren, repeated. Discontinuance of play is mandatory. The golf course is closed when this signal is sounded.

**Resume Play** - One prolonged note of siren. However, should you have any concern for your safety you should always exercise your right not to resume play.

In any event, you should always exercise your own judgment in deciding whether to continue play or not. Do not rely upon the lightning detection system or the siren.

**Lightning is deadly!**

# Practice Facilities

Once you have checked in and taken care of shopping or purchasing some last-minute necessities in the pro shop, it's time to turn your attention to your game.

The practice putting green is available for practicing and building confidence in your putting before going out to play.

Some golfers call this the *driving range,* but I would like you to think of it as the practice range instead.

One of the big mistakes golfers make is to only practice their drives before teeing off. Ideally, you should start with your shorter clubs—like wedges and 9-irons—to loosen up and develop rhythm and feel before progressing to mid and long irons and then your woods. Driving should be the last thing you do before teeing off. I'll cover this in Chapter 17.

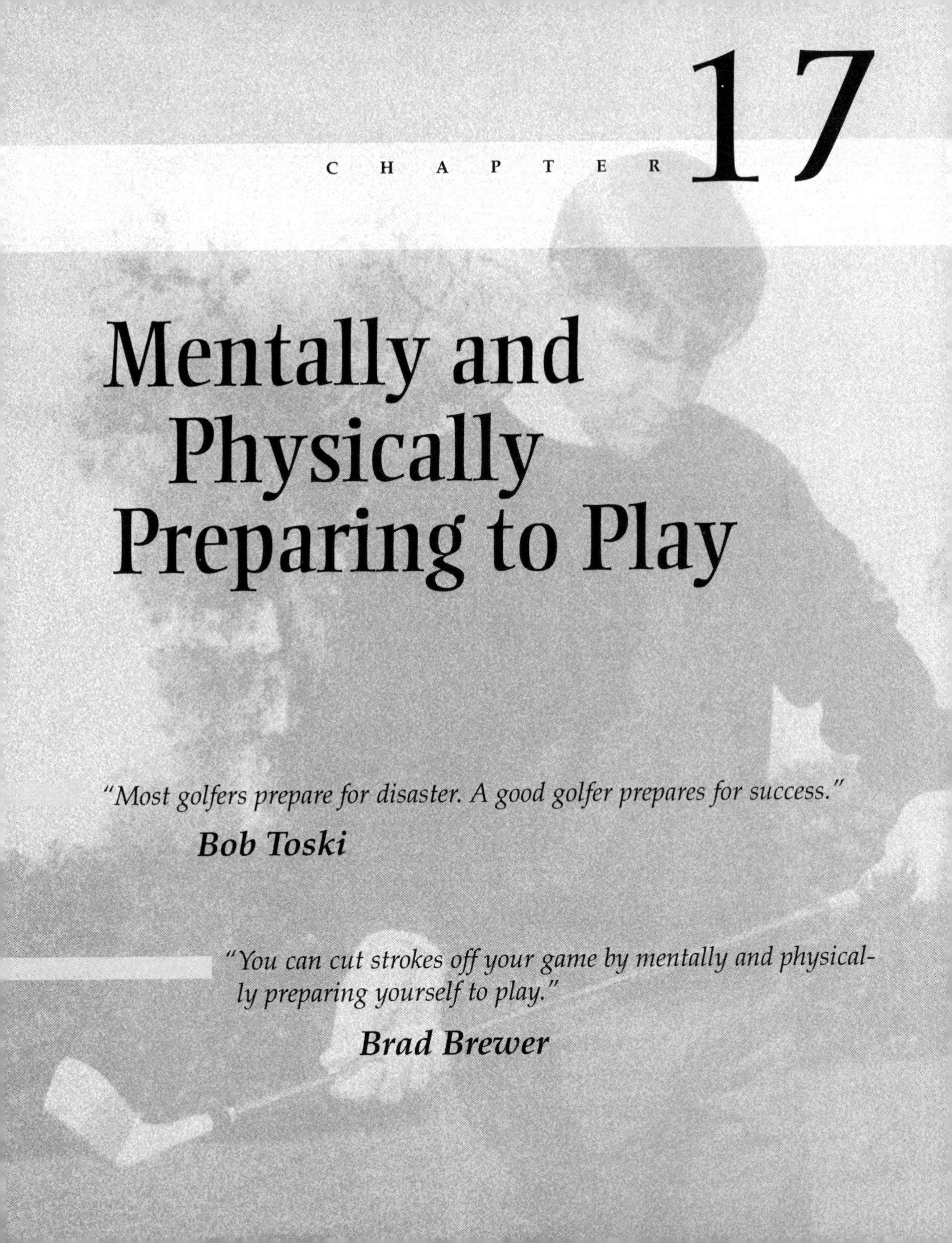

CHAPTER 17

# Mentally and Physically Preparing to Play

*"Most golfers prepare for disaster. A good golfer prepares for success."*

**Bob Toski**

*"You can cut strokes off your game by mentally and physically preparing yourself to play."*

**Brad Brewer**

**H**ow much time do you usually give yourself to prepare before heading to the first tee? Unfortunately, too many golfers arrive at the golf course within 15 minutes of teeing off. They rush around, grab a soda loaded with sugar—thereby hyping themselves—which makes it even more impossible to get out in front of everybody and tee off. It usually takes them 3 or 4 holes to relax and they have probably destroyed their opportunity to shoot a good score.

I suggest that you arrive at least 30 minutes before your tee time. It's a quality 30 minutes that you'll be investing for the benefit of the next four and a half hours of your life! Those 30 minutes will prepare you mentally and physically to get the most out of your round. So, if you want to visit the pro shop or have a snack, plan on coming to the course a little earlier.

# Pros Get Nervous Too

By the way, it's not only amateur players who get nervous before teeing off—many pros confess to having "butterflies" on the first tee every week. While you may feel unsure of your game and embarrassed to have others watch, a pro's nervousness is more like that of a race horse wanting to leave the starting gate. Stuart Appleby plays on the PGA Tour and says: "I look out at the fairway in front of me and I just can't wait to get it going."

If you have the opportunity to go to a professional event, look for your favorite player about one hour before his or her tee time. Players have their own routines and they follow them just about every time they play. Their preparation may even have started before coming out of the locker room, perhaps with a visit to the physical fitness trailer that has become an important part of the PGA and LPGA Tours. Their routines send them to the first tee ready to play their best. Familiar routines help them feel confident and prepared to start scoring right from their first tee shot. Now let me help *you* set up a routine that can improve your game and fun on the course.

# Stretches to Get You Loose

I suggest doing some light stretching before hitting any balls on the range. Here's a routine that I like to follow.

## Club Above the Head Stretch

Grab your club with both hands and stretch your arms up, extending them completely above your head.

Gradually try to stretch your arms behind your head, keeping your arms straight. This stretches your shoulders, arms, and down into your chest. Repeat a few times.

## Club Rotating Stretch

Hold the club in a parallel position about hip high in front of you. Your stance should be as wide as when you hit your driver.

Keeping your head centered, rotate around your trunk slowly, feeling the stretch as you go back. You'll feel your hips and shoulders rotating, stretching out the abdomen and hips.

Rotate slowly around to the other side. As you begin to feel more limber, increase the speed of your rotations to about the speed of your golf swing. Repeat a few times.

## Club Bending Stretch

Using the same driving stance as in our last stretch, hold the club parallel to the ground about waist high.

Bend from the waist, keeping your back straight.

Stretch down as close to the ground as you can get. This stretches out the calves and hamstrings. Repeat a few times.

## The Shoulder Stretch

Standing straight reach one hand above and behind your back placing it between your shoulder blades.

Grab your elbow with your other hand.

Pull your elbow backwards, stretching out your side and shoulders. Repeat a few times.

Repeat the stretch for your other shoulder.

## The L Stretch

Make an "L" with your forearm by bending your elbow. Place your other hand so it cups your elbow.

Stretch your elbow across your chest.

Repeat the stretch for your other elbow. You'll feel the stretch in that hard-to-get- to region in your shoulder blades.

## Relaxer Stretch

If this were a video, you could see how I am making little semi-circles with my arms as I relax, trying to get as loose as possible.

## Back Rocker Stretch

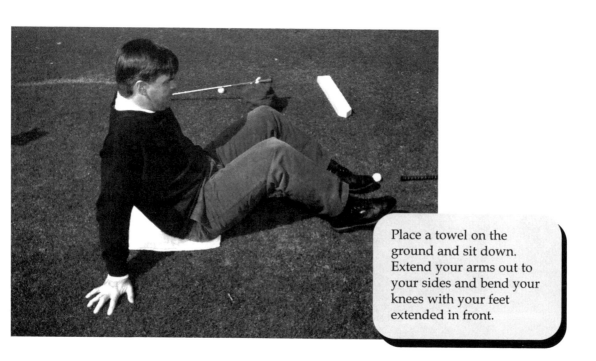

Place a towel on the ground and sit down. Extend your arms out to your sides and bend your knees with your feet extended in front.

Reach both hands under your thighs, grabbing the back of your thighs.

Roll back and forth, loosening up your lower back. This helps you get nice and limber.

## Heavy Club

The Heavy Club, available at some pro shops or golf specialty stores, works very well if you don't have a lot of time to get loose before you play. It looks like a driver but it's weighted in the clubhead and usually comes with a molded grip.

The camera has been slowed down so you can see the movement of the weighted Heavy Club as I swing down.

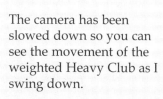

You can see the movement of the Heavy Club going up and towards my follow-through position. Make some nice fluid swings, allowing the weight of this training aid to help loosen you up.

## Swing Several Clubs If You're Short on Time

Swing two or three clubs together, if you don't have enough time to loosen up by stretching. Try to make some swings allowing the weight of the clubs to get you limber, just like a batter in the on-deck circle in baseball.

# Warming Up on the Range

Most courses today have a practice range for your long game. It may be called a driving range, but don't warm up your game just by hitting drivers. The first thing you should do is set up a practice station.

## Practice Station: Everything You'll Need to Prepare Yourself to Play

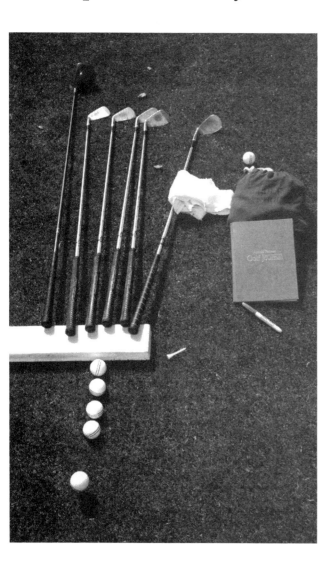

Brad's list for your practice station:

1. Practice balls
2. Tees
3. Golf Journal
4. Pen
5. Wet towel
6. Six clubs for practicing

## Try a Modified "Through the Bag" Warm-Up

Here are the clubs I suggest you use to warm up with.

Practice using these six clubs, beginning with your wedge, and then continue in the following order: wedge, 9-iron, 7-iron, 5-iron, 3-iron, driver.

## Hit Five Balls with Each Club

You don't need to hit bags of balls. Instead, hit five balls with each club, beginning with the wedge and working your way to the driver. I suggest starting with the wedge to get a good feeling for rhythm and tempo.

Hit five balls with each of the six clubs, beginning with your wedge.

Having everything organized and ready at your practice station makes it easy to follow a good warm-up routine.

## Start Focusing on Your Pre-Shot Routine

As you progress toward your long irons and driver, start focusing a bit more on the actual shot you're going to play. Don't make the mistake of just going to the range to bang a lot of balls. Instead, visualize your shot and then follow your pre-shot routine that you use on the course. This will make your practice seem more like playing. When it's time to go to the first tee, you'll feel in the flow of your game. Here's a good pre-shot routine that can help you focus on your shot.

Stand behind the ball and pick out your target.

Keeping your eye on the target, begin your address position by placing your club behind the ball and setting your back foot.

Complete your address by placing your front foot so that both of your feet are parallel to your target line. Using this routine creates the same feelings and focus that you will have when on the course.

## Keep Your Practice Clubs Clean

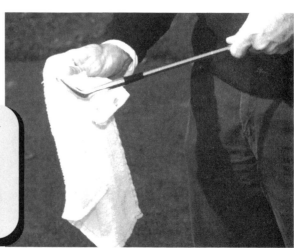

Use a damp towel to clean your clubs as you finish warming up. The grooves will be clean and the club will look good as you address your shots on the course.

## Keeping Control of Your Emotions

One of the things I like to do before heading over to the first tee is to spend a couple of minutes focusing on relaxing myself. I don't want to run over to the tee all stressed. Here's an easy way to relax and help yourself feel more comfortable.

Take some deep breaths. Inhale through your nose.

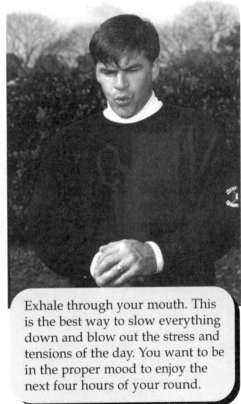

Exhale through your mouth. This is the best way to slow everything down and blow out the stress and tensions of the day. You want to be in the proper mood to enjoy the next four hours of your round.

# Mental Preparations

You've stretched, warmed up, and hit shots as you focused on your target. If you have time, it's always nice to concentrate on your strategy for playing the golf course, especially if you're playing a course for the first time. Look at the scorecard and yardage book and get a feel for how the holes are laid out and how you might play them.

# A Few More Preparations before Playing

Try jotting down some notes in your journal as you plan your strategies for playing the course.

## BRAD EXPLAINS

*PGA Touring Pro Duffy Waldorf has the most uniquely marked ball of anyone. His wife draws beautiful intricate, artistic designs on his golf balls. If you visit a PGA Tournament and watch Duffy play, you'll see what I mean.*

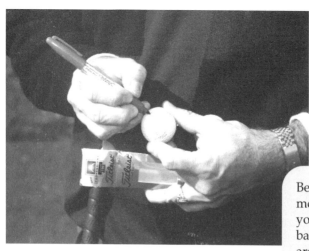

Before playing, take a few moments to distinctively mark your balls. This helps identify your ball on the course. If two golfers are laying a Titleist 3, the unique markings will identify the ball.

My distinctive marking is a smiley face. It's a reminder to have a good positive attitude and to have a fun day. Some golfers just use dots or other markings. Choose one that means something special to you.

Before heading to the tee, I make sure to protect myself with sun screen. You can get a burn even on a cloudy and windy day.

# Practice Your Putting

Usually the practice putting green is close to the first tee so I suggest making that your last stop on your way to the first tee. Don't work on mechanics, just work on developing rhythm and tempo. I suggest trying this routine to get you ready to hole a few more putts when you get to the course. I use three balls to practice with.

I'm using a shaft under my arms to help me get a feel for a one-piece motion. It's a sensation I like to have because it helps me line up correctly and develop the rhythm for a one-piece stroke.

I'll putt three or four balls with the shaft under my arms.

This part of my routine is to help me establish the feeling of rhythm and tempo. I'm not concentrating on getting the ball in the hole yet.

# Develop a Feel for the Speed of the Greens

I'll start off with some fairly long putts as I begin developing a feel for the speed or pace of the greens along with my rhythm and tempo.

This downhill breaking putt allows me to judge the speed it takes to get the ball to the crest of the hill before gravity takes over and feeds the ball to the hole.

## See the Ball Go into the Hole

I like to conclude my putting practice by sinking a few from about four feet. I want to see the ball go into the hole.

I like to putt from every angle so, with my three balls, I try to spoke them at different breaking positions. I feel sometimes that practicing my putting with my left arm only helps my stroke.

# This is What You've Been Waiting For!

I hope you're like me and can't wait to get started. I'm set up and ready for four hours of fun and challenges.

The first drive of the day, but my practice routine has prepared me mentally and physically for the round.

# Brad's Coaching
## Tips

1. Be sure to allow yourself enough time to mentally and physically prepare yourself to play. Allow at least 30 minutes before your tee time.

2. It's not usually a good idea to work on something you may have read in
   a magazine or seen on TV before playing. Save working on something
   new for practice sessions. My high school coach, Pat Shortridge, used to
   always remind me before a big match: "Brad, remember to dance with
   the one you brought."

# PART 5

# Let's Start Cutting Your Score

*Without changing anything in your golf swing, you'll learn how to immediately start cutting strokes from your game. Grid Golf is an easy-to-learn method of keeping your ball in play and out of hazards or penalty situations.*

*You'll become a master of the sand and learn how to hit the trouble shots the pros hit. All golfers get into trouble and face challenging lies. Pros know what to do and so will you!*

# CHAPTER 18

# Grid Golf: Keeping Your Ball in Play

*"In baseball, you hit your home run over the right-field fence, the left-field fence, the center-field fence. In golf, everything has to go right over second base."*

## Ken "Hawk" Harrelson

*"Grid Golf will reduce the high number of penalty shots usually incurred by mid- to high handicap golfers, effectively lowering your score. Grid Golf also creates scoring opportunities for low handicap golfers as it factors in pin placements, wind, and shot preferences."*

## Brad Brewer

# H

ere's what Grid Golf can do for you:

1. Save strokes before you even tee off.
2. Take advantage of your current game.
3. Enable you to look at the golf hole like never before.
4. Keep you out of trouble as you eliminate penalty shots.

If there were a Golf Tip Hall of Fame, the first and most illustrious inductee would be "Keep the ball in play!" Simple to understand, although you may find it hard to do. Is there anything more frustrating than seeing a beautiful golf hole in front of you and not be able to enjoy it because you're either searching for a ball in the woods or watching it drop into the pond? Golf course architects want you to admire their work, but they didn't expect you to visit every remote location on a hole. Before you even tee the ball up, I recommend that you really take a look at the hole. Many score cards have a diagram of each hole or you can buy a yardage book at the pro shop.

## BRAD EXPLAINS

*A yardage book features a map of each hole you'll be playing. The map shows the shape of the fairways and the direction to the green. All hazards, like sand bunkers, trees, and water are illustrated. Out of bounds, where it applies, is also shown. Yardage figures are provided for measurement so you'll always be able to tell how far you are from the green and how many yards away from any of the hazards.*

Instead of worrying about the trouble that lies ahead, take a deep breath, look around and admire the beautiful course you're playing. Let's make this a really interesting example by using one of the most difficult par 4 holes in golf: Bay Hill's 414-yard 18th hole. Did I mention that you'll also find the notorious Devil's Bathtub waiting for you about halfway down the right side and extending to the front of the green?

A Scuba diver surfaces with one of the many balls that fell victim to the clutches of Bay Hill's notorious 18th hole, called Devil's Bathtub.

# Mapping Your Route

Be honest now, when you looked at the diagram, did you mainly look at all the potential trouble spots? That's natural, but to start cutting some strokes off your game, I want you to look at each hole and its diagram and see opportunity instead.

Just as the yardage book features a sort of road map to the hole, you need your own customized road map that takes advantage of your current game. As your swing improves and the shape of your shots change, you will be able to take a different route to the hole. Let's refer to this approach as Grid Golf. Here's how four golfers with different skill levels can effectively use Grid Golf to cut scores.

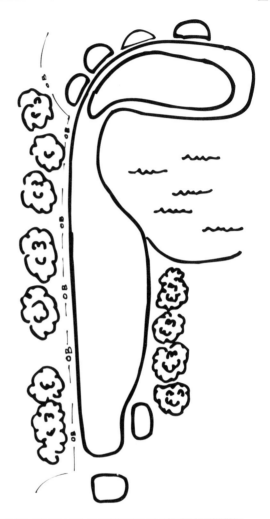

### BRAD EXPLAINS

*The real objective of Grid Golf is to teach you to keep your ball in play. It will reduce the high number of penalty shots (usually incurred by mid- to high handicap golfers) effectively lowering your score. Penalty shots come from lost balls, out of bounds, and lateral hazards. By visualizing a grid super-imposed on the hole in front of you and factoring in the shape of your current shot, Grid Golf will help you learn where to tee the ball up and aim it more effectively.*

*Grid Golf creates scoring opportunities for low handicap golfers. Depending on the changing variables—wind, weather, pin placements, and how you're playing that particular day—you can use and rely on Grid Golf to provide aiming points that will help you adjust.*

## Player A

This is how a pro would play the hole. To make it even more difficult, we'll put in the traditional "Sunday pin placement." During the annual Bay Hill Invitational held each March, the hole is set on Sunday to the right side of the green. If pros are short, splash! If they're too long, bunkers behind the green make it difficult to get close to the pin because the green slopes away toward the rocks. Using Grid Golf, here's how they would play the hole.

I've drawn in two grids, one for the drive and one for the approach shot. When you compare the width of the grid a pro would visualize to that of a high handicap amateur, you'll realize that these grids are fairly narrow.

The pro wants to birdie this par 4 hole.

- The pro wants his ball in the right center of the fairway, feeling this will provide the best location to hit the second shot to the pin on the right side. This will require hitting a left-to-right fade. For his second shot, he starts his ball 10 yards inside the out-of-bounds trouble on the left and fades it back perfectly.

- Using the grid as his guide, the pro tees the ball up at the right center of the tee box. He plans on starting the ball outside the left side of the grid, fading it back into the exact landing spot he wants—a 270-yard drive leaving 155 yards for the approach.

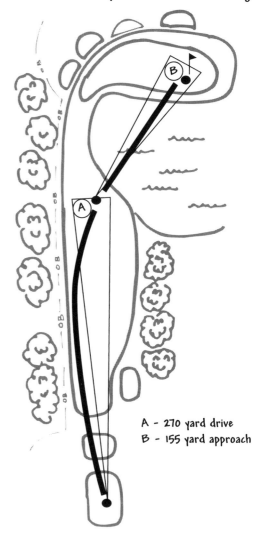

Player A
Professional
• can work the ball either direction
• chose to work away from OB & to the flag

A - 270 yard drive
B - 155 yard approach

- Instead of seeing the water hazard and wide green ahead of him, the approach shot grid is close to the hole on the right but provides more room on the left. If the pro can land his ball on the green within this grid, he has a good shot at birdie.

- Using the grid as a guide, the pro stays on the left side of the grid and his ball lands and rolls to the middle of the targeted landing area, well within range for a birdie putt.

## Player B

Our next player is a low handicap golfer and can have a handicap ranging from 0 to 10. A draw, the right-to-left ball movement, is this golfer's stock shot.

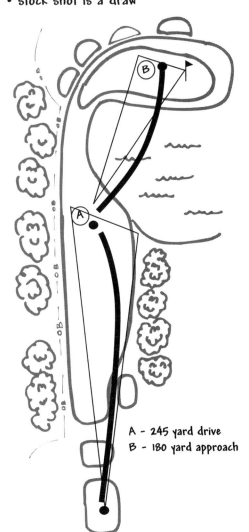

**Player B**
Low handicap 10 - 0
• stock shot is a draw

A - 245 yard drive
B - 180 yard approach

- Player B's grid is wider and starts at the right edge of the fairway because of her preference to hit a draw.

- Preferring to play a draw, Player B tees the ball on the far-left side of the tee box, giving herself that much more fairway to work with.

- Player B wants to take the out of bounds on the left out of play and, by aiming at the right side of the grid, knows the ball won't be able to draw back far enough to go out of bounds.

- Had Player B not used the grid and aimed down the center of the fairway, her draw could have gone out-of-bounds on the left, costing a one-stroke penalty.

- The 245-yard drive is safely in the center of the fairway. Even if she had not hit her best shot here, Player B would have been on the right side of the fairway, a little shorter but still in good shape. The grid provided a safe margin of error.

- Player B's draw would make it difficult to go for the pin with a 180-yard second shot, so her grid is aimed to the center of the green.

- The shot is aimed to the right of the grid and draws safely to the middle of the green. With that pin placement not favoring her style of play, Player B should have a reasonable expectation of making par on this hole, but still has a chance of making birdie.

- Grid Golf helped Player B avoid penalty strokes and navigate smartly to have a chance at birdie.

## Player C

Our Player C is a mid-handicap golfer (11 to 20). As with many golfers in this category, the fade or a controlled slice is the tendency.

- Player C's tendency to hit shots from left to right suggests he visualizes a grid that almost stretches across the complete fairway. Where he tees the ball and aims will be extremely crucial to keeping out of trouble.

- Player C wisely tees it up on the right side of the tee box, giving him the entire left side of the fairway to work with.

- By aiming the shot at the left side of the grid, this player's ball will start to the left but fade back toward the center of the grid 225 yards down the fairway. Even if he didn't hit his best shot, the ball would still be safe in the left center section of the grid.

- Had Player C aimed down the center of the fairway, he would have faded or sliced into the trees on the right. That would have cost him a shot to extricate himself from that predicament rather than use the stroke to go for the green.

- Player C is an aggressive player and wants to go for the green. He will need to take plenty of club to play smartly and carry the ball to the back of the green. Being short means—splash!

- The 200-yard approach shot is aimed slightly outside the left grid boundary to give it plenty of room to move back toward the center. The grid was aimed to the left center of the green to help avoid some of the bunkers behind.

- Having a chip shot from the back of the green and the opportunity to get it close enough to putt for a par, or even hole the chip, is a wonderful reward for this aggressive yet smart golfer.

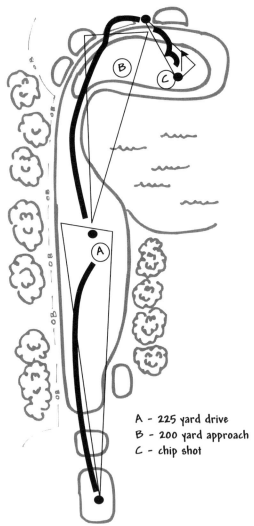

## Player C
Mid handicap 20-11
- stock shot is fade or controlled slice
- takes plenty of club to carry to back of green
- chipping back is good bailout

A - 225 yard drive
B - 200 yard approach
C - chip shot

## Player D

Our high handicapper (21 and up). Like most golfers in this skill category, Player D tends to slice or pull the ball. The grid will be very beneficial if he or she takes the time to plan some strategy and use the grid while playing this challenging hole.

Losing a ball in the water or having to hit out of the trees is not much fun. Grid Golf can help any golfer in this category avoid losing strokes unnecessarily. If you are in this category, you should have a goal of making bogey on this hole. You may do better, but bogey would be a good score and is attainable. Stand behind your ball and visualize a grid to help make that a reality.

- Player D's grid extends the full width of the fairway and even the first cut of rough.

- Player D should tee up on the far right side of the tee box to have the entire fairway to work with.

- By aiming to the left grid, which in this case extends to the left edges of the fairway, the ball will slice back to the right sharply but still land in the fairway. Notice how much room the ball has to work its way back.

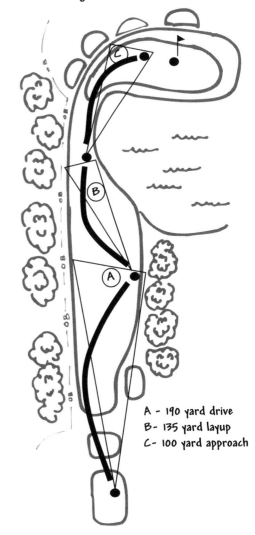

**Player D**
High handicap 21 & up
- slicer & puller
- layup for second shot saves major strokes
- use the entire grid for third shot

A - 190 yard drive
B - 135 yard layup
C - 100 yard approach

- If the grid is not used and Player D aims at the center of the fairway, the next shot (if the ball is found) will be in the trees or on the adjoining fairway on the 16th hole. The grid may have saved player D two strokes on the drive.

- Player D smartly decides to play a lay-up shot of about 135 yards rather than just hit it as far as he or she can, realizing the tendency to slice would cause a lost or wet ball. The grid avoids the Devil's Bathtub as the shot is aimed to the left of the grid but slices back to the far right side. The grid provided a safety margin, avoided the water, and saved at least one more stroke.

- Faced with a 100-yard approach to the green, Player D's grid is aimed to the center left of the green. The shot should be aimed outside the left grid boundary as a safety margin. This actually uses the entire green because player D's slice could then actually end up closer to the hole as it slices back in.

- Even with Player D's current game, a chance to make par on this extremely challenging hole is a wonderful reward for smart play. The grid took into consideration the shape tendencies of the shot and the distances Player D can hit various clubs.

# Now You Try It

Use the same hole map and draw a grid that can help your game. You may even want to sketch out some holes on your home course and draw in some grids. Here are some keys to help you decide where to tee the ball.

- If you have a tendency to slice the ball big time, tee it up on the far right side of the tee box and aim to the left boundary of your grid.

- If you hit big hooks, tee it up on the far-left side of the tee box and aim to the right side of your grid.

- Adjust your tee position to reflect your ball flight or shot selection tendency.

- Generally speaking, if you want to draw the ball, begin at the left center of the tee box.

- Fades should be teed more to the right of center.

- Always play your shots away from hazards. Every golf hole has them, as well as a safe bailout area. You will save strokes if you study the hole before you pull the trigger.

- If you are playing for a good score, don't let your ego talk you into a poor course management decision you'll later regret.

Without changing your game, Grid Golf will help you save strokes. Even if you're playing a water hole and end up in the sand away from the more severe trouble, remember these words of wisdom from golfing immortal Bobby Jones: "The difference between a sand bunker and water is the difference between a car crash and an airplane crash:—you have a chance of recovering from a car crash."

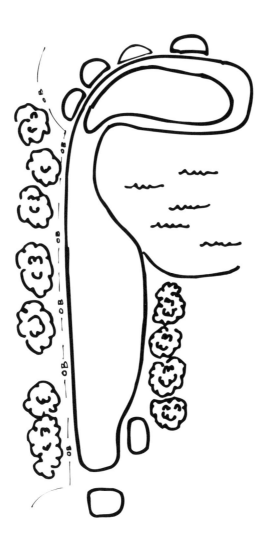

# Golf Course Strategy

*"It's a compromise between what your ego wants you to do, what experience tells you to do, and what your nerves let you do."*

**Bruce Crampton**, Senior PGA Tour player,
on concentration in golf

*"Just as with so many other things in our day-to-day lives, we need to have a plan before starting out on any endeavor. So, make it part of your routine to plan a strategy for every hole you play before even pulling a club from your bag."*

*Brad Brewer*

**L**ower scores are the main objective of playing better golf. Most golfers—without even improving the quality of their game—could shave some strokes just by thinking their way around the course instead of mechanically reacting and hitting shots. Try this approach:

- Before teeing off on every hole, visualize exactly how you want to play it. Decide on a strategy and commit to it. Do the same thing for each and every shot you face on the hole.

- Be sure and match your strategy to your skill level.

- When deciding which club to use, be realistic about the distance you regularly hit it. Many golfers make the mistake of under-clubbing themselves because they selectively remember only their best shots. That can cost you strokes!

- When in trouble, assess the risks and rewards of pulling off a shot. Being conservative rather than taking a risk of pulling off a miraculous shot can sometimes save strokes. If you say to yourself, "I hope I can play it," that's a good indication that a safer shot is indicated.

- Consider weather conditions and adjust accordingly.

- Once you commit to hitting a shot, never second-guess yourself. Second-guessing results in tentative play. Staying positive builds confidence.

# Plan Your Strategy for Each Hole

Just as with so many other things in our day-to-day lives, we need to have a plan before starting out. Make it part of your routine to plan a strategy for every hole you play before you pull a club from your bag. Focus on exactly how you want to play the hole, from your drive to the club you prefer hitting into the green. Did you know that most pros actually play the hole backward when planning their strategy? Most pros prefer hitting a full wedge into the greens. Their strategy for each of the  previous shots takes this into consideration. Which of the short clubs do you confidently feel gives you the best chance of consistently getting your ball close to the hole? Plan backward from the distance you most like to hit that club.

If you're a good wedge player, you may not need to force yourself to reach the green in two—if your wedge gets you close enough to have a makeable putt for a par. Don't try to force extra distance from shots that could adversely affect your timing, leaving you with difficult lies or in trouble. That costs strokes. Play to your strengths, not your weaknesses!

## Match Your Strategy to Your Skills

All of us would love to birdie every hole we play but we have to be realistic in assessing our skills when developing a strategy for playing a hole. We have to carefully consider each and every shot we play. Remember, a 300-yard drive counts the same as a tap-in putt.

The legendary Bobby Jones once said: "It is nothing new or original to say that golf is played one stroke at a time. But it took me many years to realize it."

## Risk vs. Gamble

Do you know the number one cause for most high scores shot by weekend golfers? Poor decisions! Hitting shots that are more of a gamble than a risk and not understanding the difference between the two.

When facing a shot that you know you have hit successfully nine times out of ten when hazards are present that could cost you a stroke, that's a risk. If you only hope you can pull off the shot, that's a gamble. Try not to fall into the trap of taking needless gambles while unrealistically expecting to make career shots. You may get away with it occasionally but, just like most gamblers, you've lost far more than you've won.

## Commit to the Shot

Have confidence in your ability to successfully hit any shot you attempt. Committing to the decision you've made and not second-guessing yourself before hitting it gives you a positive feeling and a much better chance at success. If you're confident, your mind will only be filled with positive affirmations and you'll be free to see the successful completion of your shots before you even hit them.

# Visualize Every Shot before You Hit It

Jack Nicklaus, considered the greatest golfer in the second half of the twentieth century, is an absolute master of visualizing every shot he hits before even addressing the ball. As part of his pre-shot routine, the Golden Bear stands behind the ball, picks out his target, and sees the ball's flight right to the targeted landing spot. Your mind is an incredible computer! Visualization can become a reality if it's combined with mastery of the basic fundamentals.

You won't have to concern yourself with confusing swing thoughts. Instead you will be able to fill your mind with positive thoughts and positive images. Isn't that a lot better than thinking: "I hope I don't lift my head on this 3-wood." So, just like Jack Nicklaus, be confident and positive, stand behind your ball, and visualize it flying through the air toward your target!

# Reaction Stage and Recovery Time

The other positive trait Nicklaus has is to react to his shot and then recover before visualizing and playing the next one. If you've watched him play on television, you may have heard him talking to himself while reacting to the shot. Then he takes time to let his mind relax and recover. While walking to the next shot, he looks around and thinks of other things before arriving at his ball. He picks out faces in the crowd or admires the scenery instead of castigating himself for a less than perfect shot, if that were the case. All golfers need to pace themselves to provide a break time for the mind. It's unrealistic to expect it to stay focused intensely throughout a round.

1. Pick out your target.

2. Visualize your shot.

3. Hit your shot.

4. React to your shot.

5. Recover and relax as you walk or drive to your next shot.

# Develop a Good Pre-Shot Routine

I think it's important to develop a good pre-shot routine that stays pretty much the same for every shot you hit. You'll find that it streamlines your thought process, making you feel more comfortable and at ease. Have you seen the pros on TV go through the same routine on a very short putt that they did with a longer one? All golfers should develop routines that are right for them. Here's an example.

1. Plan your strategy for the shot, commit to it, and pull your club from the bag.

2. Swing the club a few times, getting the feel for it and the type of swing you want to make.

3. Stand behind the ball, picking out your target. Also pick an interim target, like a leaf on the ground that is closer to you and on line with the actual target for aiming purposes.

4. Once your target is selected, visualize the exact shot you'll hit. Hold a positive mental image of the ball flying directly toward the target and landing on it.

5. Walk up to the ball and take your address position in the same way every time.

6. Waggle the club to relax, check your target, and fire!

C H A P T E R 20

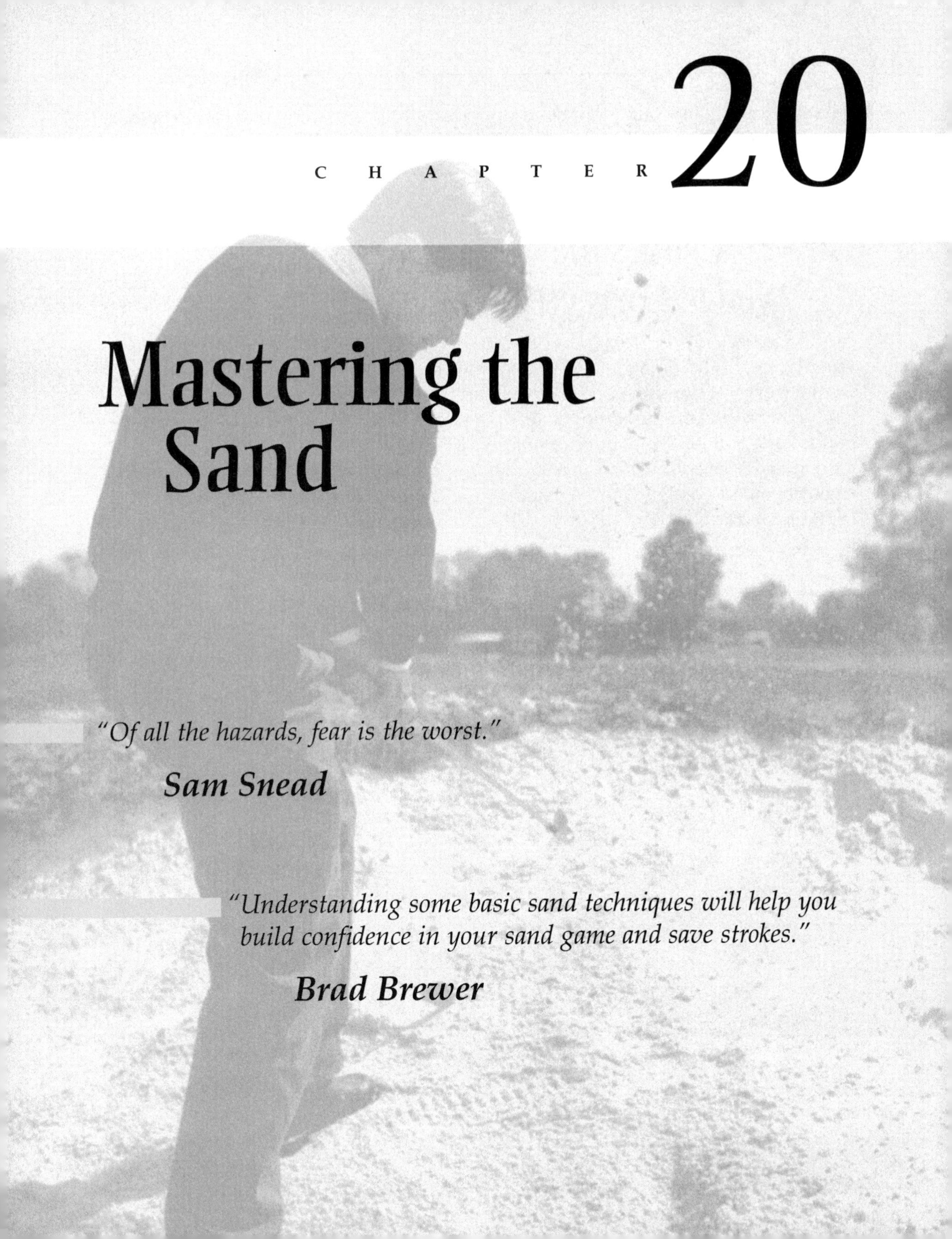

# Mastering the Sand

*"Of all the hazards, fear is the worst."*

***Sam Snead***

*"Understanding some basic sand techniques will help you build confidence in your sand game and save strokes."*

***Brad Brewer***

**L**anding in a bunker or sand trap is not the worst thing that can happen to you on a golf course. You haven't lost your ball in the woods or watched as it disappeared into a pond. So think positively and get the ball up on the green.

# How to Use a Sand Wedge Correctly

The first step in becoming a better sand player is to understand how the sand wedge works. It's designed differently than the other clubs in your bag. The sole rests closer to the ground than the leading edge. This is what we refer to as the bounce of the club. The bounce of our wedge keeps the leading edge from dragging in and accelerating during a shot. If you don't already own a sand wedge, I suggest you add one to your bag so that you can begin making the bunker a friendlier hazard.

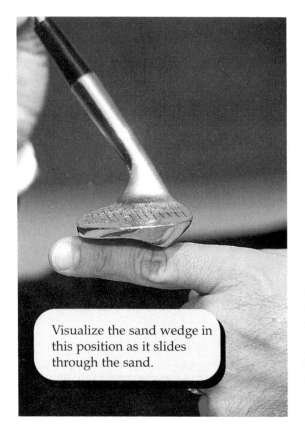

Visualize the sand wedge in this position as it slides through the sand.

As I slide the sand wedge through the sand, see how shallow the path is. The club slid over the sand instead of digging into it.

A quick wrist and a toed-in clubface set dig the club deeper into the sand. Compare this photo with the photo on the preceding page.

This is more of a digging angle of attack for the sand wedge. You would only dig deeply into the sand for balls that are buried.

# Setting Up for the Sand

All sand shots require some adjustments from your regular stance.

Normally, you want your feet to be on a line parallel to the target. In the sand, you want to open your stance similar to that of a pitch or chip shot. This open position allows you to slide under the ball, ensuring that the clubface doesn't close down and dig in.

The ball is positioned off my left heel. See how the clubface is open and hovering above the sand. When in a bunker, the club must not touch the sand at address or you must take a one-shot penalty.

Aim the clubface slightly right of your target and open your stance. Rest assured the ball will follow the path of your sandblast and not the aim of your clubface.

## Splash the Sand

This down-the-line view shows my open-to-the-target address position. The open clubface will help the bounce work correctly and pop the ball up over the steep bunker face.

This down-the-line view shows my open-to-the-target address position. The open clubface will help the bounce work correctly and pop the ball up over the steep bunker face.

# Don't Hit the Ball, Let the Sand Do the Work

You don't have to make contact with the ball for it to get out of the bunker; instead, the sand pushes it out. Set the ball off your front foot and aim your club between two to four inches behind the ball. The club enters the sand first, before sliding under the ball. I'll use a practice donut to illustrate my point. This is a wonderful practice drill for you to try too!

To practice hitting the sand, not the ball, I'm putting the ball in a practice donut. These are available through our Academy.

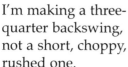

I'm making a three-quarter backswing, not a short, choppy, rushed one.

See how the club-head is sliding through the sand and under the donut and ball in this face-on view.

In this exact moment of impact, you can see the slight splash of sand and the back of the donut just starting to rise as the sand begins to push it up and out.

Sand, ball, and donut are pro-
pelled out of the bunker.

I complete my follow-
through, finishing the shot
high with my knuckles to
the sky instead of abruptly
stopping.

## The Paper Cup Drill

Here's a great drill that helps you develop the feeling of hitting the sand, not the ball. You can make your own paper cone or use a cone-shaped paper drinking cup. The main thing is to relax and concentrate on hitting the cone out of the sand, not the ball.

Place the paper cone and ball down into the sand.

This is how it looks as you address the ball.

Make a three-quarter backswing.

The clubhead slid through the sand and under the cone.

You can see how the bottom section of the cone is wrapped on the club-face as the ball flies out of the bunker.

Complete your follow-though.

# Digging for Buried Lies

A buried lie presents a challenging golf shot. If you've hit a "fried egg," here's the correct approach for getting the ball out of the bunker. You'll have to dig it out.

This is a classic example of a fried egg; the ball is the yoke and the crater is the white part. I'm pointing to the outside of the crater where you want the clubhead to dig into the sand.

As you take your address, close the clubface so it looks hooded and is aiming left of your target.

Make the backswing more vertical by setting your wrists early because the clubface needs to enter the sand with a sharp descending blow.

Digging into the sand won't permit a complete follow-through.

The digging club pops the ball out of its "breakfast mess." Expect the ball to naturally run farther when it hits the green due to the low trajectory and lack of backspin.

## Be Realistic and Save Strokes

While you always want to aim at your target, this lie would be too challenging to attempt a shot. The main goal of bunker play is to get out of the bunker. Don't waste a stroke trying an impossible shot.

Playing the ball to the side and away from the hole is a smarter shot. The ball will be out of the bunker and you can chip it close. Being realistic and playing smarter is a definite stroke saver for any golfer.

## Don't Forget to Rake

It's good golf etiquette to rake the practice bunker so it's ready for the next person. We all belong to the worldwide fraternity or sorority of golfers and this is one way to show respect for each other and the course.

# CHAPTER 21

# Challenging Lies

*"I expect to make at least seven mistakes a round. So when I make a bad shot, I don't worry about it. It was just one of those seven."*

**Walter Hagen**, one of only five men to have ever won the Grand Slam of Golf

*"You may not have hit your ball dead center in the middle of the fairway, but you can save strokes by knowing what to do when you're presented with a challenging lie."*

**Brad Brewer**

Unlike other sports, golf's playing field is always changing and forever challenging. Every golfer, regardless of ability, is going to face challenging lies every time he or she plays. While everyone "oohs" and "ahhhs" at long drives, pros really save strokes by knowing how to adapt and recover from uphill, downhill, and side hill lies and blocked target shots.

You may not have hit your ball dead center in the middle of the fairway, but you can save strokes by knowing what to do when you're presented with a challenging lie. You may not make birdie or even par, but any stroke saved is one less on your card.

# Uneven Lies

Golf course architects design courses to test our skills. Many times during a round you may hit a quality golf shot and still be faced with an uneven lie. Here are some examples you will run into:

- Ball above your feet at address
- Ball below your feet at address
- Having to play a shot from an uphill slope
- Having to play a shot from a downhill slope

## Ball above Your Feet at Address

The ball is above my feet. I'm choking up on my grip to compensate because an elevated ball is closer to me than one at a normal address.

A ball with an uphill lie has a tendency to pull to the left, so compensate by aiming a little right of target.

## Ball below Your Feet at Address

A ball below your feet will have the tendency to push right, so aim a little left of your target.

Set up with your weight more on the left side and swing smoothly, staying in balance.

## Playing from an Uphill Lie

The angle of the hill will naturally add loft to your club and make your ball go higher with less distance. Select a club with less loft: a 5-iron in place of a 7-iron, for example.

Shoulders should be parallel to the natural slope of the ground at address.

Finish high as you follow through up the slope of the hill. You will probably be hitting off your back foot due to your weight not being able to transfer up the hill. I recommend trying to play a cut shot so the clubhead doesn't close early and make for a low hook. I'll show you how to play a cut shot later in this chapter.

# Playing from a Downhill Slope

The angle of the hill will naturally de-loft your club, making your ball go lower. Select a club with more loft, like a 7-iron in place of a 9-iron.

Choke up slightly on the club.

Shoulders should be parallel to the ground at address and you will feel more weight on your forward leg as a result of the slope.

Widen your stance, positioning the ball more towards the center. Your wrists should set up earlier during the backswing to clear the slope.

I've just impacted the ball and want to swing the club down the slope with a low follow-through. I try to hit a draw or hook from this type of lie, causing me to stay down and let the clubhead cover the ball.

# Pick Your Way out of Fairway Bunkers

Sometimes an off-line drive lands you in a fairway bunker. Because you're still pretty far from the green, you need to hit a shot that gives distance if you want to save a stroke.

Choke up on the grip slightly as you dig into the sand for stability. Play the ball back in the middle of your stance to ensure a clean hit of the ball first before your club touches the sand.

A good pre-shot routine before stepping into a fairway bunker is to practice picking a leaf off the fairway. Then step into the bunker and pick the ball off the sand.

Take one extra club and make a three-quarter backswing for more control. You want your swing to feel very much like a sweeping motion, going back and through where you are picking the ball off the top of the sand.

Picking the ball displaces very little sand. Your ball will have length and accuracy as it heads to your target. Being a little thin is a good miss from the fairway bunker. A fat shot is death!

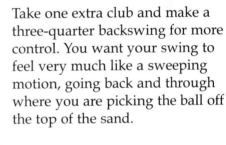

# Working Your Shots Around Trouble

Sometimes we are blocked out directly between our ball and the target. Learning how to work the ball around the trouble is an easy shot to master once you understand the technique and have a chance to put it to practice.

## Hitting a Draw

When you hit a draw, the ball starts out to the right of your designated target and draws back to the left. If you're left-handed, this is reversed. You can hit a draw around trouble or give yourself a more advantageous position for any of your wood or iron shots. The draw is accomplished by making changes in your address position and then allowing your swing to respond to the address changes.

The photos illustrate that to hit a draw I aim the club at the target and close my stance so my body is aimed to the right.

As the dotted line shows, my swing follows the position of my body more inside to out. With this simple adjustment, my clubhead will impart a right-to-left topspin on the ball.

As I release through, I want to feel the toe of the club turning over.

## Hitting a Fade

Hitting a fade or cut shot starts the ball to the left and then cuts it back toward the right. This is a controlled fade—not the slice that 85 percent of golfers are trying to straighten out. Learning how to hit a fade is a good way to understand that the club cutting across the ball imparts left-to-right sidespin on it.

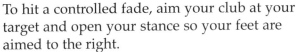

To hit a controlled fade, aim your club at your target and open your stance so your feet are aimed to the right.

Your swing follows your address position, as illustrated by the broken line, and the clubface impacts the ball from outside the target line to across the ball and back to the inside.

Try to create the feeling that you're dragging the heel of the club through impact. This helps keep the face open to ensure a left-to-right ball flight.

# The Putting Chip

If you miss the green and find your ball in the second cut of fringe or in the medium rough just off the green, you might want to try the putting chip. It is an easy shot to play and the ball comes out much softer with less effort than your usual chipping technique. Since you want to avoid getting caught in the rough, the putting chip offers less clubface to drag. Using your putting stroke for the shot lessens the tendency to get wristy for a normal chip. So if you're within 15 feet of the green, give it a try. Club selection is important and depends on how far you want the ball to roll after it lands on the green. A 5-iron will roll farther than a sand wedge.

Start by taking your normal putting grip and address. Eyes are over the line the ball takes to the hole. See how the shaft has naturally become more vertical.

Address the ball off the toe. Notice how being more vertical has lowered the toe and raised the clubface (right) limiting the area that can get caught in the grass. A normal address increases the area and the chances for trouble (left).

Develop feel by putting a ball about the same distance as your putting chip.

Take that same feel to a position off the green and try to emulate that feeling as you try the putting chip. Stroke down and through to pop the ball up.

# Mental Stroke Savers on the Course

- Stay relaxed and reduce your muscle tension.

- Gather in all the information you can before making your decision.

- Decide to play a shot you know you can pull off.

- Total commitment—no second thoughts!

- Visualize success.

- Follow your consistent pre-shot routine.

- Take aim and fire.

- Always use positive self-talk!

# Golf Is a Lifetime Sport that Starts with the Family

*Golf is a sport that has been passed down through the centuries from generation to generation. Now it's your turn as you learn how to have fun playing golf with your family. Lines of communication will flourish between parent and child, once you understand the special methods of teaching Brad and his wife Wanda use with their own children. "High-fives" all around!*

*If you have competitive juniors with a burning desire to take their game to the sport's highest levels, you'll find some wonderful information on what's involved and how to help. Maybe your competitive junior will be the next Arnold Palmer, Tiger Woods, or Karrie Webb!*

# The Joys of Teaching Your Children to Play Golf

"Some of my earliest memories are of riding around the club on a tractor with my father. When I was three, he made a special set of golf clubs for me, and then taught me how to hold them. I was lucky; I learned to hold a club the right way when I was young so the proper grip has always been second nature to me."

**Arnold Palmer**

"The traditions and history of golf have been passed down through the centuries from generation to generation. Now, as a parent, it's time to take your place in the lineage of the sport by introducing your children to golf. As you do, the quality time spent together will hopefully build family closeness, fortified with praise and encouragement. You're providing your children with a sport and memories they will enjoy for a lifetime."

**Brad Brewer**

**T**eaching a child to play golf can be one of the most rewarding experiences of your lives. As you introduce your young golfer to the game, you're taking the first step toward building a lifelong relationship—a perpetual source of incredible happiness. I can't think of another sport where a parent and child, or a grandparent and child, can bond as close together by sharing an activity and enjoying it with one another. Golf is a unique game that will continue on through a lifetime.

My father and I are at an age in our lives where it's my turn to have the children and he's become the grandfather. All of us play together and continue to have an activity where common interests are shared. Age doesn't limit our ability to play or curtail the enjoyment we receive from the game or from each other. It's neat to be able to have that experience.

Playing golf as a family is an activity we do on Sundays, after church. From our youngest child of 1 1/2 years to our 15-year-old teenager, as well as the other children in-between, golf gives everybody a chance to get out into the fresh air, play on the green grass, and use up some energy.

My youngest "junior golfer," Bradley Jr., age 18 months.

# Golf Brings our Family Closer Together

In today's modern society, with such a generation gap between interests, golf brings us closer together as a family. It's the bond that cements our family relationship. We're friends, not just grandparents, parents, and children. I've found that golf also ensures that my children are learning quality things about life:

1. How to play by the rules
2. The importance of honor and integrity
3. Proper etiquette
4. The importance of history
5. Good competition and sportsmanship

History is an important aspect in our lives and history is an important part of the game of golf. Golf teaches the traditions of the game: how to dress correctly, how to have good manners on the golf course, how to show respect to others—all while being competitive at the same time. Not many sports offer all this. That's why golf is such a great game as well as a neat sporting activity you can teach your children. And children love to learn golf, if you introduce the game to them properly.

History doesn't have to be boring either. Tiger Woods, whom your juniors will identify with, is already a huge part of golfing history. Show them pictures of his fist-pumping wins and compare that to Arnie's charge at Cherry Hills in 1960.

# Teach by Example and Make It Fun!

The best way to start your children playing golf is to have them watch you, even at a very young age. Let them observe your enjoyment. Golf is fun and, to effectively teach them to play, you are going to have to make it fun for them too. I can't stress this enough. Keep these two points in mind:

1. Make it fun.
2. Make it an activity that's enjoyable to them.

Kids can enjoy golfing in the backyard!

A chance for quality time with their father, mother, or both together while playing golf is enough to intrigue even very young children. It will boost their interest and get them excited about being a part of this sport. Once you've kindled that spark of interest, be careful not to squelch it. I've seen a lot of mistakes parents make in trying to teach children. One is not taking into consideration a child's attention span.

I look forward to the quality time I spend teaching my kids to play. I surprised Bradley with my funny new hat.

It didn't take long before he wanted to wear the hat. It's all part of making golf a fun experience.

Dressed and ready to play!

Our 5-year-old daughter Tori obviously enjoys my funny new golf hat. Find ways to surprise your junior golfers as you teach them. Tori is now intrigued to learn more about Scottish caddies.

# Understanding Your Junior Golfer's Attention Span

If you're out there working with a junior, each little person you're working with has a different attention span. It depends on the child's age and I can't decree that an 8-year-old has a 45-minute attention span or that a 15-year-old can concentrate for an hour and a half. It depends on the age and the individual. I've seen some 8-year-olds who can practice for four hours and some 15-year-olds who spend 15 minutes at golf and then they're done! Never push a child, but you do want to keep the child motivated. Don't make golf work, because as soon as it starts becoming work, children get turned off.

If you're introducing a five-year-old to golf, I recommend a maximum practice time span of 15 to 20 minutes. During that time you've got to keep it very active, very flowing, with little actual instruction. Make it something they can see. It's much more effective to teach kids visually than to verbally instruct them. Most importantly, don't overwhelm them with too many drills. You know how deadly that can be for your own game!

# Keep Drills to a Minimum—Let Them Have Fun!

Golf instructors have so much information, so many drills and exercises for any situation, that we have to be careful not to overwhelm our students.

Can you think of a more visual way to encourage your kids to coordinate their golf swing to hit an object than by hitting a paper cup full of water?

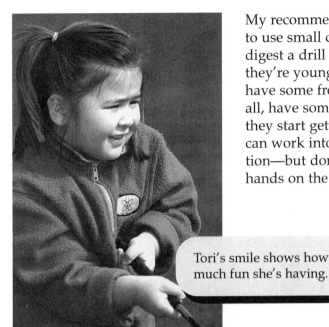

My recommendation for teaching children is to use small doses, allowing them to really digest a drill or an exercise one at a time. If they're young, limit the drills. Allow them to have some freedom and flow and, most of all, have some fun when they first start. Once they start getting the ball up in the air, you can work into getting a good hands-on position—but don't wait too long to get those hands on the club correctly!

Tori's smile shows how much fun she's having.

Let children work at their own pace—don't slow them down too much. Golf is a game of patience and although you want to instill patience in your juniors, they are not wired that way yet. Patience can be learned as they get into their pre-teens and teens. At ages five to eight, slowing down the pace is an off switch. Keep it quick and active. Use drills and exercises that turn into fun games and, most of all, keep the motion flowing.

# The Joy of Rewards for Both Parents and Children!

Rewards are very important when you're working with your juniors. Praise them lavishly. When they get the ball up in the air, it's "high fives" time. It doesn't have to be a candy bar or a present, just some positive feedback. You're giving them some gratification for a job well done. Getting encouragement from Mom or Dad is the biggest reward in the world and it can carry forward into other aspects of your parent-child relationship. You're opening and developing lines of positive communication. Does that have a lasting effect on your child? You bet!

Tori gets one up in
the air.

"High fives" are a great
form of encouragement.

We'll always remember Tiger Woods in the 1997 Masters coming down the 18th fairway. His thoughts weren't about the green jacket, symbolic of the Masters Championship. Instead, he searched out and found his father Earl Woods behind the green. It still brings tears to my eyes as I recall this touching and significant moment in golf history. His father gave him the biggest of all rewards—a hug, symbol of approval, encouragement, and love. Just as it did with Tiger, who started playing golf at a very young age, it begins with the feedback—"You did a great job!" Give your children encouragement that they are doing a great job, even though they might not think so. Little doses of "Yeah! That's great!" keeps them going. Encouragement and praise are the building blocks for success!

## The Joy of Teaching One of My Own Junior Golfers

I started working with my own junior golfer, Bradley Jr., when he was 14 months young. That's when I gave him a golf club. He's knocked every table and lamp and, from time to time, his sister's shins have bruises. But when he hits the golf ball, I clap and give him high fives. When I come home and walk through the door, the first thing he does is grab his golf club, look for the ball, and get ready to whack it. As I give him some gratification, he looks forward to that feedback, that communication of approval from me. We've already conditioned that response in

"Let's hit some balls, Dad!"

him. He's already turned on to the game, motivated and stimulated. I have to be extremely careful not to do anything that will change that attitude. I have to be sure to keep him motivated, the way he already is. It can be that simple!

Lou Holtz, the former Notre Dame coach, made a speech and someone asked him a question on how he motivated the "Fighting Irish." He said, "I don't have to motivate my team, these guys come to me motivated. I've just got to make sure that I don't de-motivate them." Now that's all I have to do with Bradley Jr.

# Keep the Learning Process in Proper Perspective

It's easy to get children stimulated, but after that you have to be sure you're doing the right things to keep them there. You can provide the emotional support and give them the tools and resources they need to take the game to whatever level they desire to take it to. That's an important key. Make sure that it's their level they want to take it to, not your level. Unfortunately, some parents start seeing little Tiger Woods, Arnold Palmer, or Annika Sorenstam in their kids and start thinking: "Hey, this kid's got potential. My kid can be the game's next greatest superstar." Those parents make the crucial mistake of overwhelming their child. Then, it gets to the point where kids start feeling the pressure and think Mom or Dad is trying to push them to be something their parents want them to be, instead of what they themselves are.

## Encourage Juniors to Compete at Their Level

Golf is a mental game that starts becoming a mental game at a very young age. Going beyond the recognition we give our kids, pats and hugs are the early rewards of competition. Play for a coke, play for a quarter. Give youngsters a goal to work toward. This will help their competitive juices at a young age. I think that's important—after all, life is competition.

I guarantee that if you told five eight-year-olds, "Okay, we're going to putt the next five holes for a coke," they would try their hardest. They are going to give their all attempting to win. It's not the coke as much as their internal drive. Kids get fired up and want to be the one to get that win.

# Fun Activities to Try with Your Juniors

In building relationships with your children, keep it fun and keep it active. Make sure the drills you give them are fun drills to do.

## The Ten Ball Drill

"Let's get started!"

Bradley helps line up the balls.

Line up about ten balls in a row on tees—that's very important. Try to put your child into a position so that he or she is pretty close to aiming down the target line. Don't get specific, just put their feet where they're in a good position and a nice stance away from the ball. Place their hands on the club in a position where they have a chance to swing the golf club. Don't get too technical with proper grip positions—they're not going to maintain those positions anyway!

As you help youngsters with this drill, try to encourage motion, try to get a flow of motion started. Allow them to go ahead and swing as quickly as they want, letting them hit the balls in rapid-fire succession, one after another—bam, bam, bam. This is great fun for younger children while the constant swinging motion creates clubhead speed along with hand/eye coordination, breeding the sensation of the club hitting the golf ball.

When you help kids create a sense of activity that they enjoy, they think it's cool. They want to see how quickly they can knock all the balls off the tees. This becomes a positive, fun-filled experience that begins teaching key elements of the golf swing in an enjoyable way.

An ineffective method that will quickly turn them off is to say: "I want you to work on your grip and work on your setup." Start your kids off that way and you will definitely bore them. Kids don't have the patience to sit there and listen—they want action!

Keep the game active at this young starting point and they'll think golf is pretty neat. You may be busy putting balls on tees for the first couple of lessons, but encourage your kids: "Yeah, that's great!" They'll get tired out after awhile and wear off some excess energy, making it a little easier to get them to bed that evening. Well, we can all dream, can't we!

## Try Larger Balls

Give them small attainable goals. Instead of hitting a small round ball that's 1.68 inches in diameter, get them to hit a big ball first. Put out a couple of large round balls—spongy balls, a ball that is going to take off when they hit it, make some noise, and go a nice distance. Let them whack the heck out of it!

This is an entertaining way to teach kids how to hold onto the golf club with a fairly correct hand position. The club is going to move a bit, so they naturally adjust their hands to a point where they are semi holding on to it correctly. You've avoided explaining the boring details of holding onto the golf club with Vs going to the right shoulder.

Not all that bad an impact position. See how Tori has naturally transferred her weight forward and is facing the target.

Tori's backswing as she prepares to hit a large round ball.

Even Bradley Jr. can enjoy the fun of hitting the larger ball.

# Encourage Natural Clubhead Acceleration!

You'll get to the point where your kids are making good, repeating, accelerating golf swings. If you start working on mechanics first, I think you hinder the ability to develop a flowing motion. I recommend first teaching them naturally to accelerate: Hit it hard, go after it. From there, you can tone them down and teach them how to have foundation and stability in their swing. Bring down their acceleration to a point where it's manageable—but give them the maximum capacity first. Don't give them any barriers as to how hard they can hit the ball. Let them rip at it! I learned this way and so did Arnie, Jack, and a young man named Tiger.

Our 10-year-old daughter, Carli, enjoys whacking the ball into a wall as hard as she can. This is a wonderful drill for her to work on her acceleration while having fun.

As you progress with your juniors, they'll get to an age where they are hitting the ball in the air pretty much every time. This is when you can show them how to stabilize their address, get their grip more neutral, and keep their head steady. Keep that acceleration to a point where they can maintain their foundations without setting up any barriers for them. Let them go at it as hard as they can. In due time, kids find their medium acceleration where they can control the direction and the distance. Their ability to discover it depends on their unique strengths, their fundamentals, and how developed they are as to how they accelerate. I think going at it with simple logic will get better results.

## Build a Practice Station

Kids are competitive. As they get older, try to establish a practice station that helps them get into good correct address every single time. Place one club on the ground for the alignment of their feet to the target and another club to show their correct ball position. This serves as a reference so that they learn to put themselves into a pretty good address position every time. Building this station helps them learn consistency.

Bradley is helping set up a practice station for his sisters.

See how I've put down one club that points at the target and another that shows where Tori should place the ball in her stance. The practice station will be a steady reference that will eventually help her develop a consistent golf swing.

# Use Familiar Teaching Aids

Some really great teaching aids to teach kids golf come from other familiar areas, like the noodle used in swimming. I love the noodle because it's a familiar object—my kids play in the pool with it. When they see the noodle, they think of fun. Put the noodle down on the ground to show your kids that the path of the golf club is not really a straight line. It has a curvature to it. As you turn away from the ball, the club swings back and up in a semicircular motion. The noodle helps because it's a positive visual reference.

For the few dollars the noodle costs it has a multitude of uses in teaching. You can build a station with it. Use it for teaching acceleration as your youngsters try to swing it back and forth, building a swishing sensation. If you're working with younger juniors, say, "This is an elephant's trunk swinging back." Trying to emulate the elephant's trunk helps develop rhythm and tempo. Gradually encourage them to swing faster and faster. Swinging the trunk back and forth will create a good accelerating motion.

Bending the noodle visually shows Carli the semicircular path a club should take.

Carli is hearing the whooshing sound the noodle makes as it's being swung down from the top of her backswing. She's having fun developing rhythm and tempo as indicated by the bend in the noodle.

# Taking Your Junior Golfers on the Course

Bradley Jr. has his pencil and is ready to keep score on our family golf outing.

When you go on the golf course with juniors, let them play a few holes or hit shots along the way. You can instill etiquette and respect for other golfers by making it a game. Make them conscious of some of the rules and some golfing etiquette—but don't make it all rules out there. Instead, inject examples that will teach playing by the rules. For instance, even though you may be keeping up with the pace of play, you might just want to pull aside one time and let the group behind you go through. Show the juniors how important and courteous it is to let another group play through. Show them how you wave them through as you pull off to the side so as not to interfere. That's part of the game.

## Games Can Teach How to Take Care of the Course

As you're playing a golf hole, make it fun for kids to find fairway divots. Call it a divot treasure hunt. Teach them the importance of keeping the course in good shape. Be a good role model for your children. If you're driving by a piece of paper that's blowing on the golf course, pick up the paper, even if you have to go out of your way to do it. Demonstrate, by your actions, that if we all pitch in, we will always have a beautiful playing field to enjoy.

I always use Arnold Palmer as an example. He will walk out of his way to pick up a piece of paper. If you don't bend down and pick up a piece of paper or cigarette butt lying on the ground when you play with him, you feel pretty guilty as he fills up his golf bag or cart. By the end of the round he looks like the "trash master." Be a good example yourself!

I'm showing my eldest daughter, 15-year-old Kenna, how to fix a ball mark on the green. I show them, by my own example, that golfers should fix two ball marks on every green.

My kids love filling in divots. In Florida, we have to fill the divots in with a sand and seed mixture. My kids can't wait to grab the scoop on the golf cart when they discover a divot. Kids love doing stuff like that. Challenge them: "See how many divots you can find in the next five minutes." Remember, don't slow up play as you do this. (Kids also love to help you rake sand bunkers.)

Tori has found a fairway divot and is replacing the turf.

Look at the fun she's having jumping on the divot to make it stay in place. This game is a great way to teach your junior golfers how to take care of the course.

# If You Take Your Kids to the Course, Give Them Your Attention

Make the experience on the golf course an enjoyable one. I can't stress this enough: Don't take your younger kids to the golf course and make it a Dad or Mom practice session. Give them all of your attention. Make sure it's an activity that's meant for them. One of the mistakes I see is parents who bring their juniors to the golf course, get them set up, buy the golf balls, and ignore them for the next hour.

Can you guess what happens? After the first 15 minutes, the parents—who are diligently working on their own games, such as implementing a new swing technique—will find the kids starting to interrupt them: "Dad, I'm hungry!" or "Mom, I have to go to the bathroom!" or "I'm thirsty."

The parent usually responds: "Not yet, we just got out here." The simple reason for the interruptions is that the child thought he or she would be spending time with Mom or Dad and that's not happening. Dad just built him a little station and, for all intents and purposes, has indicated: "There, don't bother me. Let me work on my game."

The station and golf balls become a non-talking baby sitter. Don't make that the golf experience for your child. It will turn them off. Make sure they're watching you watch them. You're becoming part of their experience out there.

Determine the purpose of your practice session. If you really need to work on your game, I suggest leaving a family golf outing for another time. Don't try to mix the two until the child is off and running on their own. Even then keep a watchful eye open and offer encouragement.

When Wanda and I take our junior golfers to the course, we spend the time together as a family instead of just parking the kids with some balls.

My friend Bill Damron did it right. When his two sons were capable of practicing on their own, he would work on his game for about 15 minutes and then stop and walk over to watch them hit a few, make a comment, and then walk back. He'd let them go for another half-hour and then walk back to check on their progress. His sons are Robert and Patrick Damron. Robert is now on the PGA Tour and Patrick is a star on the Wake Forest University golf team.

## Some Great Practice Ideas

If you want to practice your game with your child, here's a suggestion. Let your child hit a shot and then you hit a shot. Alternate shots back and forth. The beauty of a practice session like this is that your child is emulating what he or she sees.

In some circumstances, like losing your temper after a bad shot, you may not want that to happen. You can show them something demonstrate it, and then they can try. You get practice and your child learns from you. I think it's a very effective way to work with a junior.

### Allow Your Child to be the Instructor

Here's another suggestion that works from a visual standpoint and gives you important quality time together as a family. Let your child take the role of your instructor when you're hitting golf balls. After you complete your swing, ask: "What did you see?" Your youngster is learning by looking for good fundamentals in your golf swing and undoubtedly will try to copy it. As your child becomes your coach, he or she is beginning to develop an in-depth understanding of the golf swing.

# Taking Your Rightful Place in the Lineage of Golf

The traditions and history of golf have been passed down through the centuries from generation to generation. Now, as a parent, it's time to take your place in the lineage of the sport by introducing your children to golf. As you do so, you will build family closeness and provide your children with a sport and memories they will enjoy for a lifetime.

# Brad's Tips for Your Young Junior Golfers

1. Make the learning experience fun.

2. Keep the action flowing.

3. Don't work on too much technique; allow kids the freedom to make swings.

4. Build a practice station for consistency.

5. Use familiar objects as teaching aids like large balls and Styrofoam noodles.

# CHAPTER 23

# Junior Golf

*"I always thought Tom was a good man and a good player. I don't think it took winning a major to make him one."*

**Tom Kite Sr.**, after his son won the 1992 US Open, his first major

*"Some of the junior golfers your kids play with today will be their friends when they reach their 60s and 70s. They'll be the friends your kids may do business with or compete against all of their lives."*

**Brad Brewer**

During the past few years, I've gained a great deal of insight in working with competitive juniors. The Arnold Palmer Golf Academy, in close association with Saddlebrook, an extraordinary resort north of Tampa, Florida, has established a unique junior boarding school. Talented boys and girls from 11 different nations are enrolled in a nine-month private boarding school. They receive their education in the morning and we work with them in the afternoon, training them on a daily basis.

These young men and women play in the top junior tournaments. Our goal is to help take their games to the next level—collegiate golf; if they desire, they can eventually get into a position to play on the Tours, if that's something they wish to achieve. Although they come to us inspired and motivated, we help them organize themselves. Like most juniors, they can be kind of "all over the place." We help them set attainable goals. Otherwise, they can become so driven that they work themselves right into the ground. They want success now; their expectation levels are very high and they may not have patience. We keep that level high but put into perspective the reasonable time frame it will take to accomplish specific goals.

# Does Your Junior Enjoy Competition?

You may have a junior who has already shown signs of enjoying the competitive side of golf. Maybe it's just playing with a friend for a coke or a sleeve of balls, but he or she had fun and enjoyed the challenge enough to tell you about it. Here is a golden opportunity to open the lines of communication and provide a source of positive encouragement.

# Positive Ways to Help
## Your Competitive Junior Golfer

There are some very positive ways to encourage your budding competitive junior without making the mistake of pressuring your youngster into competition. For instance, never force kids to practice if they don't want to practice. It's much more effective to expose them to situations where they can learn from what they observe. Taking your junior to watch a competitive junior event in your community can inspire any youngster who has shown interest in competitive golf.

What's considered a junior event? Maybe it's a high school match or AJGA tournament in your community. Your junior can see the organization of a junior event and all that goes on there: the scoreboard, the first tee, how the juniors are announced, how they tee off together. Watching the young players coming in on the 18th hole with the crowd that gathers around the green is an atmosphere that can really inspire your junior to go on to the next level.

### BRAD EXPLAINS

*Let's make the distinction between a junior who has just started playing and one you have been working with for a while. If he has just started, wait until he looks forward to going out to the golf course and practicing with Mom and Dad. At that point, your junior has reached the level where he is hooked!*

They'll also see how disciplined the young players are in practice and how focused these young adults become when they get on the golf course. Explain the importance of a good attitude, although sometimes juniors do lose their patience and emotional control. Explain how this hurts their ability to become good quality golfers.

## A Golfing Role Model

Once your juniors start playing competitively, that's the time to bring them to top-class amateur and professional events. Even if you have to travel a few hours to see a tournament, it's well worth the effort. Let them meet some of the professionals and collect an autograph. A practice round provides an even better opportunity to meet the players; then they are relaxed and approachable.

You may find that juniors can get attached to a golf role model, like a professional player. This can be motivating—having an idol at this age can be an important learning source. They can see and read about their chosen golfers to discover what makes them tick and what they've done in their careers to position themselves to get to where they are. They can learn about their practice habits, see which tournaments their role models enter and track performance, learn about the

goals they set and, perhaps even more importantly, observe their golf swing. At this stage, juniors learn so much from what they see: They're at a visual age and very good at emulation. If they have a role model to emulate, it's amazing the difference it can make in how well they do.

## Use Video

Watch golf on TV. You can share the thrill of competitive golf with your junior and listen as the commentators provide insight into the game. It also gives youngsters a chance to follow their professional heroes.

Use your video camera to tape your swing and your junior's swing. Tape your drives and include some of the drills. Be sure to tape some swings on the course when you play. There can be a big difference between what happens on the course and how you swing in practice on the range. Be sure you use the same good habits on the course as you practiced on the range.

I recommend not getting too technical or specific in your analysis on the course. Take the same encouraging and supportive role you did on the practice range. You and your junior can compare each other's swings—this becomes an additional learning experience. The child can be the coach and say, for example: "Dad, I see you're picking up that golf club a little early. You need to work on that good one-piece take-away." As your junior is helping you, he or she is going through a learning analysis.

Tape a touring professional from a televised tournament, perhaps the one your child likes the best and watch his or her swing. Look at golf magazines together to check out various swings. Compare your basic fundamental positions on tape to the model you're looking at. This is excellent visual feedback. It's super important to not overdue the technical positions. Instead, look at the fundamentals: the grip, address position, maintaining a steady head, one-piece take-away, and acceleration.

Many people are buying digital video cameras. If you also buy some of the computer golf instructional video software that's available, you can compare your earlier swings with your current swing side by side—a big advantage. Now you can really show the progression and it becomes a nice library to have. Maybe someday your young junior will be another Tiger Woods or Karrie Webb and you'll want all these early videos to put together a great commercial!

## Positive Use of Drills

Drills can demonstrate your progress better than tapes of your golf swing. Juniors may say: "Why am I doing this stupid drill? I don't like it because it's not really hitting a golf ball." A video can show how the drill is making their golf swing look better. This sells them on the drill because they can see the difference. You can't dictate to children—you have to sell it to them.

If you are coaching your junior, don't take this approach: "If I tell you to do it, do it!" If you want to coach your junior, you need to relieve yourself, temporarily, from the parent/child relationship. Focus on selling this young person the same way you would a client or colleague in business. He or she will have to buy in on it and believe it. Children may say they will, but experience shows they won't.

Use video as a motivating tool for the drills. Show the progress and give praise. Don't use it as a way to criticize, as, for example: "I can't believe you're still doing this." Instead say: "Look at the progress you've made during the first part of your take-away." Re-enforce it by adding: "What I see is progress and what these drills have helped you accomplish." It's motivating, it's inspiring when they can visually see progress. They may not see it in their ball flight yet, but if they can see the progress they've made on video, it can be a huge uplifting experience.

## Be a Visual Coach

Eliminate all verbal babble with your junior. Adults communicate mostly through verbalization. Most juniors don't have the patience for that kind of communication—it's kind of a generation gap thing. If you sometimes feel you have communication problems with your kids about other subjects, this is the reason. Keep your words and thoughts very specific and as minimal as possible—almost as if you're speaking to a person from another country who doesn't have a great knowledge of our language. This has been one of my challenges in coaching a few of our Saddlebrook juniors. Try visual demonstration techniques using as many visuals as possible to give them a kinesthetic feel.

## Inspire with Traditions and Etiquette

Teach safety and etiquette as you work together. For example, on the driving range, be as quiet as possible working together so that other people can concentrate. You may even realize that some rules you may not have at home are important on the golf course. The difference between what to wear to the course and what is acceptable school dress can be huge!

Introduce some of the traditions by letting them hit an older type of club to get the feeling of what it was like. Go to the library and check out some golf history books. Show them the great old courses like St. Andrews and the legendary golfers of the past. Don't bore them with it—help the history of the game come alive. Your juniors are now part of the history of the sport.

Explain how important the USGA and R&A are to golf. Go over a *Rules of Golf* book and quiz each other as to what the ruling would be on a specific case that you make up. Your junior is going to be responsible for carrying on the game. Help them appreciate belonging to this worldwide fraternity or sorority. Juniors love the idea of belonging to something.

# Advanced Junior Training

What age is advanced? I've seen eight-year-olds who are ready to take on Seve Ballesteros. These kids are gifted! They're shooting in the mid-70s and hitting golf balls, as pure as can be, with a perfect swing every time. They're chipping and putting with the best. However, it depends on the individual. Generally, I would say 12 years old. This seems to be the age when their body maturity gets to a level where juniors can start hitting golf balls the extended distances required to play a championship-length golf course. Mental maturity is also important. Their mindset must allow them to focus for an extended period of time and become competitive enough to take it to the next level.

## Select a Good Swing Coach

The first thing I recommend in working with an advanced junior is to make sure he or she finds a good swing coach. Choose a local PGA teaching professional to help you assess what fundamentals your junior needs to improve the swing. Then, take on the same motivating role you did when your youngster first began. Unless you're a true expert in the biomechanics of the golf swing, I suggest getting an expert's assistance.

Your junior doesn't have to take lessons on a daily basis. You can be the coach in between, making sure he or she stays on track and focuses on the specific things that need working on. Keep youngsters fired up and having fun without pushing.

## Help Identify Goals for Your Advanced Junior

Help juniors define their goals. Start by listing areas to work on for their golf swing or the things they want to work on in the scoring zone. Define and list the areas that need improving, such as mental discipline and physical training.

## Set Up a Tournament Schedule

I believe it's best to set a tournament schedule that works in waves. Begin by choosing the most desired events. Place them on the calendar with no more than three weeks of tournaments in a row. These tournament weeks are when you want your junior to peak in performance. How do you do this? The same way Olympic trainers have organized their athletes' training periods for decades.

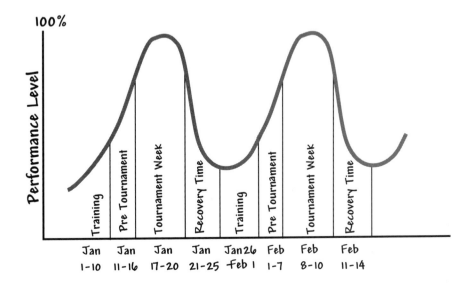

Begin each period with a minimum of one week that is designated for fundamental development and physical conditioning. Eat well, train well, and work on mechanics! I call the second period pre-competitive. It focuses more on playing and less on swing thoughts. Work on positive affirmations and goal setting for the coming events. Map out strategies, how they will play the courses, and what shots should be practiced.

The third period is tournament competitions. The best thing is to sleep and eat well and conserve energy off the golf course. Stay positive and supportive during this important period. Remember, it should be fun! The fourth period is the final phase of the wave—the downward swing—recovery, the getaway from golf time.

## Developing Other Interests Helps Juniors Compete

It's important for juniors to get away from golf now and then. One of the biggest challenges with our juniors at Saddlebrook is that their desire for success burns so intensely. At the Academy, they are in a constant competitive environment with one another. Coming from communities around the world where they were the best, they're all challenging to be the best with us. It's a very competitive environment that could become intolerably stressful if we didn't build in other activities and interests. We teach them how to recover and relax with other interests and activities, creating balance in their lives.

Juniors can easily become unbalanced—they become miserable and go into a slump or even quit the game. No one wants this to happen and, consequently, I consider developing a better training schedule and enjoyment of the game along with other non-golf-related interests. This becomes vital to their future.

I suggest a variety of activities for high school students. Golf is usually a seasonal sport. For the other months, allow them to enjoy other activities. Very often these other sports are fun and provide cross training that will build up strengths juniors need to enhance their golf game.

## Keep a Golf Journal

It's a good idea to teach juniors to keep a journal. We teach our juniors to use one for keeping their records and stats for greens in regulation, fairways hit, sand saves, putts per hole, and putts per round. These represent areas where you can set goals. Keeping track of tournament scores, making notes, writing down strategies of the courses they are going to play, and keeping all this information in an annual journal is great practice and it's fun to look back on their progress.

Any lessons taken from a professional or any advice that helped their game is part of the information to record in their journal. The junior should digest the material and then write it down in his or her own thoughts. Years from now, they can pull out the journal to help remember the thoughts and actions that were the keys to success!

## Video Journal

Along with the written journal, it's good practice keep a video journal for your juniors. The videos will record the progress of their golf swing and document the progress certain drills helped them make. Sometimes old swing flaws return and a video journal is a visual reminder of how they were corrected.

# Physical Training

When I was a junior golfer, I was advised not to swim or lift weights. The fear was that bulking up would ruin my natural swinging motion. Obviously you don't want to bulk up too much. However, cross training is greatly responsible for improving top golfers' performance over the last 10 years. Most college golf programs now train their players to be athletes. They work out with the other athletes: running, stretching, and lifting weights. They're training themselves for maximum strength, flexibility, and endurance to take their game to the next level.

Juniors need to condition their bodies and minds. Being a mentally tough competitor involves eating tough, sleeping tough, and physically and mentally conditioning tough. I recommend reading Dr. Jim Loehr's book *Mental Toughness Training for Sports*.

When we discuss advanced juniors, these are the individuals who are taking their golf from a recreational level to a competitive level. Once they do that, it becomes a different sport. Now he or she is a competitive athlete. That requires thinking, training, and participating with a competitive athlete mind-set in order to move their success to the next level.

If you analyze the success of the top players of the game, they've all learned how to do this through practice and their years of experience. That's why it's so important for juniors to observe and get to know more about those golfers who have become successful throughout their careers. These top performers have sacrificed and done the extras that the average person would never do. That's a big part of making them so unique. Of course they are blessed with a high level of talent too.

Their desire and the discipline to push that talent to the next level by working harder beyond what people of the same talent level are willing to do, make the difference. That separates the great ones from just the good ones. Desire is the fuel that allows this to happen. I've listed some good books for you to read on this very important subject in the Resources.

## Consult a Good Physical Trainer

It's a good idea to consult somebody in your area with the knowledge to help your junior's physical training. He or she must have an understanding of what the sport requires. A trainer can put together an exercise program that your junior can follow. Trainers help your juniors build their bodies correctly for golf while at the same time helping prevent injuries.

## The Champion's Mentality

When you get to a certain level, the game becomes significantly mental. It comes down to your ability to concentrate, stay in focus, and remain calm in pressure situations. Learn how to really motivate yourself on demand. Learn how to use positive self-talk. These are skills we are not born with—they have to be learned. You have to train these skills the same way you train physical skills on a daily basis. Using positive affirmations, positive self-talk, and a good visualization practice of what your golf swing looks and feels like when playing your best, (while at the same time knowing what those sensations are) are the mark of a champion.

Golfers sometimes get into that special zone that permits their talents to naturally shine through. But what we often don't understand is how to get back into that special zone again. It's usually different for everybody, but some things are similar—feeling relaxed and calm. Champions don't feel nervous or uptight when performing at their best. Instead, they're having a great time! They don't want their competition to end; instead, they want to keep playing forever. Champions are confidently aggressive and want to win!

Writing down how they feel when playing their best, in their own words, is the first step to training juniors how to get to the zone. Suggest they look at those notes along with their attainable and long-term goals on a daily basis to instill good positive thoughts. The champion mentality encourages positive self-talk: "I love to compete. I want to have that 10-foot putt to win the tournament. That's what I strive for." They may not believe it at first but, after a while, if done during every single round, it becomes a part of them. Teach your junior how to become a positive motivator and not a defeatist who says: "I stink. I hate this game!"

I use Touring Pro Mark McCumber as an example. Mark, to be honest (and he would agree), does not have the most fundamentally sound golf swing. He has great hand/eye coordination and great mental discipline. I've played with Mark and he's the best self-talker around. He can drive it 20 yards to the left and say: "All right, Mark, I can get it out of the woods from there, no problem."

On his next shot, if he were to hit it into the right rough, he would say: "At least I didn't hook it this time." I've seen him hit it on the green from there and 1-putt for a par. Mark is a champion who constantly keeps a positive attitude and comes up with positive affirmations to keep himself motivated. He does not allow negatives to take over. Instead, he constantly tells himself something positive, enjoying the challenges of each shot instead of bemoaning the bad shots.

These traits are learned and trained during the junior golfer years. Mark's attitude allows him to grind those potential 75s into 70s—that's the difference between winners and everyone else.

## Available Competitions

In Chapter 2, we looked at the road to success that professional golfers usually have in common. I suggest consulting that portion of the chapter for some suggestions as to the type of junior tournaments they entered. If your junior wants to pursue competitive golf, your very own hometown is the best place to start. Consult your local pro or high school athletic department. Call your newspaper for a listing of sources for local tournament organizers.

An APGA Saddlebrook class.

# PART 7

# Brad's Guide to Consistent Golf: The Swing Glossary

*If you want to develop a consistent golf swing that powerfully sends your ball on-line to your target, this part of the book is your permanent reference. Build your swing on the five fundamentals of:*

- *Grip*
- *Address*
- *One-piece take-away*
- *Steady head*
- *Acceleration*

*The pros constantly work on these fundamentals in their practice sessions. You'll find drills and exercises to help create new feelings so that these fundamentals become part of you. As you address the ball out on the course, you can think about the target you want to reach instead of the fundamentals of the golf swing.*

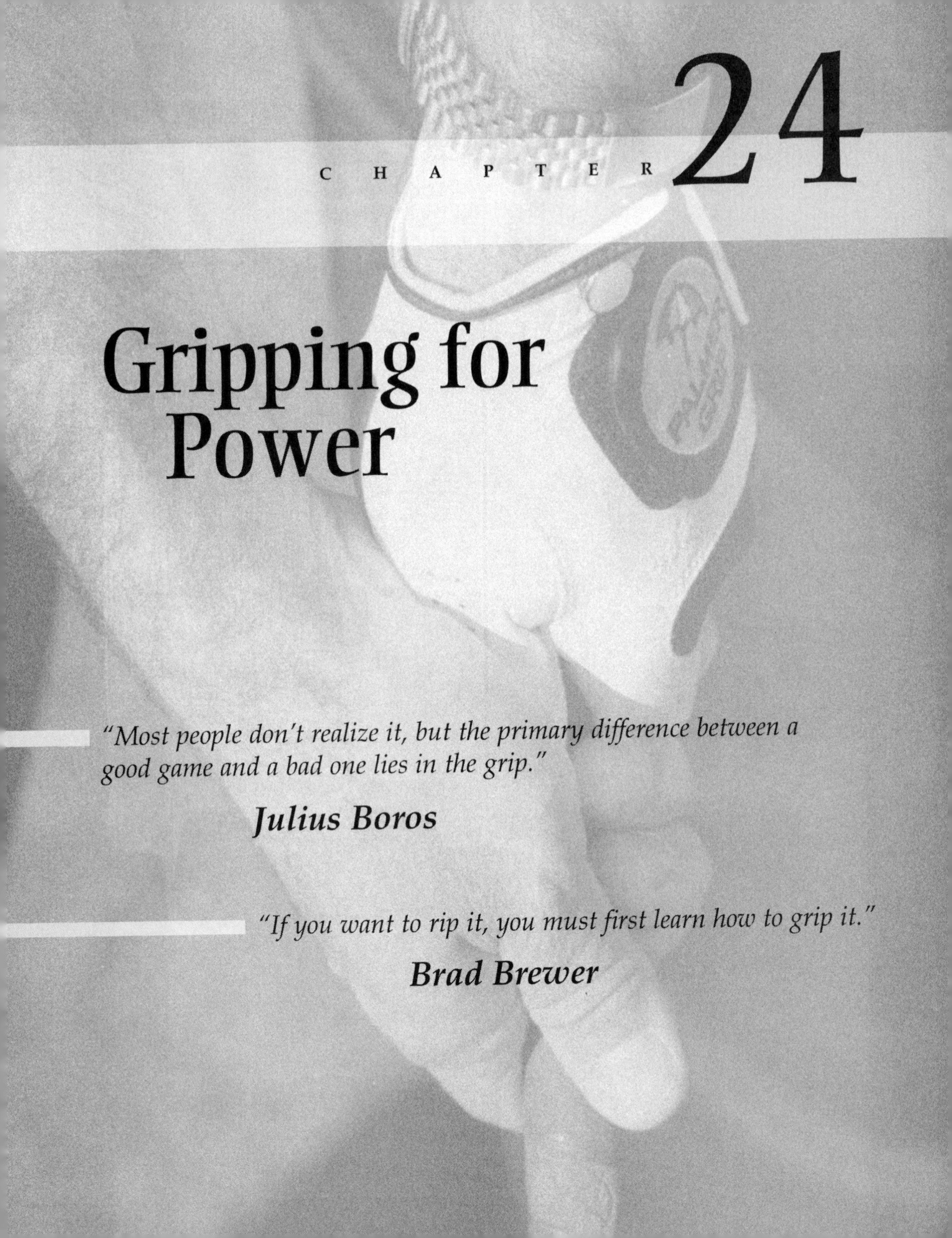

CHAPTER 24

# Gripping for Power

*"Most people don't realize it, but the primary difference between a good game and a bad one lies in the grip."*

***Julius Boros***

*"If you want to rip it, you must first learn how to grip it."*

***Brad Brewer***

T he first fundamental point for a great golf swing is a good grip. It's important to have both hands working together in a neutral position. The photo on the left shows you how it should look in a mirror or in your video if you're a right-handed golfer. The photo on the right shows a left-hander's correct neutral grip.

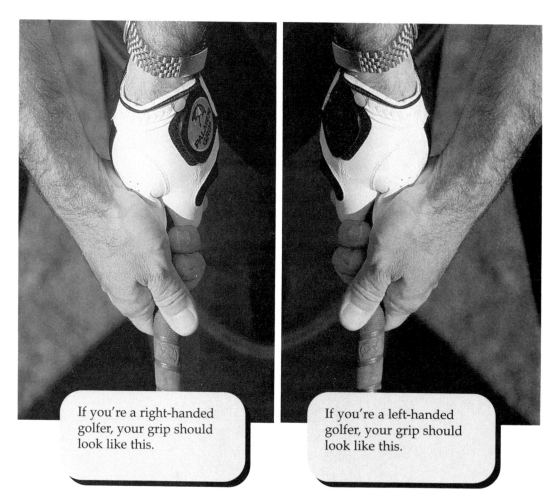

> If you're a right-handed golfer, your grip should look like this.

> If you're a left-handed golfer, your grip should look like this.

Even touring pros have to constantly check their grips. Let's work together to establish the proper neutral grip you'll need to improve your game. A word of advice, don't just read about the grip and try remembering it when you're on the course. Your home is a great place to practice your grip and a few other fundamentals. I'll demonstrate the grip for right- and left-handed golfers—after all, this is "Golf for Everybody."

**Right-handers**: I'm holding the club in the air as I rest it on my left palm, leaving a half-inch of the *butt end* (top of the grip) uncovered by my hand. See how the club takes its position between the second knuckle of my index finger across the fingers and into my palm. The base of the palm's heelpad will be able to rest on top of the club.

**Left-handers**: I'm holding the club in the air as I rest it on my right palm leaving a half-inch of the *butt end* (top of the grip) uncovered by my hand. See how the club takes its position between the second knuckle of my index finger across the fingers and into my palm. The base of the palm's heelpad will be able to rest on top of the club.

## Back to Basics

A great way to practice at home is with a short club. You can either have your local pro or a club maker put a 5-iron clubhead on a cut-down shaft along with an exact duplicate of your customized grip. The total club length should be about two feet.

The close proximity of the clubhead to the grip is a great teaching aid. You'll learn how the clubface has to square up naturally at the time of impact with your ball. If you work on your grip at home, it will feel natural when it's time to play. That's one swing thought you can eliminate.

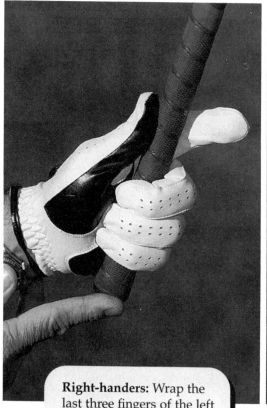

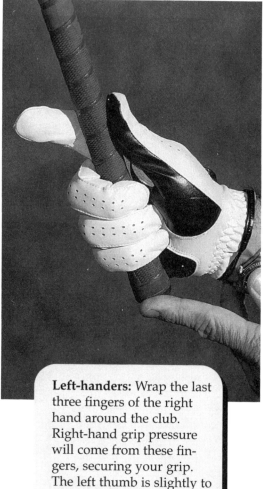

**Right-handers:** Wrap the last three fingers of the left hand around the club. Left-hand grip pressure will come from these fingers, securing your grip. The left thumb is on top of the shaft and slightly to the right of center on the shaft.

**Left-handers:** Wrap the last three fingers of the right hand around the club. Right-hand grip pressure will come from these fingers, securing your grip. The left thumb is slightly to the left of center on the shaft.

**Right-handers:** Allow your left index finger to wrap around the grip, but remember, the responsibility for left-hand grip pressure has been placed in the last three fingers of your left hand.

**Left-handers:** Allow your right index finger to wrap around the grip, but remember, the responsibility for right-hand grip pressure has been placed in the last three fingers of your right hand.

# Time for Brad's Grip Check

You can quickly see if your hand has properly gripped the club by checking the "V" made by your thumb and index finger when the club is held in front of you.

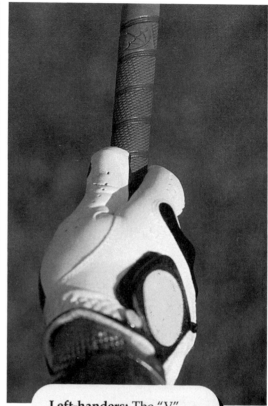

**Right-handers:** The "V" between the thumb and index finger of your left hand should be pointing to the inside of your right shoulder. Does your left-hand grip look similar to my grip position? If not, please start again, but don't just adjust it at this stage.

**Left-handers:** The "V" between the thumb and index finger of your right hand should be pointing to the inside of your left shoulder. Does your right-hand grip look like mine in a good neutral grip position? If not, please start again, don't just adjust it at this stage.

It's important for you to begin at step 1 so that you can become aware of the proper way to position your neutral grip.

# Completing Your Grip

Now that you've correctly placed the fingers of your gloved hand on the grip, please follow along as we add your other hand. I'm demonstrating the Varden or overlapping grip. Once again, you'll find photos for right- and left-handers.

### Brad's Positive Thoughts

*Even though you are separately putting your hands on the club, try to develop the feeling that both hands are working together as one, in unity.*

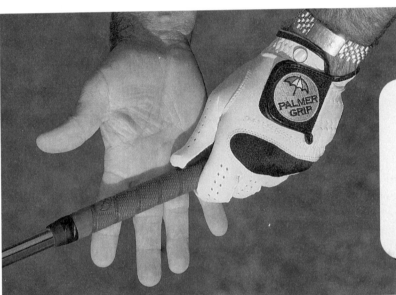

**Right-handers:** Place the club across the middle fold in the right hand's fingers. Slide your hands together until the pinkie of your right hand overlaps between the index and middle finger of your left hand. This is what we call the Vardon or overlap grip.

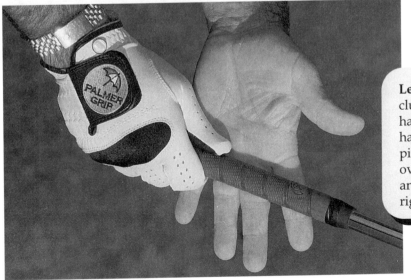

**Left-handers:** Place the club at the base of the left hand's fingers. Slide your hands together until the pinkie of your left hand overlaps between the index and middle finger of your right hand.

## Swing Killers

Avoid the common tendency and mistake of gripping high in the palm. When you grip in the palm, your hand must shift away from the proper neutral position to a swing, destroying overly strong right-hand position. For most beginners, this feels good, as if you have control of the club. But in actuality, it will restrict your maximum power and accuracy.

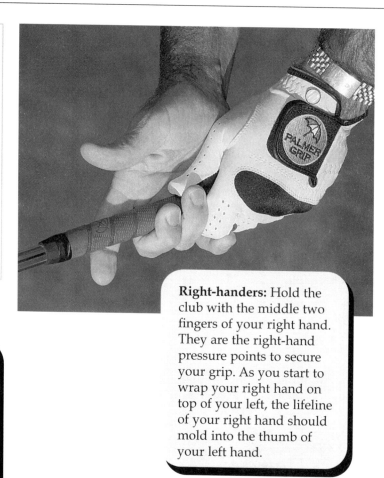

**Right-handers:** Hold the club with the middle two fingers of your right hand. They are the right-hand pressure points to secure your grip. As you start to wrap your right hand on top of your left, the lifeline of your right hand should mold into the thumb of your left hand.

**Left-handers:** Hold the club with the middle two fingers of your left hand. They are the left-hand pressure points to secure your grip. As you start to wrap your left hand on top of your right, the lifeline of your left hand should mold into the thumb of your right hand.

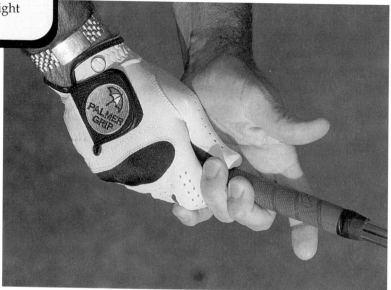

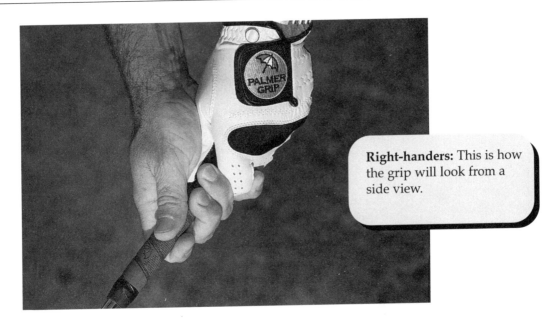

**Right-handers:** This is how the grip will look from a side view.

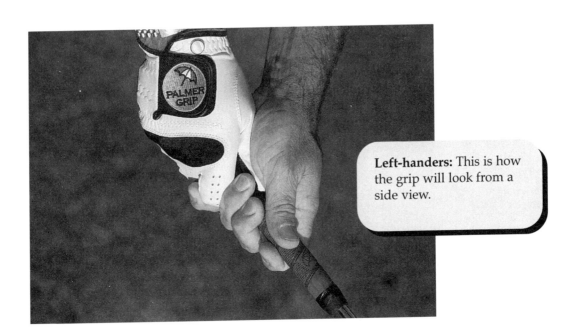

**Left-handers:** This is how the grip will look from a side view.

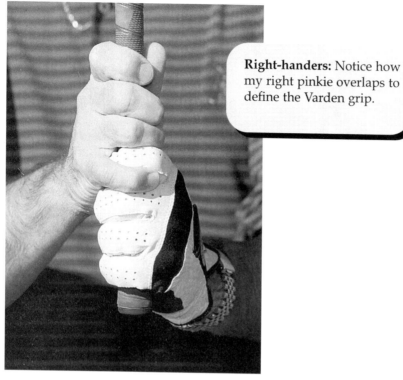

**Right-handers:** Notice how my right pinkie overlaps to define the Varden grip.

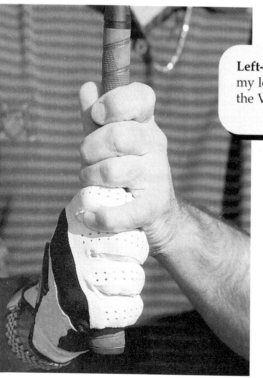

**Left-handers:** Notice how my left pinkie overlaps in the Varden grip.

# Time for Brad's Grip Check

Now that you've gripped the club with both hands, here's how to check to make sure you have a good neutral grip.

**Right-handers:** The "V" formed by the right thumb and index finger (not the crease of the glove) should be pointing to the inside of your right shoulder. If it seems to be pointing toward the outside of the shoulder, correct your right hand by moving the club more into your fingers and out from the palm of your right hand. Should it be pointing more to the center of your body, adjust your right-hand finger position until the "V" points to the inside of your right shoulder.

**Left-handers:** The "V" formed by the left thumb and index finger (not the crease of the glove) should be pointing to the inside of your left shoulder. If it seems to be pointing toward the outside of the shoulder, correct your left hand by moving the club more into your fingers and out from the palm of your left hand. Should it be pointing more to the center of your body, adjust your left-hand finger position until the "V" points to the inside of your left shoulder.

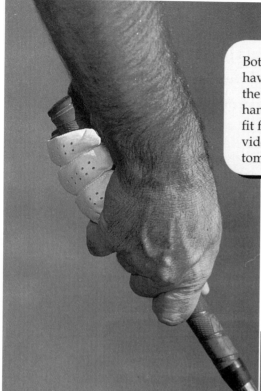

Both right- and left-handed golfers should have about a half-inch of the club visible at the butt end. This guarantees that your hands are holding the grip circumference fit for the size of the hand. Chapter 8 provides additional information about customizing your grips.

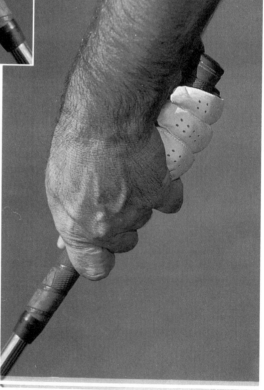

# Brad, How Firmly Should I Hold the Club?

Actually, the question should be, "How relaxed can my grip be?" The amount of pressure needed to hold the club is just as vitally important to a good golf swing as the position of the hands. Ideally, it should be just firm enough for you to feel the clubhead at the end of the shaft. Do you remember the pressure points I demonstrated earlier? That's correct, the last three fingers of the left hand and the middle two fingers of the right. If you play left-handed, it's just the opposite. The key is to apply just enough pressure at those points so the club doesn't fly out of your hands—but loose enough so you can gain maximum acceleration.

Here's a good drill to help develop the feel of just the right amount of pressure. If you get too tight with your hands, you won't sense the feel of the clubhead—too loose and the club will fall over.

Hold your club up in front of you so that you take all the pressure off the shaft.

You can get your hands feeling nice and soft on the club by balancing the weight of the clubhead as you rotate your wrists, making semicircles. Release your grip pressure enough to create a smooth flowing motion. If you tighten up your grip pressure, notice how rigid you become and how small your circles are. This is what happens to your swinging motion with excessive grip pressure.

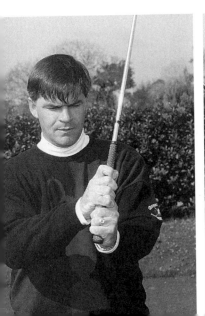

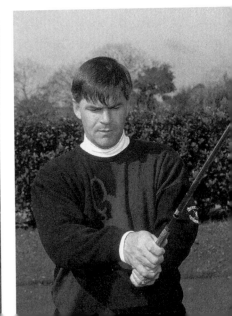

## Pick the Right Grip!

The previous photos illustrated the correct way to grip your club with the overlapping grip. It's also referred to as the *Vardon grip*. However, you have several other choices available because the main objective is to find a grip that feels comfortable and natural to you.

If you have large hands and long fingers, the Vardon grip may be for you. It seems to help prevent your fingers from getting too involved holding onto the club. However, if you have smaller hands with shorter fingers, the *interlocking grip* may be better suited for your game. It's used by many of the players on the LPGA tour and by the legendary Jack Nicklaus.

Some players also choose the *ten-finger or baseball grip*. The hands do not overlap at all so all ten fingers are gripping the club. If you've played a lot of baseball you may feel more comfortable with this grip, so give it a try.

The St. Andrews grip is an excellent grip for seniors because it helps encourage more flexibility in the wrists. Gene Sarazen won his Major titles using the grip first developed by the caddies at St. Andrews and then taught by Alex Morrison, one of the most famous and controversial teachers in the early part of the 1900s. My good friend and mentor Dick Tiddy still uses it. Dick is very much a "feel" player and says this grip allows him to feel the club setting and releasing through the ball.

All of these grips should have one very important trait in common: They all must be neutral grips, meaning the "Vs" of the hand should be pointing to the inside of your right shoulder if you play right-handed or to the inside of your left shoulder if you play left-handed.

### HISTORICAL HIGHLIGHT

Harry Vardon may have been one of the purest strikers of the golf ball who ever lived. Winning six British Opens, he dominated golf at the beginning of the 20th century. Along with James Braid and J. H. Taylor, the three were known as the *Great Triumvirate*. Even though Vardon popularized the overlapping grip and history linked his name to it, Johnny Laidlay, an amateur player of high renown, is believed to have actually originated it. It's still the most popular grip used on the professional tours.

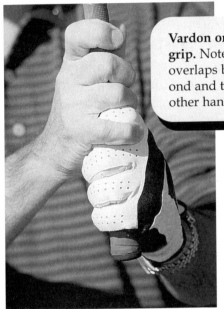

**Vardon or overlapping grip.** Note how the pinkie overlaps between the second and third fingers of the other hand.

**The interlocking grip.** Note how the pinkie interlocks and wraps around the second finger of the other hand. This provides some additional control if you have smaller hands and shorter fingers.

**St. Andrews grip.** Similar to the interlocking grip, but note how the thumb of the gloved hand is wrapped around the shaft. As this provides more wrist flexibility, it's an ideal grip for senior players.

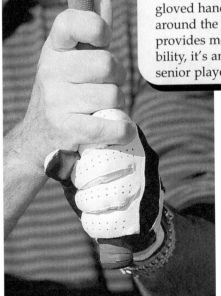

**Baseball or ten-finger grip.** See how all ten fingers are in contact with the shaft? Some golfers find this to be an ideal grip. Try it, it may work for you.

# Brad's Drills for Developing and Maintaining a Consistent Grip

Now that you've learned the correct way to grip the club, here are a few drills that will help you maintain it. The tendency is for elements of your former grip to sneak back in. Drills help establish new *Feel Feedback*, allowing you to feel more comfortable with your new grip.

## Tee for Three Drill

Using a tee as part of this drill will help you with the last three fingers of your gloved hand. Since there is a tendency to subconsciously change your grip back to your former grip when you address the ball, this will help you maintain correct position. You'll also find it an excellent drill for feeling the correct grip pressure throughout your swing.

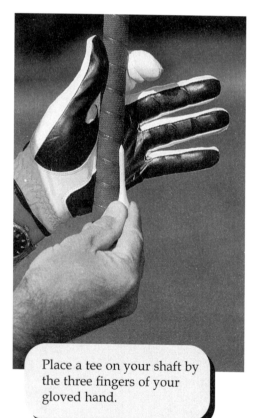

Place a tee on your shaft by the three fingers of your gloved hand.

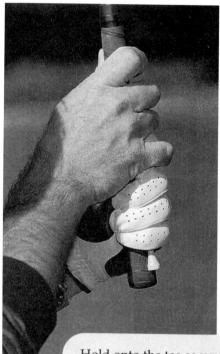

Hold onto the tee as you wrap your fingers around the grip. Now address the ball and make your swing.

If the tee falls out while at address, you re-gripped. If it fell out while making your swing, you have a tendency to let go of the club with the last three fingers.

Practice using the tee and you'll quickly adapt to your new correct grip. With a good neutral grip, you'll be well on your way to a new consistent golf swing.

## Tee-V Drill

It's very common to re-grip when you address the ball just before the take-away. The problem is that golfers almost always shift their hands into different positions. This will destroy your swing even before you make it. Here is a good drill to check your hand positions using a tee and the "V" of your un-gloved hand. It doesn't require buying an expensive training device to develop a consistent grip.

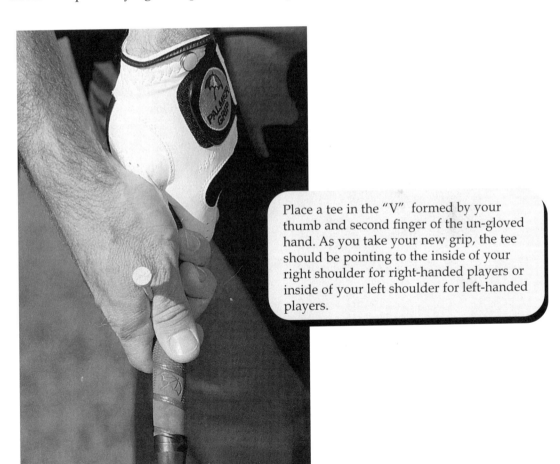

Place a tee in the "V" formed by your thumb and second finger of the un-gloved hand. As you take your new grip, the tee should be pointing to the inside of your right shoulder for right-handed players or inside of your left shoulder for left-handed players.

Some golfers have a tendency to want to strengthen their grip by moving their thumb under the shaft. This position spells disaster for your swinging motion. However, by pinching the tee between your thumb and second finger, you'll be able to create the new feeling of keeping your "V" to the right shoulder.

## Relaxed Grip Drill

This is an easy way to check your grip pressure. You'll quickly understand that holding your club too tightly restricts the free-flowing movement you'll need for a powerful and consistent golf swing. Have a partner help by holding onto the clubhead as you extend the club out.

Have your friend try to gently pull the club away. If your grip pressure is too tight, your arms will remain close to your body, resisting the pulling away. Could you make a free flowing swing with too much pressure like that?

This is an example of creating the feel of excellent grip pressure. As your friend gently pulls the club away, your arms should be able to extend straight out in front of you.

### FEEL FEEDBACK

*Concentrate on what the pressure of your grip feels like in the bottom photo. This is a good feeling to have throughout your swing. You want the sensation of allowing centrifugal force taking the clubhead away from you on your downswing. A relaxed grip allows this to naturally happen.*

*If you've ever seen another golfer developing a chicken wing look as they swing, one of the reasons is a tight grip restricting the swing. Unfortunately, this takes the club on a slice producing an across the ball outside-to-inside swing path, common to 85 percent of golfers.*

Walking down the fairway during a round with Arnold Palmer at the Oasis Golf Club, Mesquite, Nevada.

Brad and Michael Jordan. Golf gives you the opportunity to meet new friends.

Playing with Arnold Palmer during a Tournament in Sanctuary Cove, Australia.

Brad with rock star Huey Lewis.

Seeing your swing is a great teaching tool.

FALL 1996

# THE SCORE CARD

## THE ALUMNI NEWSLETTER OF THE ARNOLD PALMER GOLF ACADEMY

▶ **Palmer Leads U.S. to Victory**

**Play from the Wet Rough**

**Gripless Red Hots!**

▶ Academy Alumnus, Tom Harmon and caddies Pat, Patrick and Paddy watch APAI Director Brad Brewer tee off at Tralee Ireland, the Arnold Palmer-designed course voted "number one" by the APGA group.
*See Ireland story, page 2.*

Brad teaching at a Corporate Golf clinic.

A Sunday golf outing with his family.

# Address Position

*"Why don't you aim more to the right?"*

**Ben Hogan,** when asked by an amateur player for advice on
why he was hitting his shots to the left.

*Addressing the ball properly is not a mystery. Only four
very simple components are required: posture, head position, alignment, and ball position.*
**Brad Brewer**

Just as you can't build a magnificent building without a solid foundation, the same is true for your golf swing. Putting yourself in a good address position, the second of our five fundamentals, is vital if you want to be able to make a good natural swinging motion. Without good posture, alignment, and ball position, it's very difficult to swing the club at maximum clubhead speed and have the ball move toward your target.

# A Good Address Position

The key at address is to get into a good athletic position. You want to be able to consistently make the natural swinging motion time after time. If your set-up is not correct, your entire swing will require all sorts of needless compensations rather than performing its true function—sending the ball powerfully toward the target with the greatest of ease!

Take a moment to look at what a good address position should look like. Get a feeling for the athletic posture, spine angle, width of stance, ball position, and alignment. I'm checking my set-up on the course with two clubs on the ground (in the next two photos) but we'll work on the address for various clubs back on the practice range.

Face-on view and down-the-line view of a good address position.

# 5-Iron Address

- The width of the stance should be just inside your shoulder width.
- Ball position is about two inches off the left heel, the bottom of the swing arc.
- You should be able to draw a line from your left shoulder down your left arm straight through your shaft.

This is an excellent starting point to make a one-piece take-away, the third of our five basic fundamentals.

I suggest you build a practice station that allows you to consistently work on your address. I'm using some pointer boards but you can use clubs. Lay one club on the ground parallel to your target line to line up your feet. Position another club that's perpendicular to the first one to consistently position your ball.

5-iron address position.

## FEEL FEEDBACK

*In your 5-iron address position you'll feel your weight toward the right side. The weight should be felt on the balls of the feet. You'll feel your right shoulder tilted a little underneath your left at address—unless your right arm is six inches longer than your left!*

Down-the-line view for 5-iron address.

- Feet, hips, and shoulders aimed parallel to the target line.
- Hip girdles are pushed back slightly. Spine angle tilt from the waist and a high chest create a good straight line. No slouching forward!
- Arms hang down naturally from the shoulders. Let gravity take care of that. Don't reach away, let them hang down naturally at set-up. They will be under your chin.
- Look down at the golf ball, keeping your chin up. Don't tuck your chin into your neck or you won't be able to turn your shoulders under your chin. Beware of the "turtle neck" syndrome.
- Knees flexed to your balance point, feel the weight distribution on the balls of your feet.

If you are in perfect posture, you should be able to draw a vertical line that begins inside your shoulder, intersects your knee, and continues down to the balls of your feet. If you're looking at your address on a video freeze frame, hold a ruler on the screen to evaluate your address position.

## Swing Killers

If the vertical line that begins at your shoulder is too much toward your toe, you're tilted forward too much, causing your balance point to be toe-weighted.

If you're not tilting forward enough or if too much of your knee is on the right side of the line, your balance point will shift too much into your heels. Either error will directly affect your take-away path: You'll be searching for the best path to keep you in balance. Have a friend check you at the range by holding a club to simulate the line—you'll quickly know exactly what the fault is in your posture and can get back into swing balance.

## Wedge Address

- The width of stance is narrow.
- Feet, hips, and shoulders are open slightly to the left of target.
- Ball position is still off the inside left heel, but the open stance has made the chest move more in front of the ball causing the ball to look further back in the stance.

Accuracy with the wedge is extremely important and the open position becomes a "governor" allowing only a half to three-quarter backswing. It also encourages better acceleration through the shot and more of a descending angle of attack. A 5-iron, by comparison, requires more of a sweeping angle of attack.

- Feet, hips, and shoulders slightly pointed to left of the target line. This position restricts making a full pivot away, limiting you to a half to three-quarter swing, depending on how much you open at address. The resulting steeper angle of attack coming down and through will help you hit crisper and more accurate shots.
- Hang your hands down naturally from your shoulders. The open position makes it appear that they are close to the thigh.

Wedge address position.

Down-the-line view of address for your wedge.

### FEEL FEEDBACK

*If your wedge address position is correct, you should feel about 60 percent of your weight on the inside and ball of your left foot and 40 percent on the inside and ball of the right foot.*

## Driver Address

- Wider width of stance than a 5-iron. The right foot is moved back so the base is slightly wider than shoulder width because the driver requires a wider swing arc and more foundation for the bigger swing action.
- Ball is two inches off the left heel.
- You should be able to draw a line from your left shoulder down your left arm straight through the shaft.

Your chin is swiveled slightly to the right when you set up at address for your driver. This gives a little more room for a big wide shoulder turn as you begin your take-away. Don't move your head to the right, feel as if you've swiveled it.

Driver address position.

- The right foot is slightly inside the target line so the feet, hips, and shoulders are slightly aimed to the right of the target. This makes it easier to make a bigger, wider turn going away, creating more of a draw position.
- Allow your arms to hand down naturally from your shoulders. As you address the ball, you should be able to see just the top of your left forearm over the top of your right forearm. You should see a little bit of bend in your right elbow.
- Look down at the golf ball, keeping your chin up. Don't tuck your chin into your neck or you won't be able to turn your shoulders under your chin as you swing back.
- Knees should be flexed to keep a good balanced foundation.
- Hip girdles are pushed back slightly, which causes the proper straight back position.

Down-the-line view of driver address.

You should be able to draw a vertical line that begins inside of your shoulder, intersects your knee, and continues down to the balls of your feet. If you're looking at your address on a video freeze frame, hold a ruler on the screen to evaluate your address position.

**BRAD EXPLAINS**

*As you set up for your driver, you'll feel a little more weight on your right foot than you did with your 5-iron. (The weight should be felt on the inside or balls of the feet.) This is because of your wider base. You should feel around 70 percent of your weight on your right side if you're set up correctly at address.*

# Drills to Help You Master the Address Fundamental

Now that you understand what a good address position consists of, here are some drills to incorporate into your practice. Some of them can be easily done at home.

## Hip Set Drill

This drill helps you develop the proper posture position.

Start in an upright position, chest parallel to your target. Hold a club in both hands and put it across your belt buckle.

Push back with the club and feel as if you're keeping your chest up. You'll create a good address position with the hip girdles moving back and up, setting the proper spine angle for address.

## Arms Hang Down Drill

Once you've set a good spine angle, you need to develop the feeling of your arms hanging down from your shoulders.

Let gravity take over, allowing your hands to hang down naturally from your shoulders. Clap a few times to get all the tension out and you'll have a good natural position. There should be between one to one-and-a-half hand lengths between your hands and the front of your thighs.

## Alignment Drill

This is almost a fail-safe way to set up with proper alignment.

Place a board or a club on the ground to get your aiming point. I'm pointing to the club I've put on the ground that's parallel to it. This will help me align my feet, hips, and shoulders parallel to the target line. If you ever have an opportunity to attend a PGA or LPGA Tour event, visit the practice tee and you will see the alignment drill put to good use by almost every player.

## Alignment Check

A good alignment check is to first set up at address with your feet, hips, and shoulders parallel to the target line. Hold another club across your shoulders and swivel your head to the left. (Don't swivel your body, just your head!) You should be able to look down your parallel to the target line without seeing your left shoulder. Have a partner or caddie help you out with this one.

## Ball Position Check

I really suggest building a practice station on the practice tee. Along with a target line marker, set up the boards or club perpendicular to each other. One shows your parallel target line for aligning feet, hips, and shoulders while the other is a ball position aid.

Your ball should always be positioned so that it is located at the bottom of the swing arc for the club you're using. The next three photos show the positions for 5-iron, wedge, and driver. Notice the ball is always about two inches off the left heel, but the width of stance is adjusted for the clubs used. Longer clubs sweep through the ball and need a wider width of stance. When using shorter clubs, like those used in the scoring zone, a slightly opened and narrower stance encourages the half to three-quarter swing you'll need for a more descending angle of attack.

- Approximately two inches off left heel.
- Feet apart, inside shoulder width.
- Feet (along with hips and shoulders) parallel to the target line.

### SWING KILLERS

*If your alignment is off, you will inadvertently be hurting your game. Even pros have to constantly work on their alignment and address fundamentals. Being slightly out of alignment at address can make a huge difference after the ball travels 200 yards.*

5-iron ball position.

Wedge ball position.

- Approximately two inches off left heel.
- Stance narrower than 5-iron stance.
- Feet (along with hips and shoulders) slightly aimed to the left in a slightly open position.

Driver ball position.

- Approximately two inches off left heel.
- Widen stance by moving right foot so stance is slightly wider than shoulder width. This allows a big, wide swing arc.
- Back foot is slightly back from parallel target line so that feet, hips, and shoulders are aimed slightly right of target.

## Understanding How Far Away the Ball Is Drill

The length and lie of the golf club dictates how far away the ball is from your address position.

Your address position doesn't change. Let the length and lie of the club dictate how far away the ball is. Don't change your address position. Notice how I've maintained my spine angle and that my hands are hanging naturally from my shoulders.

# The Pre-Shot Routine

The most direct route toward a repeatable correct address position is to combine the various elements into a pre-shot routine, just like the pros. A routine that's so simple you can duplicate it each and every time you address the ball. As you watch the pros on TV, notice how each one has developed his or her own unique pre-shot routine, right down to the same number of wags of the clubhead before beginning their swings.

You can and should do the same thing. Your pre-shot routine will become comfortable and familiar, helping increase your confidence levels. When you're confident in your ability, it's difficult for pressure to creep in, especially on the first tee. Here's a good example of an efficient routine.

Stand behind the ball and pick out your target. (Remember, golf is a target sport!) Walk in smoothly to the ball, keeping your eyes focused on your target.

For a straight path to the target, position the clubhead first to your target.

Align your feet, hips, and shoulders in a parallel position to that target line. Get comfortable with a few waggles of the club to keep the tension out. Allow the feelings you've worked on while mastering the address fundamental to take over, and you're all ready to make a nice natural swinging motion.

# Brad's Coaching Tips

1. Set an attainable goal for developing a correct address position.

2. Practice your address at home and on the practice range.

3. After you've done some of the alignment drills in this chapter, hit five balls working on each fundamental and then hit five balls thinking about your target.

4. Use your pre-shot routine for the balls you hit on the practice range and play real shots that you know you will face on the courses you play. Make your practice fun!

5. Work on the first two fundamentals of grip and address before making any swing changes. Once you've mastered the first two, you may find that the motion may have fixed itself.

# CHAPTER 26

# The Swing

*"Sam's always been smart enough to know that the way to ruin his swing would be to start getting too complex about it. He's kept his thinking simple."*

**Dr. Cary Middlecoff**, 1956 U.S. Open Champion, commenting on golfing legend Sam Snead

*"It's important to balance working on your mechanics and fundamentals with the real objective—getting the ball to the target."*

*Brad Brewer*

E ver since the dawn of the game, golfers have been in search of the perfect golf swing. Countless books have been written on theory and technique. The swing has been analyzed by the best minds in the sport and by computer models. The result of all this research: There is no correct swing that every golfer needs to imitate. Like your own fingerprint, every swing is uniquely different in a very similar way.

Raymond Floyd has a funny but true quote about the swings of his fellow pros: "If a great golf swing puts you high on the money list, there'd be some of us who would be broke." Fred Couples says: "As far as swing and techniques are concerned, I don't know diddly-squat."

# Five Fundamentals for a Good Golf Swing

While their swings may differ, the great players of the game have something in common: They've mastered the five basic fundamentals of a good golf swing.

| | |
|---|---|
| 1. Grip | Correctly holding the club |
| 2. Address | Posture, alignment, and ball position |
| 3. Take-away | Path the club and arms take during the start of the swing |
| 4. Steady head | Head position during the swing maintains the original relationship to the ball formed at address |
| 5. Acceleration | Sequencing of motion as the clubhead smoothly increases speed throughout the swing |

I can't put enough emphasis on how important it is to master these five fundamentals. Forget about technically analyzing various positions in your swing—that's a trap far too many golfers fall into. Spend some quality practice time working on five easy-to-understand fundamentals and allow the rest of your swing to take care of itself. *Each golfer's individual swing will reflect their physical ability, age, body type, and style of play.*

Arnold Palmer's swing is different from Payne Stewart's. The looping swing of Jim Furyk is far different from Tiger Woods' swing. All good swings are not "cookie cutter" duplications of each other. But, keep in mind that they do share the five fundamentals.

# My Swing

Let's use my swing as an example to illustrate the five fundamentals. We've already covered the importance of grip and address in separate chapters, along with some drills to help you master them. I'll refer to them briefly, but I'll concentrate more on (1) take-away, (2) steady head, and (3) acceleration.

## Address

- Athletic balanced position
- Straight spine angle from the hips to the tip of the head
- Slight flex of the knees
- Alignment with feet, hips, and shoulders parallel to the target line
- A line drawn from the inside of the shoulder should also intersect the knees and extend to the balls of my feet
- Line goes from the inside of the shoulder and down the shaft to the ball
- Shoulder-width stance shown is for a mid-iron
- Ball two inches off left heel
- Head position behind the ball, chin tilted to the right side providing room for the shoulders to rotate under and around the steady head

## One-Piece Take-Away

This is the moment of truth as we coordinate the movement of many independent body parts into a smooth one-piece motion. If you begin with a good grip, correct address, and the one-piece take-away, you are well on your way to having a good repeating golf swing. Many of your faults will be corrected as a result of mastering the first three fundamentals.

- The triangle of hands, arms and shoulders are swinging the club away in unison (one-piece).

- As this occurs, the hips and left knee naturally pivot to the right.

- You can see a bit of natural weight transfer that loads up in the right leg as a result of this one-piece take-away.

- The head has stayed steady in this part of the swing. This defines our swing's maximum extension from a fixed axis.

- You can see the same triangle I had at address as I'm swinging back with my hands, arms, and shoulders in unison.

- My wrists have stayed passive and not set the club too early in the swing.

- This good extension is going to allow the widest swing arc and coordination of all the muscles into the golf swing.

## Continuation to the Top of the Backswing

- At this point, the momentum of the club is naturally setting up the wrist hinge, along with the pivot away with the body taking the club to the top.

- The approximate 90-degree angle set by the forearm and the wrist demonstrates a good hinging motion that happens only when your grip and grip pressure are good enough to let this natural setting become part of the motion in your golf swing.

## Top of the Swing

- Everything is coordinated into a full coiled-up backswing.

- The hands are in a good high position.

- Left arm has swung into a position that works across the chest and above the right shoulder.

- The club has been swung up in a comfortable position that leaves room between the right elbow and the side.

- You cannot see the shaft pointed left or right. It proves I've arrived at the top in a good one-piece motion that will allow me to start down and have the club swinging back to the ball, in a very simple way, without having to re-route anything.

- The hands are high over the right side.

- The shaft is parallel to the ground as a result of my shoulders being turned a full 90 degrees or slightly more.

- My hips have been naturally pulled into about a 40-degree turn. Some people will have more or less, depending on their flexibility.

- I'm in a good coiled position with all the weight held on the inside of the right leg.

Everything that you're seeing and reading about in the top of the backswing occurred naturally because my grip, address, and one-piece take-away allowed it to happen. I'm only pointing out the degrees of turn to show what can happen naturally just by mastering the simple fundamentals.

Often, the swings I see my students make are incredibly complicated. Instead of developing distance-producing acceleration, their swings are inefficiently compensating for faults with grip, address, and take-away. They have to make incredible adjustments just to get back to the ball. Master the five fundamentals and you'll really enjoy playing consistent golf.

## Swinging Back to the Ball

- Start back to the ball from the ground up.
- Motion begins with the knees and hips starting to unwind and moving back to the left side.
- This transfers the weight to the forward side.
- As a result, the hips, shoulders, and arms begin to uncoil.
- The hands have been pulled down to about shoulder height but the club has yet to release, as indicated by the position of the shaft.
- The shaft is pointing to the left, which indicates naturally swinging the club from the inside. If we were incorrectly swinging the club from the outside, the shaft would be more vertical.

## Acceleration

The last of the five fundamentals is acceleration. Acceleration naturally occurs through a chain of events in the swing. It begins from the ground up and then naturally and fluidly gathers momentum as it works down in to impact and beyond. You want your top acceleration point to be at the impact zone, not at the top of the backswing in the transition.

A lot of amateurs go after the ball too hard from the top of the swing, releasing the angle of the forearm and the shaft early, throwing it out trying to get to the ball quickly. This loses total control of the clubhead angle of attack and their power.

- The transitional view seen from the front.
- You can see a little more dynamics in the lower body as it starts to initiate the downswing.
- Because the lower body begins unwinding first, initiating the forward motion, you'll notice the good angle set between the forearm and the shaft, indicating the club has not been thrown from the top.
- There is good delayed wrist cock. I'm not trying to delay it—it's happening naturally by letting the lower body be the leader instead of the hands casting.
- The head is steady and continues to stay as close to its original position as possible.

## Steady Head

Maintaining a steady head in your golf swing is one of the five fundamentals. In order to have a repeating swing, you need a consistent reference point with your original address position. Imagine your head as the fixed access or the center of your swing. The path of the motion depends on your head's stability. If it moves in any direction, so does your entire swing!

If we want to swing back to our original address position, we need to maintain a steady head throughout the swing—or have a lot of talent. The head does not actually remain rock steady; there is some slight movement in all great swings. However, all good ball strikers feel that when they are swinging their best, their head is as steady as the Rock of Gibraltar. When they are swinging poorly, they feel it moving all over the place.

Jack Nicklaus feels that keeping a still head is his one consistent swing thought that has worked time and time again throughout his career. Arnold Palmer would tell you today that it is the number one fundamental to good golf: "If everybody were to steady their heads, the highest handicap would be 18." Read instructional books written by the game's greats: Ben Hogan, Sam Snead, Bobby Jones, Gary Player, Tom Watson. All address the importance of maintaining a steady head for great golf. And so do I!

# Impact

- I've returned almost identically to my original address position.

- The hips are slightly turned to the left more than they would have been at address, showing that I am accelerating through the ball and not at it.

- At this point, the natural releasing of the golf club is happening as a result of good fluid acceleration.

- The stored power is being exploded into the back of the ball.

- The spine angle and knee flex we had at address is almost identical at impact, due to maintaining a steady head throughout the entire golf swing.

- The same straight line we had at address, on the left side, has returned at impact.

- Good firm impact position.

- The hands are leading the clubhead into the impact zone. If your hands pass the clubhead before impact, you have decelerated. This will cause a loss of power and path.

- A lot of flex in the shaft from good quality acceleration.

- Notice how the head has stayed back and allowed the natural centrifugal force of the clubhead to swing out completely to its full extension point.

# Continuing to Follow-Through

- A full extension of the arms working down the line.

- Hips and shoulders are naturally unwinding with the momentum of the golf swing.

- No jumping off the right side took place. That causes excessive lower body motion and loses the spine angle we set at address.

- The shoulders are rotating on the same pivot axis I had at address. The right shoulder is working down and through instead of around and high.

- Keeping the head steady has allowed a full extension of the right arm and the shaft. The centrifugal force at the end of the club is pulling me through to a full extension.

- The triangle of the hands, arms, and shoulders is a mirror image as it was on the first part of the take-away.

- It may look as if I'm leaning to the right, but the weight has been pulled into the left side.

- The knee flex and steady head are allowing me to pivot my hips back to the left side.

## Swing Killers

If someone tells you to keep your head down, that could be a swing killer. Keep your head steady but allow the natural motion of the follow-through to pull you all the way through the shot. If you try to stay back too long, it tends to make you decelerate, flipping the club through the shot. Allow the full extension of your follow-through to pull your head up. Then you can enjoy those long and straight strikes heading toward the pin.

- The line shows I have stayed on a good swing plane throughout.
- The head is beginning to be pulled forward with the entire body.

- The natural acceleration of the swing carries you through to a well-balanced finish.

- At the finish, about 85 percent of your weight should be balanced on your left leg.

- Your hips and chest should be facing toward the target.

- Your hands should end up quite high, as they were at the top of the backswing.

- The shaft should be comfortably working across your back.

- Your eyes are tracking a great shot.

- Your entire body is saying, "Wow, that felt great!"

# Brad's Swing Drills

Now it's time to start working on your new swing. I hope that you began by working on the first two fundamentals, grip and address. Here are some drills to help develop the new feeling for your swing.

## Body Pivot Exercise

This is a wonderful exercise that shows you how little your body has to do in a proper golf swing. Do it slowly as you develop a feeling for the natural transfer of weight to the right side on take-away and over to the left side on your forward swing. Also work on maintaining a steady head as you rotate back and through.

I suggest doing the exercise a few times slowly to begin to develop the feel for the swing. Next, slowly rotate back, and when you reach the top of the swing, begin accelerating from the ground up at the same tempo as a regular swing. You may want to videotape yourself and check your positions.

Place a shaft across your chest and cross your arms. Hold the shaft tight against your chest and shoulders. Begin with a good athletic address position and proper spine angle.

Maintain a steady head as you rotate back around your fixed spine angle. Feel the weight begin to transfer to your left side.

1. Rotate back and the shaft of your club will point to the ground, as in this photo, at the top of your golfswing. This is a good coiled position with all the weight on the right side. Your transition back to the ball should start from the ground up with your lower body.

2. Feel the weight transferring to the right side as you approach impact. Try to establish the feeling of a steady head throughout the swing. In this position, it's behind the ball as it was at address.

3. In this post-impact position, you should feel your right shoulder working under instead of around, as it might have if you had started your transition to the ball from the top part of your body instead of from ground up. See how the hips have opened slightly to allow room for the arms and club to swing through.

4. Rotate through to a balanced finish position.

## Broom Sweep Release Exercise

This exercise will help develop the feel of a one-piece take-away as it builds strength in your hands, arms, and the big muscles in your back and shoulders.

Use a broom as a club. Set up as if you were about to tee off.

Sweep the broom back. You will develop the feel of a one-piece take-away as you swing your hands, arms, and shoulders back in unison. Maintain the feeling of a steady head throughout the swing.

Let the momentum carry the broom to the top of your swing as your wrists naturally hinge.

Begin your unwinding to the ball from the ground up. When you get to the impact zone, your weight will naturally transfer over to the right side. Your steady head will allow you to rotate around your spine angle as you sweep through the ball.

Sweep through to the finish position.

## Point Tee to Ball Drill

This drill will help increase your proper timing and acceleration. It will also indirectly achieve an inside-to-square swing plane that will promote a draw.

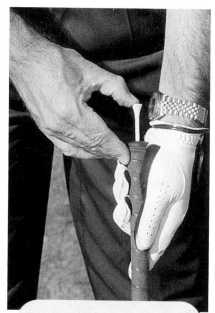

Using a mid-iron, place a tee in the hole at the end of the club.

After setting up in a good address position, swing the club back at half speed and stop at the top of your backswing.

Make the change in direction from backswing to downswing by planting the left heel and left side firmly on the ground. Feel the pull on your left arm and the butt of the club moving down toward the ball. Try to develop the feel of driving the tee in the butt end of your club toward the ball until you pass your right hip.

## Connection Drill

This is a great exercise to help you focus as you feel a one-piece kind of motion with the hands, arms, and shoulders allowing you to accelerate with a feeling of unity and balance.

Use a towel or headcover for this drill.

Place it in your left armpit and hold it firmly against your chest with pressure from your left arm. Take a good address position.

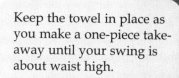

Keep the towel in place as you make a one-piece take-away until your swing is about waist high.

Feel your head remaining steady as you swing forward to waist high. Develop the feeling of your feet, hips, and shoulders pivoting in the swing.

## Draw Back Drill

This is an outstanding drill that promotes a full turn and reduces picking up the club on the take-away. It will help you develop the feel of an inside approach to the ball.

Address the ball normally to start.

Draw your right foot back one foot behind the left.

Make your one-piece take-away and continue to the top of your backswing so that your back faces the target.

On the downswing, keep the right foot drawn back and allow the weight to shift fully into the follow-through. A great way to feel the club swinging from the inside on the forward swing.

# Dumping Practice!

It's important to balance working on your mechanics and fundamentals with the real objective—getting the ball to the target.

I suggest you hit five practice shots thinking about mechanics and the feel of what you're doing.

Eliminate all mechanical thoughts. Try to get a feeling that you're on the course, and hit five target reaction shots.

Pick out a target and realistically decide on the type of shot you know you can hit. Focus on reacting to that target and let your natural abilities take over. Don't think of every fundamental lesson at the same time, because you'll end up tying yourself in knots. Improvement really kicks in when the fundamentals become a natural part of your swing.

## Perpetual Motion Drill

Begin this drill with five balls on tees. It's difficult to show in still photography, but hit all five in succession, only pausing long enough to move forward to address the next ball. The object of this drill is to get some natural motion back in your swing. Swing back and through with controlled rhythm and acceleration.

# Training Aids

I believe certain training aids can be beneficial if they can help you establish feel. One training aid that is outstanding for working on every area of your game is the Natraflex mentor training glove.

The Natraflex is a glove that you slip on your hand and play a complete round in. It helps you with set-up, one-piece take-away, and develops better acceleration by assuring a proper release position with your hands and arms. It is also a muscle-conditioning glove with built-in flexors that work you out as you play and practice.

You'll find it extremely beneficial for developing the proper left forearm and hand "golfing muscles."

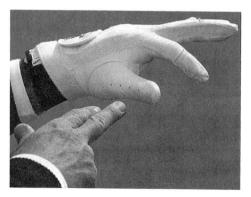
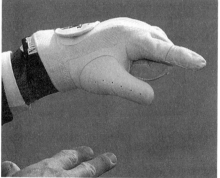

The Natraflex is a training aid that you can take to the course with you. You'll quickly develop some important feel with every shot you hit that will help your game.

CHAPTER 27

# The Scoring Zone

*"If I ever needed an 8-foot putt and everything I owned depended on it, I would want Arnold Palmer to putt it for me."*

***Bobby Jones***

*"Improving your scoring zone shots is the quickest way to reducing your scores."*

***Brad Brewer***

The scoring zone starts about 60 yards out and is the area of the course where you pitch, chip, and putt. For the best players in the world, this area represents 42 percent of their game. As your handicap increases, that percentage goes up. It's the area of the game that PGA Tour professionals practice the most. Unfortunately, it's totally neglected by most amateurs during their practice sessions.

If you want to improve your handicap and your scores in a short time frame, this is where you need to start—it's the quickest way to save strokes in everybody's game. That 3-foot putt counts the same as a 300-yard drive and, if missed, can become very frustrating.

The average high handicap golfer averages 40 putts or more per round. Compare that to the touring professional average of 29. Improving your short game will allow you to get closer to the hole and sink more putts. The scoring zone, in my opinion, begins about 60 yards from the hole.

# Chipping It Close or In!

We'll start with chipping, the shots that are played from just off the putting green. You can use a variety of clubs from a 5-iron to a wedge to chip with. Choose your weapon based on how far you want the ball to run to the hole after landing on the green. Your club choice depends on your distance from the edge of the green and then the distance to the hole: 5-irons will run farther than wedges. You want the ball to become a putt as soon as possible. If you apply this simple philosophy in your chipping game, you will soon benefit from more consistent distance control and many more playable misses in general.

Be sure and pick out a line to the hole, then determine your target landing spot. Make the one-piece stroke I'll help you with shortly, then watch your ball land, roll, and get close to or go into the hole.

## Chipping Keys

1. A good neutral grip. Same as your full swing, but grip pressure becomes even more important. The lighter your grip pressure, the better touch and feel you'll have for your club.
2. Choking down on the club.
3. Narrowing the stance.
4. Slightly opening up the feet, hips, and shoulders.
5. Swing back and through in a one-piece motion.

## Choking Down on the Grip

- Gains control of a squared clubhead position throughout the stroke.
- More feel for the club you're swinging.
- Limiting your swing arc allows better control of distance allowing you to control the smooth acceleration of the club.

## Address Position

Face-on view.

Down-the-line view.

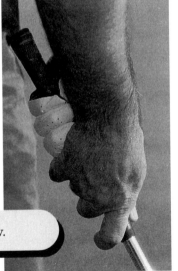

- Stance is narrow and open to the target line.
- Play the ball approximately two inches off your left heel.
- Hands set-up slightly forward of the ball.

- By choking down on the club, you naturally go into more of your putting position.
- Tilted over more at address, your swing plane becomes more vertical.
- Your feet, hips and chest should be open to the target. (Aimed slightly left for right-handers and aimed slightly right for left-handers.)
- The open position will keep your hands forward of the clubhead and the ball throughout your stroke. This promotes a sweeping angle of attack.

## Chipping Action Sequence

Here's what a one-piece chipping stroke looks like. Review your chipping action by taping your swing, then comparing it to mine.

As I begin to take the club back, notice the straight line going down the inside of the left shoulder running down the shaft. My hands are marginally in front of the ball because of the open stance and the ball is positioned two inches off the left heel. More weight sets upon the left side naturally.

First part of the take-away. The triangle formed between the shoulders, arms, and hands moves the club back in a one-piece unit.

The backswing: Minimal wrist action if any.

## FEEL FEEDBACK

*You should feel as if you're brushing the grass through impact and allowing the ball to naturally roll up the face of the golf club. You can practice that feel by taking a small broom and making the same stroke.*

Forward motion is a mirror image of the backswing. One-piece back and one-piece through makes it easy to control a smooth and fluid acceleration. Just as my clubhead is about to impact the ball, see how I've returned to exactly the same position as when I just started to take the club back. Hands are slightly ahead of the club assuring a clean crisp contact of the ball in the middle of the clubface every time. Post impact: Triangle still together tells the story of a good one-piece action throughout the swing.

Follow-through. The same hand, arms and shoulder motion has carried me to my follow-through.

# Brad's Chipping Drills

Here are some very simple drills to help you condition a good technique needed for chipping correctly.

## Golf Ball Toss Drill

This is an outstanding drill to help you learn distance control in your chipping action.

Put a golf ball in your right hand.

Lob it underhand toward your target, developing a feel for the chipping motion. Try lofting it with different trajectories, feeling how your motion increases with higher trajectories.

## Brush and Wedge Drill

This drill provides the feel and visuals of chipping with a smooth brush stroke. Begin by choking down as you hold a broom and a wedge together as I am.

As you brush the broom back, the club follows with a sweeping one-piece take-away motion.

You'll hit consistent chips around the green if you sweep away with your stroke. Here the club follows the broom's lead. The ball will roll up the face of the club and nice clean contact with the ball is the result.

## Flamingo Drill

One common problem I see with many golfers having trouble with their chipping is too much lower body motion. An important key to better chipping is to stay steady with your lower body. This drill will keep your weight on your left side because you hit shots with your right heel raised off the ground balancing on your toe—similar to our famous Florida flamingos.

Take your normal address position, but lift your right heel off the ground. Make a one-piece swing with your hands, arms, and shoulders working together and you'll see how the raised heel restricts your lower body movement, keeping the weight on your left side.

## Two Club Chipping Drill

Developing the feel of the all-important one-piece motion is this drill's major benefit. Golfers have the incorrect tendency to slow down their arm swing and then flip their wrists as they hit chips. The drill objective is to stroke back and through in a one-piece motion without the extended club hitting your left side.

Overlap the grip of your chipping club with another club that is extended with its clubhead pointing up.

Make a good one-piece sweep-away with your hands, arms, and shoulders maintaining the triangle shape formed at address.

Swing forward, brushing cleanly through impact without having the club's extension hit your left side.

Continue on to your follow-through. The extended club kept your arm swing accelerating and did not allow you to get wristy.

# Pitching

When you find yourself farther out from the green and require a longer approach shot than a chip, it's called a pitch. The ball has to have more loft to it to cover the longer distance and land softly so that it doesn't run too much. You can hit pitch shots with pitching wedges, sand wedges, and lob wedges. The built-in loft dictates which one is appropriate for the distance needed to the pin. Usually the pitching wedge is used for longer shots, the sand wedge and lob wedges are used when you are closer to the green. If you have a chance to play in Scotland, you might want to pitch with a 7-iron so that the ball can run a little farther after landing.

## Pitching Keys

- Address position is similar to a chip. Club aimed at the target.
- Choke marginally down on the club, depending on your distance. This limits the length of the shaft, allowing you to have better control of your distance. For a longer distance, don't choke down as much. For shorter pitches, you can choke down the grip very close to the shaft.
- Open your stance with your feet, hips, and shoulders aligned to the left of your intended target, similar to the way you chip.
- The ball should be approximately two inches off the inside of your left heel.
- Match your swing going back and through. If you're swinging the club back halfway, for example, follow-through halfway, keeping an even tempo in-between.

Many golfers make the mistake of swinging the club too far back when hitting pitch shots. Then they have to decelerate their club coming into the shot attempting to hit it the correct distance. This causes a lot of fat chunky shots or thin sculled shots—ugly any way you look at it.

Think of your swing as a clock and swing from 3 o'clock to 9 o'clock. Practice accelerating smoothly through the shot with the same matched length at follow-through as you had on your backswing.

# Hitting a Pitch

The set-up is similar to a chip but because the stroke is longer, you will have a wrist set. Keep a smooth tempo as you swing the club back and forth. Accelerate through the ball matching the length of your backswing to your follow-through. Go from 4 o'clock to 8 o'clock, 2 o'clock to 10 o'clock, and so on.

Address the ball similar to a chip.

Feet, hips, and shoulders are aligned open to the target. Choke down on the club depending on the length needed for your shot.

Take the club back in a one-piece motion with your hands, arms, and shoulders, similar to a chip.

Your wrists will set naturally as you increase the
length of your swing.

Match the length of your
backswing and follow-
through. Smoothly accelerate through the ball.

# Putting

Just as with our full and partial swings, the key to becoming a good putter is in mastering the basic fundamentals first.

## Grip

I'll demonstrate the reverse overlapping grip, which is probably the most popular grip used on the Tours. It's a grip that gives you a nice snug feeling with your hands close together. You'll be able to make a unified stroking motion with this grip.

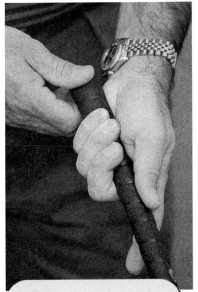

The club is more in the palm of your left hand than it would be in your regular grip.

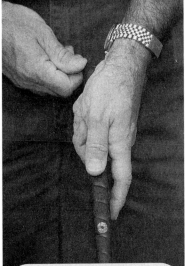

The V formed by the thumb and index finger is pointed at your left shoulder. You should feel that the hand is underneath the grip a little bit.

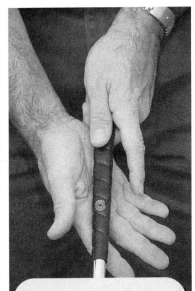

As you close the hand the V of your right hand should point to the right shoulder. As you look down at your grip, the V of each hand should point at its same side shoulder.

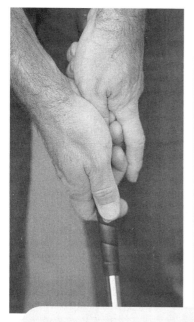 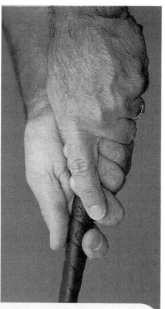

Your grip pressure should be light so that you can feel your instrument as you stroke back and forth with a good rhythmic tempo. If you can't feel the weight of the putter head swinging back and through, your hands are too tight. Keeping your hands soft will allow you to feel the weight at the end of the instrument.

All five fingers of the right hand are on the club with the thumb marginally down the inside right on the shaft. The index finger of your left hand is overlapped across the fingers of the right hand.

## BRAD EXPLAINS

*Each of us has one eye that is more dominant than the other. You can find yours by staring at an object at least four feet in front of you. Curl your right hand so the thumb touches your fingers and, when held in front, you should be able to see through the hole formed. Center your hand so you can see your target. Keeping your hand in position, close one eye. If the target is still in line and can be seen through your fingers, the open eye is your dominant eye. If the target is not centered, close that eye and then open the other one. The target should appear centered—that eye is your dominant eye.*

## Putting Address

The ball should be in the middle of your stance.

You want to align your dominant eye over the ball. I'm hanging a club down from my eye to check on the position, putting it on top of my target line.

# Alignment

Setting up as parallel to your target line as possible is the most consistent way to align yourself. I find it much easier for everyone we teach at our academies to do this but, if you have a preference for a slightly opened stance and you can sink putts with it—go with it! I suggest starting out square and then make an adjustment if it makes you feel more comfortable.

Keep your shoulders level to the ground. This is important if you want to swing back in a one-piece pendulum motion. See how I match the length of my swing back and forth. If you take it back six inches, follow through six inches.

## SWING KILLERS

*Many people tilt their left shoulder up at address too much. This makes it difficult for them to take the putter back in a one-piece motion. They end up dragging it into the ground or picking it up with their hands. Try to keep your shoulders as level to the ground as possible, at address, to avoid this problem.*

This is a close-up view of how my hands, arms, and shoulders stay together as I make a one-piece pendulum stroke.

## Pendulum Drill

- Place a club under your arms and hold snugly against your chest. The club will help you align your body parallel to your target line.
- Make strokes feeling the motion of your shoulders coordinated with the pendulum motion of the clubhead swinging.
- Maintain a steady head like all the great putters.
- Allow the putter head to swing past your head—don't come up and out of the putt early.
- Another good drill is to listen for the ball going into the hole, rather than watching it. This way, you're not tempted to raise your head.

### FEEL FEEDBACK

*As you stroke it back and through you should feel a good shoulder, hand, and arm movement all in one unison piece. After a few minutes of practice, try making a few putts feeling the same one-piece motion that has begun to become a habit in your putting stroke.*

## Putt-Tee Practice Station

Set up a practice station on the green with three tees: a tee for ball position; a tee as the governor for the length of the backswing; a tee for the follow-through. Stroke within the guidelines of the tees. You'll build symmetry in your unified stroke, back and through. It's a great way to practice, getting yourself into good putting habits.

## Tennis Ball Drill

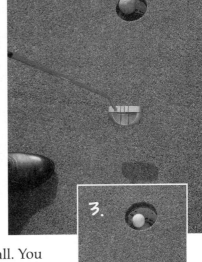

Try making five putts from two feet with a tennis ball. You must make a smooth accelerating stroke. See how the ball barely fits in the hole. After this exercise, when you putt the golf ball, the hole will look as big as a bushel basket. This really will help you with the short putts many golfers have trouble with.

## Left Hand Putting Drill

Putt with your left hand. This is good practice to help you work on stroking back and through. The back of the left hand should always be accelerating through to the hole and not breaking down. Stroking 2- and 3-foot putts with the left hand only gives you a good solid feel.

## Spoke Drill

Take five golf balls and put them at a three-foot range around the hole. Make all the putts from the three-foot range, then set them up at the five-foot range. This is an outstanding way to practice all the breaks you may find on a green: left to right, right to left, uphill and downhill.

Take five golf balls and put them at a three-foot range around the hole.

# Crystal Clear Tempo

I want to share with you the best putting tip I ever received. It came from a good friend of mine, Ian Baker-Finch, shortly after his 1994 British Open victory. We were playing golf at Winged Foot Country Club in Westchester County, New York. The greens that day were slicker than ice on a Minnesota lake in January and I was having a tough time judging my distance.

After knocking a 10-foot putt 30 feet past the hole and completely off the green, my good friend from the land down under let me in on his secret to putting fast greens. He said: "I visualize that my putter shaft is made of a very thin piece of lead crystal with a heavy putter head. I must swing the putter back and through in a very slow even pace with the head of the shaft or it will break."

Visualization can be a very powerful tool and, in this story, I went on to shoot 3 under on the back side with a total of 12 putts. I have been successful with this thought for putting fast greens many times since then. Next time you putt fast greens and you are struggling with your tempo control, try our Crystal Clear Tempo secret.

# Glossary

**Address**   Your body position (posture, alignment, ball position) as you set up to the ball.

**Addressing the ball**   Taking a stance and grounding the club (except in a hazard) before taking a swing.

**Approach**   A shot hit to the putting green.

**Away**   A player who is farthest from the hole. This player plays their ball first.

**Apron**   Slightly higher grassy area surrounding the putting surface. Also referred to as fringe.

**Backspin**   The spin of a golf ball that is the opposite direction of the ball's flight.

**Ball mark**   The damaged indented area caused by the ball when it lands on the green.

**Ball marker**   Something round and small to mark the position of your ball on the putting green. You should mark your ball to clean it and also allow your playing partners to have an unobstructed line to the hole. Markers can be purchased, are attached to your glove, or use a dime, nickel, or quarter.

**Birdie**   One stroke under the designated par of the hole.

**Bogey**   One stroke over the designated par of a hole.

**Bunker**   Also referred to as a sand trap.

**Blade**   To hit the ball at its center with the bottom edge of your club.

**Blocked shot**  Hitting a ball on a straight line to the right.

**Bump and run**  A type of approach shot that lands off the green and then rolls onto the green and toward the hole.

**Carry**  How far a ball flies through the air. If a water hazard is in front of you, you have to figure the carry to be sure you've taken enough club.

**Casual water**  A temporary water accumulation not intended as a hazard. Consult the published *Rules of Golf* for information on the relief you are entitled to.

**Chili-dip**  Hitting the ground before contacting the ball. The result: weak popped up shots also called fat.

**Divot**  Turf displaced by a player's club when making a swing. Divots must be replaced.

**Double bogey**  Two strokes over the designated par for a hole.

**Draw**  A shot that curves from right to left for right-handers and the opposite for left-handed golfers.

**Drop**  The act of returning a ball back into play. Consult *The Rules of Golf* for more correct information on circumstances where this occurs.

**Eagle**  Two strokes under the designated par for a hole.

**Fairway**  Closely mowed route of play between tee and green.

**Fore**  A warning cry to any person in the way of play or who may be within the flight of your airborne ball.

**Green**  The putting surface.

**Gross score**  Total number of strokes taken to complete a designated round.

**Ground-the-club**  Touching the surface of the ground with the sole of the club at address.

**Handicap**  A deduction from a player's gross score. Handicaps for players are determined by guidelines published by the USGA.

**Halved the hole**  The phrase used to describe a hole where identical scores were made.

**Honor**  The right to tee off first, earned by scoring the lowest on the previous hole.

**Hook**  A stroke made by a right-handed player that curves the ball to the left of the target. It's the opposite for left-handers.

**Hot**  A ball that comes off the clubface without backspin and will go farther than normal as a result. If a lie put grass between the clubface and ball, the grooves can't grip the ball to develop backspin. Understanding this, a golfer knows their ball will come out "hot" and plans for that.

**Lateral hazard**  A hazard, (usually water) that is on the side of a fairway or green. Red stakes are used to mark lateral hazards.

**Lie**  Stationary position of the ball. Also it is described as the angle of the shaft in relation to the ground when the club sole rests naturally.

**Local rules**  Special rules for the course that you are playing.

**Loft**  The amount of angle built into the clubface.

**Match play**  A format where each hole is a separate contest. The winner is the individual or team who wins more holes than are left to play.

**Mulligan**  A second ball that's hit from the same location. The shot that's tried again. Usually limited to friendly rounds.

**Net score**  Gross score less handicap.

**Par**  The score a good golfer should make on a given hole. Determined by factoring in 2 putts plus the number strokes needed to cover the yardage between the tee and green.

**Provisional ball**  A second ball hit before a player looks for their first ball which is out of bounds or in a water hazard.

**Pull shot**  A straight shot in which the flight of the ball is left of the target for right-handers and right of the target for left-handers.

**Push shot**   A straight shot in which the flight of the ball is right of the target for a right-handed golfer and left of the target for a left-hander.

**Rough**   Areas of longer grass adjacent to the tee, fairway green, or hazards.

**Shank**   To hit a shot off the club's hosel.

**Slice**   A stroke made across the ball creating spin that curves the ball to the right of the intended target for right-handed golfers and to the left of the target for left-handers.

**Stance**   Position of the feet at address.

**Stroke**   Any forward motion of the clubhead made with an intent to strike the ball. The number of strokes taken on each hole are entered for that hole's score.

**Stroke play**   Competition based on the total number of strokes taken.

**Target**   The spot or area a golfer chooses for the ball to land or roll.

**Top**   To hit the ball above its center.

# Resources

Arnold Palmer Golf Academy
9000 Bay Hill Blvd.
Orlando, Florida 32819
Phone: 800-523-5999
        407-876-5362
Fax:    407-876-0673
Web site: http://www.apga.com

Arnold Palmer's Bay Hill Club and Lodge
9000 Bay Hill Blvd.
Orlando, Florida 32819
407-876-2429

## Training Aids to Help Your Game

The "Donut"
Arnold Palmer Golf Academy
Phone: 800-523-5999

Natraflex Mentor training glove
706-846-9837

## Golf Publications

PGA Tour Partner's Club
12301 White Water Drive
P.O. BOX 3433
Minnetonka, MN 55345

Golf Magazine
P.O. Box 51413
Boulder, CO 80203-1413

Golf Digest
1-800-Par-golf

Senior Golfer Magazine
P.O. Box 37080
Boone, IA 50037-2080

Golf For Women
212-551-6925

Junior Golf Magazine
760-323-0204

## Golf Organizations

The United States Golf Association (USGA)
P.O. Box 708
Golf House
Far Hills, NJ 07931
908-234-2300

American Junior Golf Association (AJGA)
3415 Steeplechase Lane
Roswell, GA 80112
303-220-0921

Executive Women's Golf League
1401 Forum Way, #100
West Palm Beach, Florida 33401
561-471-1477

Professional Golfers Association of America
100 Avenue of the Champions
Palm Beach Gardens, FL 33418
561 624-8400

## Suggested Books

### Books by Arnold Palmer:

Play Great Golf
Go For Broke
Complete Book of Putting

*Books published by The Arnold Palmer Golf Academy:*
Arnold Palmer Golf Academy Golf Journal

## Fitness books:
The Complete Idiot's Guide to Healthy Stretching
Chris "Mr. Stretch" Verna and Steve Hosid

## Other Books of Interest
The Rules of Golf
USGA

Mental Toughness Training for Sports
James E. Loehr, Ed.D

Affirmations of Wealth
John Alexandrov

Golf is a Game of Confidence
Bob Rotella

The Winner Within
Pat Riley

Golf Architecture
Dr. A. Mackenzie

New World Atlas of Golf
Gallery Books

A Pictorial History of Golf
Nevin Gibson

Professional Club Fitting Manual
PGA of America

Get Motivated
Kara Farley and Sheila Curry

The Random House International Encyclopedia of Golf
Random House

Golf: the History of an Obsession
David Stirk

# Collectibles

British Links Golf Classics
800-348-4646

Michael Roche Historic Sculptures
847-296-9593

# Index